HOUSEHOLDS WORK

HOUSEHOLDS WORK

Productive activities, women and income in the household economy

Edited by
Duncan Ironmonger

Allen & Unwin
Sydney   Wellington   London   Boston

© University of Melbourne

This book is copyright under the Berne Convention. No reproduction without permission. All rights reserved.

First published in 1989

Allen & Unwin Australia Pty Ltd
An Unwin Hyman Company
8 Napier Street, North Sydney NSW 2059 Australia

Allen & Unwin New Zealand Limited
75 Ghuznee Street, Wellington, New Zealand

Unwin Hyman Limited
15–17 Broadwick Street, London, W1V 1FP England

Unwin Hyman Inc.
8 Winchester Place, Winchester, Mass 01890 USA

National Library of Australia
Cataloguing-in-Publication:

Households work: productive activities, women and income in the household economy.

  Bibliography.
  Includes index.
  ISBN 0 04 928068 6.

  1. Households – Economic aspects – Australia. 2. Home economics – Australia. 3. Housewives – Australia – Economic conditions. 4. Sexual division of labor – Australia. I. Ironmonger, D.S. (Duncan Standon).

339.2'2'0994

Library of Congress Catalog Number: 89–84070

Set in 10/11 pt Century Schoolbook by SRM Production Services
Produced by SRM Production Services Sdn Bhd, Malaysia

CONTENTS

Contributors vii
Preface ix

PART 1: HOUSEHOLD PRODUCTIVE ACTIVITIES 1
1 Households and the household economy — Duncan Ironmonger — 3
  Commentary: Frank Maas
2 Household productive activities — Duncan Ironmonger and Evelyn Sonius — 18
  Commentary: Meredith Edwards
3 Work in households: an overview and three studies — Jacqueline Goodnow — 38
  Commentary: Merle Thornton
4 The household economy and social class — Adam Jamrozik — 64
  Commentary: Margo Huxley

PART 2: WOMEN IN THE HOUSEHOLD
5 Women in the home — Mary Draper — 85
  Commentary: Dorothy Broom
6 Female sole-parent households — Helen Brownlee — 97
  Commentary: Maryann Wulff
7 Older women living alone — Dianne Rudd — 113
  Commentary: Elizabeth Ozanne

PART 3: INCOME SUPPORT FOR HOUSEHOLDS
8 Perspectives of fifty low income households — Jenny Trethewey — 131
  Commentary: Peter Saunders

9 Income support, the labour market and the household *Commentary*: Barbara Spalding	Bettina Cass and Peter Whiteford	149
10 The value of work in marriage *Commentary*: Ross Williams	Kathleen Funder	173
Bibliography		190
Index		201

Contributors

Chapters —

Helen BROWNLEE	Australian Institute of Family Studies
Bettina CASS	University of Sydney
Mary DRAPER	Women's Policy Co-ordination Unit
Kathleen FUNDER	Australian Institute of Family Studies
Jaqueline GOODNOW	Macquarie University
Duncan IRONMONGER	University of Melbourne
Adam JAMROZIK	Social Welfare Research Centre
Dianne RUDD	Flinders University
Evelyn SONIUS	University of Melbourne
Jenny TRETHEWEY	Brotherhood of St. Laurence
Peter WHITEFORD	Social Welfare Research Centre

Commentaries —

Dorothy BROOM	Australian National University
Meredith EDWARDS	Department of Social Security
Margo HUXLEY	University of New England
Frank MAAS	Australian Institute of Family Studies
Elizabeth OZANNE	University of Melbourne
Peter SAUNDERS	Social Welfare Research Centre
Barbara SPALDING	Social Justice Strategy Unit
Merle THORNTON	University of Melbourne
Ross WILLIAMS	University of Melbourne
Maryann WULFF	Swinburne Institute of Technology

Preface

Households work. Yet the work they do and the very large volume of economic production that results from this work are consistently ignored in national statistics.

Households employ more people for more hours in useful productive work than do business and government. However, the most commonly used national measures of employment and work exclude unpaid employment and work in households, not because it is without value, but merely because it is not paid.

The evidence from the 1974 survey of time use in Australian households is that paid work in the market economy absorbs *less than half* of all labour time used for production of goods and services; just *over half* is unpaid time used for household production — meals, clean clothes, child care, house maintenance, shopping and so on. The official 1987 time use pilot survey by the Australian Bureau of Statistics confirms the importance of the household as a productive sector — unpaid work in the household exceeded paid work in the market.

Everyone has experience of participation in the work of a household and most people experience work in several households in the course of a lifetime — with different people and in different places. In spite of this, it is not commonly recognised that collectively, each week, households produce many billions of dollars worth of economic output. Part of this misunderstanding arises from the statistical quirk that omits most of these dollars from our official measures of Gross National Product (GNP).

Clearly, a proper perspective on the *total* economic system requires a better understanding of households. Even to understand the working of the *market* economy requires an understanding of the working of the household economy — not only its well recognised role as a *consumer* of goods and services, but perhaps more importantly its role as a *producer* of goods and services. Effectively, the household competes with the market.

Despite the feminist revolution and some advances towards equal opportunity, women are still responsible for, and still carry out, most of the work done within households. Time-use surveys indicate that about 75 per cent of all time put into household productive activities is contributed by women, most of whom are also contributing time to the market economy. In addition, a great proportion of households are either female sole-parent households or older women living alone. The changing structure of households and changes in the relationships between household work and market work raise questions about the income needed to support households.

In an attempt to reach a better understanding of the working role of households a number of Australian researchers and policy advisers concerned with aspects of the household economy were invited to contribute to this volume. The contributions were first presented at a workshop on the theme 'The Future of the Household Economy and the Role of Women' held at the University of Melbourne in 1987. Each chapter is followed by an independent commentary originally given at the workshop.

The authors in this volume have been driven by their curiosity to know more about households and to enlarge their understanding, and ours, beyond the immediate personal experience of their own households. Their chapters have been brought together in three parts that attempt to provide a better understanding of how households work, a wider perspective on the role of women in the household and a discussion of the provision of income support for households.

The first part—*Household Productive Activities*—begins with an overview of the treatment of the household by economic and social researchers. It provides estimates of the contribution of the household economy to economic welfare and speculates on the interactions between the household, the market and technological change. The section provides a framework for understanding household work and also explores the conceptual framework of the household economy in relation to social class.

The second part—*Women in the Household*—starts by giving a perspective on women's activities in the home based on material obtained from a survey of women in Victoria. This chapter documents the desire of many women to have their caring and other unpaid work in the household economy accorded greater recognition, but not necessarily in monetary terms. A second chapter focuses on households headed by a female sole parent and a third is concerned with older women living alone.

The final part—*Income Support for Households*—also consists of three chapters. The first gives some understanding of a

PREFACE   xi

group of fifty low-income households. Another discusses the implications for income support policies of the interaction between market and non-market activities of members of households. The final chapter deals with a particular, but not uncommon issue. It argues that the opportunity costs of marriage should be shared after marriage dissolution and presents a practical model for providing a fairer economic outcome.

All 21 contributors—authors and commentators—deserve thanks for their assistance in the preparation of this volume. They all responded generously and with enthusiasm for the project. Special thanks are due to Evelyn Sonius, my co-researcher on household productive activities at the University of Melbourne, who has contributed much to the final shape of this volume through numerous discussions with me over the last year. I also wish to thank Betty Cross and Nicola Schumacher who assisted in the preparation of the manuscript for the publisher.

Rhonda Galbally, Director, and Louise Crossley, Deputy Director, Commission for the Future also deserve thanks for their initial support of the idea which led to this volume and their wish that it will lead to a clearer understanding of the future of the household economy and the role of women.

A final acknowledgment is due to the Australian Research Committee (formerly the Australian Research Grants Committee) for supporting the research which has led to the estimation and publication of the first input–output table of household productive activities.

Duncan Ironmonger
30 September 1988

PART 1
Household Productive Activities

1 DUNCAN IRONMONGER
Households and the household economy

Research on the household overlaps research on the family, but the focus is different. Family research tends to concentrate on the interactions between the individual members of the family, their personal and social relations and the attitudes members have to one another. The disciplinary base for family research is psychology and sociology. Household research focusses on the activities of the household as a unit, emphasising transactions between households and the other units that make up society. The disciplinary base for household research is economics.

The household as an economic unit

Of course, personal relations and attitudes play a big part in the decisions of the household as an economic unit. Altruism, rather than exchange, is the basic motivating force for the distribution of household product and income between the members. Some economists, such as Kenneth Boulding (1981), have recognised this difference, but others, such as Gary Becker (1981), have tended to ascribe to 'economic' motives too high an influence on household decisions. The sociologists Richard and Sarah Berk (1983) have written an interesting discussion of the challenge to sociology of the new home economics.

Technically, households comprise those families or individuals who live alone or together as a domestic unit for the general purpose of everyday activities. A household can consist of a single person living alone; general usage does not regard that person as a family. Again, several unrelated individuals, not regarded as a family, can live together as a household. So can two or more families. The ways in which individuals and families live and work together as households is an obvious area of research for both those interested in families and those interested in households.

The household economy

The household economy is the term for the collective economic activities of households. Sometimes the household economy is called the household sector of the economy. This sector is distinguished from the business sector, the government sector, and the foreign sector in the measurement of economic activities of a country. However, the household sector is large enough and distinctive enough in its method of operation to deserve the term 'household economy'. The other sectors of the economy can then be called the 'market economy'. Thus, the transactions between household and market are perhaps more akin to international trade between two countries than transactions between different industrial sectors of a single economy.

The two major types of inter-economy trade are the sale of labour time by the household to the market and the purchase of consumer goods and services by the household. Research on the former is usually considered as part of the *economics of labour,* and much research has been undertaken on the factors involved in labour market participation, particularly the labour market participation of women. Research on purchases by households is usually considered as part of the *economics of consumer behaviour* and there is now a huge literature on the theory and measurement of consumer behaviour.

Within the market economy itself there has been a great volume of research on the structure of the economy, and the organisation of its sectors, industries, enterprises and individual establishments. Questions about the economics of these activities have included research into the factors involved in differential rates of productivity, profitability and technological change, and the factors governing investment and growth in different industries. With the improvement of our statistics of the flows between industries, input–output analysis has become a major technique for studying the structure of the market economy.

There has also been much research into financial aspects of the market economy and in particular the influence of government finance and taxation of the operation of the rest of the economy. The impact of the government sector on the household has also been the subject of economic research. In addition to studies of the effects of different forms and levels of taxation on household spending and saving, there have been studies of the effect of taxation on the willingness of households to offer labour time to the market economy and a number of studies of the effect of taxation on the distribution of income.

Research on the distribution of income between the individuals, families and households comprising the household economy has attracted a great deal of attention from economists.

HOUSEHOLD ECONOMY 5

However, virtually none of this work has taken into account the large amount of income generated and distributed by the everyday productive activities of the households themselves. As the income omitted is of the order of one third to one half of all income, we must form the view that most research on income distribution is seriously deficient.

Research on household productive activities

This chapter sets out a broad outline of research into household activities; the following chapter on 'Household Productive Activities' explains in more detail a research programme that we are undertaking into the detailed input–output structure of productive activities within the household economy.

Perhaps the most written-about aspect of household production concerns the division of labour within the household. Much of the literature which comprises women's studies concerns itself, quite rightly, with who does the work at home. Whilst I agree this is an extremely important issue, it seems to me that the concentration on 'who does the work' has pushed into the background the enormous importance of the work itself, which is in some ways the prior issue.

Economic research concerning the division of labour would probably start from the theory that people allocate their time to different jobs up to the point where the additional benefit from an extra period of time in one job is equal to the additional benefit from an extra period of time in any other job. Since the various members of a household will probably have different productivities in particular jobs, it benefits a household to allocate tasks according to these relative productivities. Immediately there is the problem of how much time each member of the household is able and willing to supply for household productive activities. These decisions must take into account choices about time needed for all other activities, including work in the market economy, leisure and personal needs. Time is thus the major resource to be allocated by the members of a household. The limitations of the 24-hour day, 168-hour week and 8760-hour year become apparent. Given that human physiological needs absorb about ten hours per day, including eight hours for sleep, time for conscious allocation to productive and leisure activities is only fourteen hours per person per day; 98 hours per week or 5110 per year.

As Scott Burns puts it:

> Another major implication of the household economy is that money is no longer an adequate measure of our economic experience. Time, not money, is the fulcrum and measure of our experience. Although time

and money have been regarded as interchangeable since Ben
Franklin, they are not. Time is absolute; money is relative. There are
about four hundred thousand healthy waking hours in a lifetime.
Only eighty thousand of these hours are devoted to demonstrating
the identity of time and money... The hours of work done outside the
money economy rival those done inside and will soon surpass them.
Time is the ultimate unit of exchange. Money is an aberration, an
artifact of the market economy, an institution whose logical
fulfillment and destiny is to occupy less and less of our time and
attention. Yet we continue to measure our experience by its units of
exchange. This will change as the household economy rises in
importance and recognition. (Burns, 1977:8)

Productive activities in the household economy can be described in various ways. We all have our own ideas about appropriate categories of these activities — cooking, cleaning, laundry, gardening, shopping, childcare, and so on. These are the main categories, but many subdivisions are possible. For example, cooking could be divided according to the main meals of the day, cleaning according to the different rooms of the house, and shopping according to the types of goods and services purchased. Travel time involved with shopping can be regarded as a separate activity; so also can travel time involved with the care of children. There are also activities associated with the management of household productive activities such as making shopping lists, paying the bills and keeping household accounts. Subsidiary activities such as setting and clearing the table, putting away clean clothes and clean dishes, making the bed and washing the car also need to be accounted for.

Some productive activities in the household involve the maintenance and improvement of the physical capital of the household. This includes house maintenance, repair, decoration and extension; owner–building; maintenance and repair of household equipment, cars and other vehicles; manufacture and repair of clothing (sewing and knitting); and the building of garden structures, gates and fences. This investment activity by the household can be substantial. However, the most important investment activity of the household is that involved in child care — investment in human capital. The education of each generation is not entirely entrusted to the government and private schools of the market economy.

In our analysis of the structure of household productive activities we have thirteen activities:

- cooking and washing up
- housework
- other repairs and house maintenance

- other domestic activities
- education
- civic and collective activities
- child care
- travel for child care
- travel for shopping
- shopping — personal care away from home
- shopping for goods
- shopping for services
- gardening

These activities involve the input of millions of hours each year, the use of millions of dollars worth of foodstuffs, materials and energy and produce millions of dollars' worth of valuable output. Collectively, in terms of input, value added and output, household productive activities rival not only major sectors, such as mining and manufacturing, but the whole market economy itself.

Contribution of the household economy to total economic welfare

Estimates of the contribution of the household economy have been made by a number of researchers. Oli Hawrylyshun, the Canadian statistician, has provided a survey of the empirical estimates (Hawrylyshun, 1976). These show for countries such as the United States, Canada, Britain and France that in recent years the household's contribution to total Gross National Product (GNP) would be to add between 30 and 50 percent to the official statistics. Colin Clark (1958) provided estimates for the United Kingdom for the years 1871 to 1956. These showed the household's addition to GNP declining from over 100 percent in 1871 to less than 50 percent in 1956. Robert Eisner (1978) and his colleagues (Eisner, Simons, Pieper and Bender, 1982) show that the additional product provided by the household economy of the United States declined as a proportion of the total product of the other sectors from 75 percent in 1946 to just over 63 percent in 1976.

Estimates of household production in Australia were made by Graeme Snooks (1983) for the selected years over the period 1891–1981 and by Rodney Maddock and Michael Carter (1983) for selected years over the period 1911–1981 in papers presented to the First Spring Workshop in Economic History held at the Australian National University in September 1983. Snooks' estimates are not based on time-use surveys but on crude assumptions about the numbers of women not employed in the market economy. Maddock and Carter made some use of the United States' time-use data reported by Joann Vanek (1974) and of the 1976 Melbourne data obtained by Jerzy Krupinski and Alan Mackenzie (1979). Ted Gillin (1974) also made estimates of household production for some recent years in his paper on social indicators.

Our preliminary estimates for Australia in 1975–76 indicate a figure of $49 billion, which compares with a Gross Domestic Product (GDP) of $69 billion. The labour time component of household production amounts to almost $33 billion, the inclusion of which would boost GDP by 48 percent to $102 billion. Put another way, the Australian time-use survey for 1974 shows paid work of 10 billion hours and unpaid work in household production of 11 billion hours. Australian households demanded and supplied more labour for their own purposes in production within the household than they supplied to the whole of the rest of the economy.

The efficiency and effectiveness of the use of labour in the household should thus be of as much concern in relation to economic welfare as the use of labour in the 'market' economy. Household production and productivity will be determined not only by the skill and experience of household members but also by the range and type of housing, vehicles and other equipment available for use in this production.

The general methods of making and doing useful things in the household can be called the technology of household production. Household technology is thus not so much the physical equipment but the ways in which this equipment can be used; not just the 'hardware' but the combination of both 'hardware' and 'software'.

Aggregate household productivity is also affected by the structure of households. Thus, if there are 'economies of scale' as between different sizes of households, with larger households of about five or six members being more efficient than smaller households of only one or two members, overall productivity would fall if the proportion of smaller households were to increase.

The impact of changing household technology and changing household structure on total economic welfare is worth much further study. Indications are that there have been significant changes in both in the last few years. On the demographic side we have seen a decline in the average size of households. The average number of persons per dwelling in Australia declined by 16 percent from 3.55 in 1961 to 2.98 in 1981 (Australian Bureau of Statistics, 1984). In part this is due not only to a reduction in the birth rate but also to a large increase in the proportion of young people establishing their own households rather than remaining in the parental household. The dwellings occupied by these households are mostly rented so that the large rise in the number of these households was sufficient to cause an apparent decline in the proportion of Australian households owning their own dwelling. In fact home ownership at every age has continued to increase, as the age-specific home ownership data show.

The diffusion of new technology into the household economy has continued at a rapid rate in the last few decades. The concrete evidence of these new methods of household production can be seen in the equipment and vehicles in and around the home. The proportions of households with electric and/or gas cooking, hot water systems, space heating and laundry equipment has risen to the point that very few households are now without these facilities.

Furthermore, it is now becoming commonplace not only for every household to have a motor car but for every adult to have one. Cars have become essential components of the technology of most Australian households. Within household productive activities their most important role is in shopping—in transporting the foodstuffs, materials and equipment used in the household. For many households cars are also essential in child care. Cars are multi-purpose pieces of household equipment, sometimes used for production (either for the household or for the market) and sometimes used for leisure.

However, it seems to me that communications technologies are where the action is. This underlies the overwhelming importance of information in all its forms as a component of both production and of leisure activities. The distribution of printed information has gone through many different technological stages from books to newspapers and glossy magazines. All of these are still with us in appropriate niches. The distribution and networking of information through electronic means has also evolved from telegraph and telephone to radio and television.

In the last few years there has been a large increase in the information-processing capability of most households. This is not only in the number of radios and television receivers, and in the proportion of households with telephones, but in the volume of investment in sound- and picture-processing equipment ranging from record players, tape recorders, video recorders, hi-fi equipment and compact-disc players. A growing proportion of households have home computers and some of these are linked via modems through the telephone network to the electronic and computing systems of the world. Australian households have been at the forefront of some of these developments, notably in the speed of adoption of colour television and video recording equipment.

Although the continuing revolution in communication and information technology has had its greatest impact in the home through television, and this impact has been greatest on leisure activities rather than on household production, we can expect future developments in these fields to change our methods of doing things at home. They will also continue to change the ways in which the household interacts with the market economy. Perhaps the most important innovation in the next few years will be the development of much cheaper, higher volume, communication facilities to households via glass-fibre optics, replacing the existing twisted-pair copper wire.

Hypotheses about interaction between the household and market economies

This interaction can be considered at two levels—the macro-economic level and the micro-economic level. At the macro level the most important transaction between the two economies is demand for labour by the market and its supply by the household. This demand competes with the household's own demand for labour time. Thus we have the general hypothesis that production and employment in the household economy will move in a counter-cyclical way to production in the market economy. When the market is booming with a strong demand for labour, the household will do less work at home. When the market is recessed the household will do more work. Thus the 'total' economy, the sum of market and household, will be much steadier and have a smoother growth path than that shown by the figures we currently use to measure the total output and employment of 'the' economy.

Leisure time is also affected by the fluctuation in the market economy's demand for labour time. Consequently, these three competing demands for our time—market production, household production and leisure—should be considered together. Staffan Linder's *The Harried Leisure Class* (1970) is probably the most complete treatment of hypotheses about the constraints between production and leisure. The absolute constraint is time.

At the detailed micro level, the theory of household expenditure ('consumer behaviour' in the economist's jargon) tries to provide the hypotheses about the factors that govern the distribution of these expenditures amongst alternative commodities. At one level of disaggregation the main lines of research have isolated the effects of the variations in the money incomes of households and the prices of commodities, either through time or across households. Applied economic research, particularly since the systematic collection of household expenditure data by time series estimates and by household surveys, has provided empirical estimates of the income and price elasticities for most commodities. Thus we can quantify with some certainty the effects on household purchases of variations in relative prices of commodities and variations in household incomes. At another level of disaggregation, the effects on purchases of the numbers, ages and sex of household members has been studied intensively. This research has sometimes been used to devise equivalence scales to standardise purchases for these types of variation among households.

The uncertainties in our understanding of this level of interaction between the household and the market arise mainly in relation to new commodities and outmoded commodities. The rates of technological change in the attributes of household commodities, in the diffusion of these commodities among households and in consequent changes in the household production process, require much further research to fill out the picture of the rate of technological change in household production.

The household has always provided labour services to the market economy. Since the industrial revolution this has involved the household sending its members on a daily journey to the factory, mine or office to perform the services required by employers. In spite of this general situation, in some households the worker has stayed at home and provided services to employers. This system of 'outwork' has been particularly important in the clothing industry, where women have worked at home at piece rates well below the market rates for the same work in the employer's factory. The economic and social factors behind the continued operation of this system are worthy of further study, particularly as changes are being made in the industrial and legislative framework for outworkers and technological changes in communications and information processing can lead to new classes of paid work at home. It could be that a new class of exploited outworker is being created, but there may be a brighter side to this situation. Concern is growing over the environmental impact of our economic activities. The continued operation of our economic systems will require a much lower environmental impact than at present. Perhaps one way that this could come about is through the household economy providing a larger proportion of output. A reduced movement of people and goods would reduce fuel costs and pollution. For this to come about many changes would be needed both in the organisation of market production and in the household's capacity for home production.

Research on the future of the household economy

Research on the household economy will require a much greater emphasis on the measurement of the use of time. Considering the importance of the matter it is surprising that our official statistical organisation did not undertake its first pilot survey of time use until 1987. However, there have been some previous Australian studies of time use, notably that conducted by the Cities Commission in 1974, which involved collecting time diaries from almost 1500 people in Melbourne and Albury–Wodonga.

The principal problem with time use surveys is that the present method of 'data logging' requires respondents to keep written time diaries. Improved methods of measuring time use involving electronic devices are currently on the drawing board and will greatly reduce the cost and difficulty of recording whilst at the same time increasing the reliability of the data.

To get an accurate understanding of the structure of the activities of the household economy it will also be necessary to coordinate the time use surveys with surveys of the other inputs into household production—the purchases of energy, materials and equipment. Measurements of outputs will also be necessary, but these may not be as difficult as preliminary study suggests.

Beyond the fairly static model provided by the input–output table there is the goal of a more dynamic model of the household economy. This could be put together in the form of a quarterly or annual econometric model linked to a matching model of the market economy.

However, it is possible that the most useful model of the household economy will be one that is more akin to the ecological model of general systems theory. Following the lead of Kenneth Boulding (1978), this model would involve information, materials and energy as inputs rather than the economist's usual factors of production—labour and capital. James Miller's theory of living systems (Miller, 1978) may well provide the framework we need.

Exploration of policy questions about taxation, income support, service availability and need urgently requires a more complete understanding of the household economy and its interaction with the public and private sectors of the market economy. Until we have built the more dynamic models, either on econometric or ecological general systems lines, one way of exploring these questions would be to produce a series of input–output tables of household productive activities for a whole range of different types of households. These tables—for households with children and those without, for households of older people or of young adults, for farm households or city ones—could form the basis of our impact studies of the effects of policies over a wide range of issues. The main point is that these tables will provide more complete statements of the real world we are trying to understand.

FRANK MAAS
Commentary

Ironmonger's chapter is illuminating, informative and speculative—illuminating in its overview of the treatment by economic researchers of the household economy, informative as to the estimates of the value of household production and speculative regarding the future impact of technologies on the household economy.

He raises the following propositions as to the worth of developing more comprehensive analyses of the household economy:

- that by more accurately measuring the productive output of the household, estimates of national product will be enhanced;
- that by understanding the processes of production and consumption in the household—who does what, with what technology, with what inputs, and how consumption of output is allocated—our capacity to address questions of efficiency and equity will be enhanced; and
- that a better understanding of the interaction between the household economy and the market economy will enhance our capacity to address policy issues to do with taxation, income support, allocation of services and identification of need.

My comments reflect questions that focus largely on policy implications.

The first set of questions relates to definitions. Ironmonger seeks to differentiate the family from the household and makes the rather gratuitous observation that family interaction is the province of sociologists and psychologists while economists may stake out a rather exclusive claim to the study of households. As a proponent of family studies, I cannot resist the opportunity to argue that, while there are important distinctions to be made between households and families, examination of many of the economic activities of households only makes sense in the light of the understandings and analyses pertaining to family. The economic activity devoted to child rearing in the household is probably the clearest and most complicated example of myriad family-related issues determining economic outcomes such as the equitable treatment of individuals, fair tax treatment of households and the distribution of income within and between households. Families are the most common and the most interesting focus for a study of the household economy and an integrated approach incorporating both economic and other perspectives is going to be necessary to make any sense of such an endeavour.

Which leads me to the next definitional question. Ironmonger confines his definition of the household economy to economic activities within and by domestic units and he discusses extensively interactions between the household economy and the market economy. He also addresses to a limited extent the allocative mechanisms within households. He does not give much attention to economic interaction between households or of economic activity that occurs over time within households.

In the first instance significant non-market transfer of goods and services occurs between households, both on a family and non-family basis. The family dimension is again highlighted by the experience of certain individuals being part-time members of more than one household, i.e., children of separated parents.

Regarding transfers over time, investment in home renovations, etc. represents a transfer of consumption from present to the future and the allocation of returns to that investment may be significantly affected by intervening — usually family-related — events such as divorce. Consequently appropriate measures of the extent of household economic activity and the allocative outcomes of that activity should take account of a wide range of transfers.

The final definitional issue relates to differentiating household economic activity from market economic activity. Market activities can be divided into formal and informal sectors with outwork, for example, being market activity albeit performed in the household. But difficulties arise when attempting to characterise activities like the mutual exchange of services, such as child care between households, or the unpaid caring for an invalid relative. Interaction between households and the public or market sector are difficult to define when services are undertaken for no pay, such as the assistance by parents in classrooms or voluntary work for hospitals. Should these activities be deemed part of the household economy or an unpaid or underpaid part of the market economy?

The relationship between the market and household economies forms the central component of Ironmonger's chapter. He poses the hypothesis that 'production and employment in the household economy will move in a counter-cyclical way to production in the market economy'. It is clear that this hypothesis stands and the questions that then arise are difficult ones. Is it beneficial that the household economy will expand when the market is unable to provide sufficient employment for those who would seek it? If so, beneficial for whom? For those who will retain jobs and not be required to support the unemployed through tax transfers or for those forced to reside and labour in the household economy? Chapter 4 discusses the differences the class system imposes on the choices of people to participate in one or other of the economies or both. Chapter 5 focusses on the gender dimensions of that choice.

In conclusion, it is impossible to resist raising some of the policy implications of this book. If particular households and particular members of those households perform services unpaid that would otherwise be required to be paid for by households and individuals within the market economy, then is this not to the benefit of those in the market economy and to the disadvantage of those service providers in the household economy? Numerous examples come to mind, not the least being the care of children, the aged or the invalid, usually by women. And what of the desire, documented by Draper in Chapter 5 of many women to have this and other unpaid work in the household economy accorded greater recognition but not necessarily in monetary terms?

How does the household economy or the market economy, or both, address the substantial reduction in material well-being of children and women when the distributional processes of the household collapse, as in divorce? This is especially problematic when the household worker has made an early entry into that sector without credentials entitling her to access to the market economy.

Ironmonger characterises the costs incurred in raising children as investment in human capital. Yet the return to that investment goes usually to the child in later years, i.e., to another household in the future, and to society generally. Should the market economy allow those households to deduct costs incurred from market income and compensate households' losses in the household earnings?

How should the community as a whole treat economic activity within the household that produces a sizeable return for that endeavour but retains all of it? For example, the owner-built home may be lauded as an example of personal enterprise but taxes that would normally be generated by paid work by the owner and by the builder will be retained in the household. This

HOUSEHOLD ECONOMY

is on top of a lack of a capital gains tax on the home or taxes on imputed rents.

How should public policy treat the growing phenomenon of two-earner households buying domestic services (usually) at rates well below the market value and in the informal market? While the New Right would have wages set at such levels, combined with a lack of protection accorded regulated work, would the purchasers of such services accept this situation in their own case? An interesting sidelight here focusses on the moving of domestic activity into the market and the performance of it by household members who have been progressively divested of productive activity in the household. I am referring to the growth of part-time employment for secondary students in the fast-food and supermarket industries.

Finally, can rigidities between the household and market economies be removed that would allow a greater variety of combinations to be constructed by household members? It is clear that many women would prefer to combine part-market and part-household activities (as would many men) at certain stages of their lives. Alternatively would the results of such change further exacerbate class and gender disadvantage, as suggested by Jamrozik in Chapter 4? The result is probably still dependent upon the distribution of wealth within the market economy and consolidated within households.

Perhaps answers to such questions will be more forthcoming when Ironmonger constructs the ecological models he envisages. I, for one, would be interested to see the results.

2 Household productive activities

DUNCAN IRONMONGER & EVELYN SONIUS

Although household productive activities seem to involve as much labour input time as production in the market sector of the economy, they have been inadequately researched. Moreover, in order to answer questions relating to performance and future directions in the market economy it will be necessary to develop a more precise understanding of the nature and scale of productive activities which take place within the household.

For example, it has long been thought that the extent to which household equipment allows tasks to be completed with smaller labour-time inputs, the more time is available for supply to the business and government sectors of the market economy. What has not been recognised is that to the extent to which the household becomes more productive (not less) through investment in new and more appropriate technology, it is able to produce more goods and services (essentially for home consumption) from the same input of time. Furthermore, these goods and services may be more highly valued than the commodities that could be obtained by earning income in the market economy.

To provide a foundation for investigations into household productive activities we are preparing input–output tables of household activities as fully specified as possible. These will provide measures of time, materials, and energy inputs into various household types. Measures will also be obtained of the resulting product and service outputs obtained from these inputs. Currently our work involves a reanalysis of the 1974 survey of Australians' use of time (Cities Commission, 1975) into appropriate input–output matrices, alongside data from household expenditure surveys collected by the Australian Bureau of Statistics on purchases of other inputs such as food,

---

We wish to acknowledge support for the research reported in this chapter from the Australian Department of Science, Australian Research Grant Project No. A786-15397, 'The Input–Output Structure of Household Productive Activities.'

energy and other household supplies. These two primary sources of data have been integrated to produce a statement about Australian household productive activities as a whole. This chapter presents and discusses the first of these tables. Initial discussion briefly outlines the historical context in which the debate regarding household productive activities has emerged. Attention will then focus on a discussion of the methodology and the results.

Historical background

In 1974 Ann Oakley wrote: 'A housewife is a woman: a housewife does housework' (1974b:1). The significance of this statement went unrecognised by many. However, Oakley's work was important in that it opened up an area traditionally ignored by both academics and lay people alike; that is, it focussed on the previously invisible world of the houseworker.

With the emergence of the feminist movement in the late 1960s and early 1970s traditional notions of what constituted male and female roles were challenged. Feminists questioned the so-called 'natural' division of labour, which allocated men to the paid market economy while women were relegated to the private unpaid domestic sphere. It became increasingly obvious to many that with more and more women entering paid work traditional gender roles were both contradictory and inappropriate. While historically women had always formed the greater part of the reserve army of labour (called upon to make good deficiencies in the labour army proper), the rise of the women's movement witnessed a growing consciousness that the 'wife, mother and domestic labourer' role did not, and should not, constitute every woman's 'universe'.

There was growing interest in what individuals, particularly women, did in the household, and domestic labour became a new focus for debate amongst feminist and non-feminist writers alike. While many refused to acknowledge the importance of unpaid work done in the household, others argued that until women's unpaid labour was given equal status to the work done in the market economy, there could be no real move towards equality.

It is in this context that continuing interest in housework and household productive activities has developed. It can be argued, however, that many people are still unaware of what goes on in the household. For many, the household is a 'haven' from the 'heartless world' of production in the market economy, an escape from the alienation and exploitation of the workplace. Some see it as the foundation of women's continued oppression while others do not even think about it.

However, the ideology that all the 'real work' gets done in the marketplace while the 'missus' does the 'easy stuff' such as child care, financial management, chauffeuring, cooking, and so on, is a pervasive one. The question 'What do you do all day?' directed at the unpaid houseworker persists, reflecting a general lack of understanding of what is involved in household productive work. As Berk and Berk (1983) argue, many researchers have ignored '...how families meet their material needs for cooked meals, clean clothes...' (1983:375–6). This neglect led them to further observe: '...the labours of women, and household work in particular, have been typically consigned to the 'folk' forums of 'women's' pages and day-time talk shows (1983:376).

Furthermore, it is not only the productive work done by women that is misunderstood. The productive work that men and children do is also in need of analysis, as is the dual role of the growing number of women who have responsibility not only for household work but who also participate in the market economy.

Prior to industrialisation the 'family' was seen as the basic social and economic unit. Most families were large, self-sustaining and rural. They produced and processed the necessary items for consumption and for trading in the marketplace (Cowan, 1976). However, with the advent of industrialisation, the family as an economic unit diminished in importance. The household is no longer considered to be the locus of production; production is now seen to take place in the market economy.

Coupled with this has been the view that the development of technology in the twentieth century has alleviated the burden of work done in the household. While it cannot be denied that the introduction of new technology (especially electricity, sewerage, piped water and contraception) has drastically changed patterns of household productive activity (Ravetz, 1965; Cowan, 1976; Vanek, 1978; Broom, 1982) it must be stressed that with new technology came new expectations of what 'housewives' should be doing. Cowan (1976) outlines the emergence of new standards and values towards housework in the 1920s. Women were encouraged to be good consumers and managers; to invest in new labour-saving devices; and the discovery of the 'household germ' brought a whole host of new problems for the houseworker to worry about. Thus, as Vanek (1974) astutely observed, the total time spent by houseworkers on housework between 1920 and 1970 seems to have remained little changed.

During the twentieth century the household has mainly been

seen as a consumption unit, not a productive one. Many researchers have either ignored or discounted the possibility that productive activity takes place within the household. Consequently, the contribution of household productive activity to the economy at large is assigned a nil value and rarely included in calculations of national income; certainly not in the official statistics (see Ironmonger, 1988a). This has important implications, especially for women, whose contribution to society is valued in terms of hours spent in the market economy while the many more hours they spend in household activity is neglected. Pigou articulated the paradox thus:

... the services rendered by women enter into the dividend when they are rendered in exchange for wages, whether in factory or in the home, but do not enter into it when they are rendered by mothers and wives gratuitously to their families. Thus, if a man marries his housekeeper or his cook, the national dividend is diminished. (1920, fifth edition 1946:33−4)

While the function of household productive activity is to provide goods (food and clothes) and services (education, cleaning, nurturing and so on) for household members, this work remains unaccounted for in the GNP. Many writers have challenged this omission (Hershlag, 1960; Ravetz, 1965; Berk and Berk, 1983), arguing that household production and market production cannot be studied separately. They argue that they are both of equal conceptual status and thus need to be studied simultaneously, for neither one operates in a vacuum. The importance of this kind of approach is summed up by Hershlag:

A reconsideration of possible inclusion of unpaid domestic service in national accounting is important not only from the viewpoint of the legitimacy of this item in the accounting system itself, but also for the sake of proper economic analysis of total and per capita incomes, their industrial origin, their distribution, changes over the years within one economy, and comparisons with other economies both developed and under-developed. (1960:40)

We now turn our attention to the estimates of the structure of household productive activities in Australia.

Preparing input–output tables

The first major survey of time use for Australian households was conducted by the Cities Commission in 1974 (Cities Commission, 1975). The major focus of the study was on the way people in two Australian cities—Melbourne and Albury–Wodonga—allocate their time. The report contains preliminary results of personal

Table 2.1 Time budget of a day, Melbourne and Albury–Wodonga, 1974 (hours per day)

ACTIVITIES	MELBOURNE						ALBURY–WODONGA					
	Wage earning women		Non wage earning women (Housewives)		Wage earning men		Wage earning women		Non wage earning women (Housewives)		Wage earning men	
	Week Day	Week End	Week Day	Week End	Week Day	Week End	Week Day	Week End	Week Day	Week End	Week Day	Week End
Number in each cell	130	50	140	67	236	69	127	77	154	87	239	66
Normal work	4.97	0.59	—	—	6.80	1.76	4.50	1.55	—	—	6.69	1.50
Overtime	—	—	—	—	0.20	0.06	—	0.08	—	—	0.06	0.08
Breaks during work	0.64	0.06	—	—	1.18	0.25	0.58	0.10	—	—	1.38	0.37
Trips to and from work	0.80	0.07	—	—	1.04	0.16	0.43	0.13	—	—	0.60	0.16
Work related	6.41	0.72	—	—	9.22	2.23	5.51	1.86	—	—	8.73	2.11
Cooking and washing up	1.19	1.61	2.09	1.93	0.20	0.22	1.30	1.32	2.23	1.93	0.18	0.30
Housework	1.21	1.68	2.49	1.54	0.10	0.22	1.55	1.73	2.57	1.65	0.09	0.33
Other repairs and house maintenance	—	0.01	0.10	0.12	0.12	1.18	—	0.05	0.11	0.08	0.18	0.55
Gardening	0.03	0.08	0.17	0.17	0.14	0.48	—	0.17	0.28	0.28	0.11	0.42
Animal care, other domestic activities	0.18	0.19	0.29	0.26	0.16	0.16	0.26	0.25	0.39	0.20	0.18	0.35
Housework	2.61	3.57	5.31	4.02	0.76	2.26	3.11	3.52	5.58	4.14	0.74	1.95
Child care	0.37	0.27	1.23	1.46	0.21	0.16	0.43	0.31	0.92	0.75	0.18	0.21
Travel connected with above activities	0.08	0.05	0.23	0.05	0.05	0.02	0.07	0.05	0.10	0.03	0.02	0.05
Care of children	0.45	0.32	1.46	1.51	0.26	0.18	0.50	0.36	1.02	0.78	0.20	0.26
Purchase of goods	0.42	0.31	0.69	0.30	0.13	0.26	0.47	0.30	0.68	0.18	0.21	0.36
Purchase of services	0.08	—	0.02	—	0.01	0.01	0.09	0.06	0.09	—	0.02	—
Personal care outside home	0.05	—	0.04	0.04	0.04	0.07	0.04	0.06	0.05	0.02	0.06	0.03
Travel connected with above activities	0.22	0.15	0.38	0.14	0.14	0.24	0.19	0.13	0.27	0.10	0.10	0.19

Purchase of goods and services	0.77	0.46	1.13	0.48	0.32	0.58	0.79	0.55	1.09	0.30	0.39	0.58
Personal care at home	0.85	0.99	0.76	0.70	0.68	0.69	0.81	0.89	0.73	0.70	0.65	0.68
Eating	1.09	1.48	1.67	1.66	1.04	1.48	1.12	1.36	1.61	1.62	0.97	1.27
Sleeping	8.12	9.00	8.64	8.87	7.82	8.66	8.30	9.24	8.69	9.40	8.19	8.76
Physiological needs	10.06	11.47	11.07	11.23	9.54	10.83	10.23	11.49	11.03	11.72	9.81	10.71
Education	0.30	0.04	0.13	0.09	0.15	0.16	0.05	0.05	0.12	0.08	0.13	0.07
Social activities and entertainment	0.24	0.83	0.13	0.23	0.41	0.82	0.30	0.86	0.07	0.43	0.48	1.63
Being with friends	0.47	1.90	0.64	1.45	0.46	1.65	0.55	1.33	0.73	1.21	0.37	1.11
Active leisure	0.33	0.85	0.71	0.83	0.23	0.79	0.38	0.88	0.63	0.81	0.36	1.02
Television	1.08	1.21	1.94	1.69	1.51	2.35	1.37	1.50	2.02	2.18	1.56	1.86
Radio and records	0.05	0.20	0.08	0.28	0.07	0.24	0.07	0.06	0.08	0.13	0.08	0.19
Reading	0.40	0.56	0.50	0.50	0.40	0.41	0.37	0.33	0.51	0.40	0.53	0.41
Other passive leisure	0.47	0.57	0.48	0.57	0.32	0.45	0.38	0.29	0.51	0.64	0.28	0.43
Civic and collective participation	0.07	0.25	0.14	0.28	0.05	0.03	0.11	0.18	0.18	0.37	0.08	0.22
Travel connected with above activities	0.28	0.98	0.28	0.82	0.29	0.85	0.21	0.68	0.32	0.68	0.31	1.13
Free time	3.69	7.39	5.03	6.74	3.89	7.75	3.79	6.16	5.17	6.93	4.18	8.07

Source: Cities Commission (1975)

time diaries kept by 776 representative people in Albury–Wodonga and 717 in Melbourne, aged 18–69 years.

The general purpose of the study was to demonstrate that time could be quantified and used to assist planners in designing and protecting social environments. It was also intended as a companion study to the multi-national time-budget studies conducted in twelve countries in 1965–66, as reported by Szalai (1972), and used the methodology of these earlier surveys.

One person from each selected household was required to keep a diary of their different activities from midnight to midnight for one specific 24-hour period. In this diary they recorded details of the activity itself, duration of the activity, location, and other details. They also completed a pre- and post-diary questionnaire. Interviews were conducted at private dwellings in the autumn of 1974. A caretaker's flat and other apartments in a factory, office blocks and clubs, were counted as private dwellings for the purposes of sampling. However, institutions such as hospitals, hotels, prisons, hostels, barracks and boarding houses were excluded.

Table 2.1 shows one set of results from the 1974 Australian time use survey. This provides the number of hours three categories of people used in a series of activities for both a week day and weekend day. As Szalai (1972) observed, in most industrial societies the majority of adults fall into three categories:

- *wage-earning men*: employed (or self-employed) males involved in paid work in the market economy
- *wage-earning women*: employed (or self-employed) women involved in paid work in the market economy
- *non-wage-earning women*: doing no paid work, or only a negligible amount, but who are normally involved in a considerable amount of unpaid household productive work

These are the categories of people in Table 2.1 and so we have used these same categories in our input–output table.

Of the 24 activities shown in Table 2.1 we have included only those that we regard as being household productive activities and hence, we do not use the data for paid work, physiological needs and leisure activities.

Household productive activities

In our analysis there are thirteen household productive activities. These are shown as the headings to the columns of Table 2.2.

It is important to distinguish between productive and non-productive activities. For our purposes a household productive activity is one which produces goods and services for members of the household. A non-productive activity is one which an individual cannot pay someone else to do for her/him (such as sleeping, eating and exercise). Thus, while these activities are vital to individual wellbeing, they are not included in our definition of productive activities. We have also included as household productive activities two categories that the survey regarded as 'free time'—civic and collective work and education.

To calculate the total annual average number of hours in each activity for each adult category we first multiplied the weekday figure by 5.0 and weekend figure by 2.0 to give a weekly total, and then multiplied this by 52 (number of weeks per year). We have then used weights of 75 percent for Melbourne and 25 percent for Albury–Wodonga to calculate the Australian averages used in the input–output tables.

We have used ABS population data to give estimates of the 1975–76 Australian adult population aged 18–69 years, as being:

Wage-earning women	1 840 000
Non-wage-earning women	2 131 000
Wage-earning men	3 730 000
Total	7 701 000

These figures have been used to estimate the total number of hours in household productive work (the top four rows of Table 2.2). Thus, our estimates exclude hours provided by people aged 70 or more, those aged 17 or less, and non-wage-earning men.

Household expenditure data

The data obtained from the time use survey were placed alongside data obtained from the household expenditure survey collected by the ABS in 1975–76. This survey was intended as a follow-up to the survey conducted in 1974–75 for seven Australian capital cities. The concepts, definitions and general methodology were retained, however the 1975–76 survey also includes data for non-metropolitan areas.

The statistics from this survey were based on a sample of Australian private dwellings. Private dwellings included houses, home units, flats, caravans and other structures being used as private places of residence. Like the Australians' Use of Time Survey, hotels, boarding houses and institutions were excluded and thus are also excluded from our study.

Information was collected on a *household* basis rather than on selected individuals in the population. While there has been much debate over what constitutes a household we have used the definition provided by the Australian Bureau of Statistics. A

Table 2.2 Input–output of household production, Australia, 1975–76

	Dollars/Hour			Cooking and washing up	House-work	Other repairs and house maintenance	Other domestic work	Education	Civic and collective work	Child care	Travel for Child care	Travel for shopping	Shopping personal care away from home	Shopping for goods	Shopping for services	Gardening	TOTAL
								Million hours									
Total Adults	2.80			2786	2782	613	604	406	319	1424	218	568	124	963	78	492	11466
Wage earning Women	2.80			877	943	4	135	122	83	238	47	129	26	266	42	30	2941
Non Wage Earning Women	2.80			1608	1738	81	229	90	150	923	119	224	31	441	21	153	5808
Wage Earning Men	3.01			302	191	528	241	194	86	263	52	214	67	256	15	309	2716
	$/hh/w	$/hh/y	$m/y					$ million									
Food – excl meals out 10–43	27.54	1432	5957	5957													5957
Kitchen ware 59	1.62	84	350	350													350
Household non-durables 61	2.68	139	580	263	271											46	580
Household, domes services 62	0.96	50	208	52	52					52						52	208
Household appliances 58	3.67	191	794	322	332	71	70										794
Tools 60	1.02	53	221			110										110	221
Misc. services 86	4.47	232	967			483											483
Animals, animal expenses 78	1.53	80	331				331										331
Post 74	0.43	22	93				31										31
Books, newspapers, mags 80	2.09	109	452					90									90
Education fees 81	1.19	62	257					257									257
Telephone 75	2.02	105	437						44								44
Medical expenses 64, 65, 67	3.90	203	844							422							422
Medicines, pharmacs 66	1.40	73	303							151							151
Chemists goods 83	2.00	104	433							144							144
Other rec. equipment 77	4.52	235	978							196							196
Other misc. goods 84	2.64	137	571							286							286
Vehicles 68, 69	10.22	531	2211								142	371					514
Petrol, oils 70	6.17	321	1335								86	224					310
Vehicle-running expenses 71	12.90	671	2790								180	469					648
Fares and freight 73	1.89	98	409								26	69					95
Hairdng. beauty serv 82	0.96	50	208										208				208
Electricity 07	2.78	145	601	100	22	5	5	3	2	70							206
Gas 08	0.77	40	167	28	6	1	1	1	1	19							57
Liquid fuel 09	0.47	24	102	17	4	1	1	1	0	12							35

Furniture, floor covers 56	4.00	208	865	32	33	7	7	5	4	16	—	—	—	—	—	104
Textiles, furnishings 57	3.08	160	666	25	25	5	5	4	3	13	—	—	—	—	—	80
Insurance of contents 63	0.26	14	56	2	2	0	0	0	0	1	—	—	—	—	—	7
Clothing 50–55	14.35	746	3104	129	133	28	28	19	15	66	10	26	6	45	4	532
Food – meals out 44	6.10	317	1319	—	—	—	—	—	—	—	—	—	—	—	—	0
Alcohol 45–48	6.54	340	1415	—	—	—	—	—	—	—	—	—	—	—	—	0
Tobacco 49	3.70	192	800	—	—	—	—	—	—	—	—	—	—	—	—	0
Entertainment, rec servs 79	2.92	152	632	—	—	—	—	—	—	—	—	—	—	—	—	0
Holidays 85	4.40	229	952	—	—	—	—	—	—	—	—	—	—	—	—	0
TV, sound equipment 76	3.53	184	764	—	—	—	—	—	—	—	—	—	—	—	—	0
TOTAL PURCHASES (Ex HOUSING)	148.72	7733	32167	7276	880	713	479	380	69	1447	445	1159	213	45	4	13340
Housing Costs 01–06	23.65	1230	5115	279	288	61	61	41	32	143	—	1636	361	2750	222	954
Total Adults Time $million	151.15	7860	32692	7870	8088	1825	1743	1177	911	4044	621	1636	361	2750	222	32692
TOTAL OUTPUT	321.09	16697	69974	15425	9256	2599	2283	1597	1012	5634	1066	2795	574	2795	226	46986

Source: Ironmonger and Sonius (1987)

household is, thus, defined as a group of people living together as a single unit in the sense that they have common housekeeping arrangements; that is, they have some common provision for food and other essential items.

For Table 2.2 we utilised the results from Table 2.20 entitled 'Household Expenditure by Age of Head of Household, Australia' (ABS, 1977). This provided data for the commodity and service inputs into the Australian household. It also provided the average weekly household expenditure for all households. Expenditure was defined as all payments of goods and services for private use, made by all members of the selected household aged fifteen years and over.

In Table 2.2 there are 35 household expenditure classifications, excluding housing costs. Housing costs, which is the 'space' input into household productive activities, is calculated below. The numbers that appear alongside the commodity and service inputs are the original classification numbers used in the Household Expenditure Survey.

Hourly wage rates

Hourly wage rates (cents) were obtained from data produced quarterly by the Australian Bureau of Statistics entitled 'Wage Rates and Earnings'. Average figures were calculated from the quarterly figures for September 1975–June 1976 (ABS, 1976). Calculating the economic value of household activity has been much debated. We have used an opportunity cost approach whereby the hourly wage rate for women who work in the market economy has been applied to all the work done by women in the household. Similarly, the hourly market wage rates for men have been applied to men's work in the household.

Total figures for all household-expenditure items were used to calculate dollars per household per week ($/hh/w), dollars per household per year ($/hh/y), and millions of dollars per year ($m/y).

Allocation of purchases

Total purchases have been allocated to the various household activities. This has been done by allocating items necessary to produce a particular good or service into appropriate household activities. For example, in an activity such as 'Cooking and washing up' several inputs are required if a meal is to be produced for members of the household to consume, and for cleaning up afterwards. These input items include food (excluding meals out and takeaway food); kitchenware (utensils, plates, glasses and so on); household non-durables (washing up detergent); household domestic services (given that some house-

PRODUCTIVE ACTIVITIES

holds may hire someone to cook and wash up); household appliances (stove, refrigerator, dishwasher); electricity; gas and liquid fuel; furniture (table and chairs); textiles; insurance of contents; and clothing.

In our analysis we assumed that all the food purchased by the household (excluding meals out and takeaway food) was used to produce meals. This is also the case for the input of kitchenware. However, household non-durables are necessary for other activities. Thus, the total input for this item has been allocated to three activities — cooking and washing up, housework, and gardening.

Household domestic services have also been allocated to four activities. It is assumed that households may hire someone to cook and wash up, perform housework, care for children, or garden.

Our input–output table measures the household productive activities of adults. However, the data collected by the ABS includes expenditure for children. In order to take account of this we have adjusted the figures for some input items. The electricity, gas, liquid fuel, furniture/floor covers, textiles/furnishings, insurance of contents, and clothing have been multiplied by 0.6520. This is on the basis that children, who comprise 34.8 per cent of household population, also utilise 34.8 percent of these purchases.

It can be seen from the input–output table that some items do not appear as inputs into any household productive activities. These items (takeaway food and meals out, alcohol, tobacco, entertainment, holidays, and television) have been allocated as inputs into leisure activities.

It has been assumed that 'clothing' is necessary for all household productive activities. However, clothing is also necessary for leisure, physiological needs, and paid work activities. Consequently, the total millions of dollars for 'clothing' has been adjusted to take into account, firstly, the number of children using the item, and, secondly, it has been allocated to the above four categories of activities according to the number of waking hours.

Purchases of vehicles, petrol, oils, vehicle running expenses, and fares and freight have also been allocated to the four activities according to the time spent by adults in travel. In the input–output table these items appear as inputs into two household activities — travel for childcare and travel for shopping.

Child care

Child care is one of the most important household productive activities. This investment into human capital has been traditionally viewed as a primary activity for the household unit. In our analysis several items (medical expenses, medicines, chemist goods, recording equipment, and other miscellaneous goods) have been allocated as inputs to child care. However, these items are also used by adults, thus the purchases for these various inputs have also been allocated to leisure and physiological needs. One quarter of purchases for household domestic services has been allocated to child care. This is to take account of the cost of child care fees.

Results

The full details of the entries in our 1975–76 input–output table of household productive activities are set out in Table 2.2. Table 2.3 summarises the data in that table. It shows for each output —cooking, housework, child care, and so on—the composition of inputs in five major groups.

Table 2.3 and Figure 2.1 also show the relative importance of each of the major household productive activities. Cooking and washing up produced output valued at $15 425 million in 1975–76, slightly less than the value of gross product of all manufacturing industry ($15 667 million) but much greater than the gross product of agriculture, forestry and fishing ($3987 million) and mining ($3151 million). These figures illustrate the importance of household production in comparison with the major sectors of the market economy.

Table 2.3 also shows the relative importance of the major groups of inputs into household production and in Table 2.4 these inputs are expressed as input–output coefficients, showing the proportions the inputs are to each dollar's worth of output. Overall, time has an input coefficient of 70.0 percent, materials

Table 2.3 Household productive activities: total inputs and outputs, Australia, 1975–76

INPUT OUTPUT	Time	Materials	Energy	Equipment	Space	Total
Cooking/washing up	7922	6219	144	861	279	15425
Housework	8140	271	32	525	288	9256
Other repairs & maintenance	1825	483	7	222	61	2599
Other domestic work	1743	362	7	111	61	2283
Education & civic/coll.	2088	392	8	49	73	2609
Child care	4717	1208	187	445	143	6700
Shopping	4969	745	224	453	–	6390
Gardening	1496	46	–	133	49	1725
TOTAL	32900	9726	609	2799	954	46986

PRODUCTIVE ACTIVITIES   31

Figure 2.1 The household economy: Australia, 1975–76 Main activities

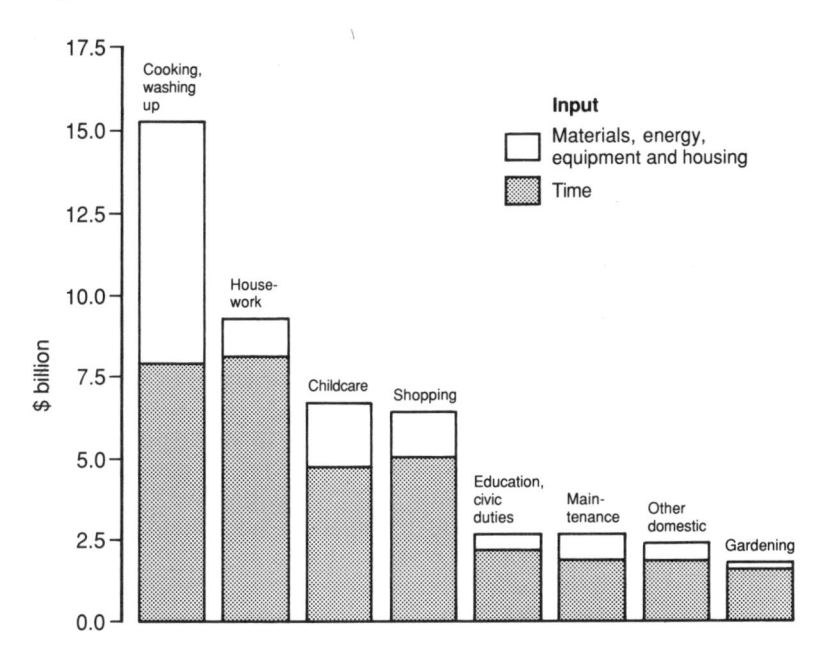

20.7 percent, capital equipment and housing 8.0 percent and energy 1.3 percent.

These coefficients vary for the different household activities; time has particularly high coefficients in housework and cleaning (88.0 percent) and gardening (86.7 percent) and materials (mainly foods) have a high coefficient (40.3 percent) in the major activity of cooking and washing up.

Table 2.4 Household productive activities: input–output coefficients, Australia, 1975–76 (condensed table)

INPUT	Time	Materials	Energy	Equipment	Housing	Total
OUTPUT						
Cooking/washing up	.513	.403	.009	.056	.018	1.000
Housework	.880	.029	.003	.057	.031	1.000
Other repairs & maintenance	.702	.186	.003	.085	.023	1.000
Other domestic work	.763	.159	.003	.049	.027	1.000
Education & civic/coll.	.800	.150	.003	.019	.028	1.000
Child care	.704	.180	.028	.066	.021	1.000
Shopping	.778	.117	.035	.071		1.000
Gardening	.867	.027		.077	.028	1.000
TOTAL	.700	.207	.013	.060	.020	1.000

The next step for us will be to use the more detailed information from the time-use and household-purchases surveys to produce 1975–76 household input-output tables for different types of households. The range of questions for which we then expect to attempt to get answers are:

- What are the differences in household productivity between households of different types and what factors explain these differences?
- What economies of scale exist in household production in relation to the number of members of the household?
- What are the effects on household productivity of different levels of investment in household equipment, including appliances, vehicles and space?
- What are the effects on household production of the skill, training and education levels of household members?
- What method of valuation should be used for household inputs of time and of household outputs of products and services?
- What are the main factors involved in household decisions about participation in the market economy?

We are looking forward to the development of a fascinating research programme.

MEREDITH EDWARDS

Commentary

Eight years ago at an Australian sociology conference in Canberra, I gave a paper on 'The Economics of Home Activities'. That paper attempted to share with sociologists what economics has to offer in analysing the productive aspects of home activities. It offered a conceptual framework of relevance to an appraisal of the Ironmonger and Sonius work: it pointed to the deficiency of the traditional economic work/leisure model insofar as it does not incorporate unpaid activities. Only with a distinction between paid and unpaid activities can the importance of time as a scarce resource be given the prominence it deserves. My paper also analysed several methods by which to value home activities.

The importance of time, particularly in the provision of child care and the different ways of valuing home activities, are two issues on which I want to comment.

As I understand it, Ironmonger and Sonius have set out to obtain a better understanding of the nature and scale of household productive activities. For this purpose the end product will be input–output tables of household activities. Although the Ironmonger and Sonius chapter does present input–output tables, it concentrates on the historical context of the debate and on the methodology. I believe that it is essential, at this early stage in the project, that the framework and assumptions are carefully scrutinised and generally agreed to before much effort is put into numerical results.

Measurement of home activities

For a study of this kind to produce meaningful results, it is crucial that the valuation method is appropriate to the purpose. This is particularly so when labour time is such an important input.

It is worth noting the reason why the national accounts do not include unpaid domestic activities since it is generally agreed to be logical to include home activities in estimates of our national income. It has been the inability to determine the appropriate valuation method and to come up with meaningful results that has led to the underestimation of our national income. Hence the importance of researchers exploring further the appropriate method for valuation of home activities.

There are several possible methods for estimating the value of the non-market activities performed at home. Three in particular are:

- the market cost approach: summing the market cost of separate services
- the replacement cost approach: estimating the cost of replacing the home manager
- the opportunity cost approach: estimating the potential earnings of the home manager (I shall avoid the term 'housewife') in the market

Two additional methods, about which I refrain from further comment, are:

- the reservation wage approach: estimating the reservation, wage or transfer earnings of the home manager; and
- the spouse paid wage approach: estimating the effective 'wage' income received by the home manager (for further details, see Edwards, 1984).

These methods for valuing home activities reflect alternative purposes: in particular, whether the measurement is of the value of services to the producer of the service, to the consumer of the service, to the unit (e.g., family) that consumes and produces, or whether measurement is in order to estimate the contribution of home managers to a country's national income.

From the point of view of the home manager, the most appropriate measure is what could be earned in paid employment or, in other words, the 'opportunity cost' approach. From the point of view of the family, the 'replacement cost' approach would be more appropriate since this reflects what it would cost the family to replace those services. (In this context it is worth noting, without further comment, that some tasks in the absence of the home manager may not be undertaken without her/his presence, e.g., making desserts). If the purpose is to measure national income, it is most appropriate to estimate the contribution of home managers by use of the market cost approach.

Ironmonger and Sonius state that they used the opportunity approach to value household activity, which, strictly, is incorrect.

Valuing the services of the home manager according to the market wage is likely to lead to an overestimate of the value of home activity because the wage rate is likely to exceed a housekeeper wage. Further, women at home are unlikely to command in the market the average wage currently received by wage-earning women. For these reasons I would consider use of a 'housekeeper wage' even though still arbitrary, as a more appropriate measure of the value of home activity.

Child care issues

The greatest difficulty I have in accepting the framework used by Ironmonger and Sonius is that it fails to confront the distinctive characteristic of the caring part of home activities. I will illustrate my argument by reference to the caring for children, but the argument could be broadened to the care of other dependent peoples.

There are several differences between caring for children and pursuing other household activities. First, there is a degree of flexibility about when most household activities can be undertaken—many tasks can be done morning, noon or evening, during the week or at weekends, e.g., washing clothes, ironing or gardening. Child care cannot be so flexibly organised since the existence of dependent children, at least up to a certain age, makes continuous care or supervision necessary.

Second, improved technology (a fact given some emphasis by the authors of the paper) does lead to increased productivity for many activities such as cooking and cleaning. However, it is difficult to envisage much enhancement in productivity from caring as a result of improvements in technology when the human input of time is the critical factor of production.

Third, some would argue that most forms of home activity can fairly easily be substituted by market purchases; substitution for parental care is much more limited, at least below a certain minimum number of hours a week.

To sum up so far, home activities other than child care permit some flexibility in when they are undertaken; their productivity can be affected by technology; and most if not all non-care home activities can be purchased fairly readily in the market. Money can be used to save time on these activities in a way that is more difficult when caring for one's own children. But there is a most fundamental difference between child care performed at home and other home activities to which I have yet to allude. That is that child care competes directly with time in paid activity— normally the two cannot be undertaken simultaneously. By way of contrast other domestic activities can be performed at times when paid work is not being undertaken.

If it is accepted that there is a distinctive difference between child care and other home activities, then it follows that in households where caring occurs, most other household activities should be regarded as complementary products to child care rather than independent of it. Historically, child care was performed alongside other essential domestic activities — the production of marketable produce from the field and in the home. Today, due in large part to new technologies, it is the other way around: much home activity is undertaken while caring for children; it is of a less tangible and marketable form and, *excluding* child care, it does not normally justify full-time activity. Because child care is a necessary activity it is not surprising that, despite new technology, the total time spent by home managers on housework over the last half a century has not changed.

An interesting related point is that the greater the number of activities undertaken simultaneously with child care, the lower the productivity that can be expected from the time input. By way of contrast, whenever child care is the main activity, productivity is likely to remain constant.

It would seem desirable to reflect the complementary relationship between child care and home activities in input–output tables, particularly in cases where child care is the major domestic function performed.

Wage-earning and non-wage-earning women

I am somewhat critical of the threefold distinction used in the paper — wage-earning men, wage-earning women and non-wage-earning women. Such a classification ignores the productive activity of men in the home. More importantly the distinction is in danger of being translated into the assumption that the home activities of wage-earning women are insignificant. Since so many women with children are found in part-time rather than full-time work, they must necessarily straddle two of the above categories. Categories relying on hours of work in market activity would appear more appropriate.

The second point I wish to make under this heading is the need for some measure of the comparative efficiency of households, in particular between the home manager who is not in paid activity and the home manager who is. In this context I want to refer to a study by Richard Berk and Sarah Berk (1979) in which there is a report on interviews with 750 households undertaken at about the time of the Albury–Wodonga–Melbourne study. In comparing employed women with women who work full-time in the home on their early morning activities, Berk and Berk reported the following:

> Unemployed wives wake up, make lunch, make coffee and then wake the children. Employed wives wake up, make coffee, drink coffee, start the dishwasher, groom, make lunch, clean the bathroom, dress, talk with their husbands, make breakfast, eat breakfast and THEN wake the children. Note that the latter complete a number of essential activities such as making breakfast, some important kinds of household work such as cleaning the bathroom and even manage to squeeze in some activities which probably have high leisure components. (1979:73)

What can be concluded from a comparison of this kind is the possibly marked difference in productivity between two households depending upon the labour force status of the home manager. It also points to the importance of time studies to back up any work done on national data such as work Ironmonger and Sonius intend to produce.

Conclusion

In this short commentary I have attempted to focus on some conceptual issues that need to be 'got right' before a serious attempt is made at estimating the relevant input–output coefficients.

I have identified issues but fallen short of solving them. There is a need to ensure that the method of valuing home activities is correct in relation to the task. There is also a need to take sufficient account of the complementarity between child care and other domestic activities and, related, the diminishing productivity of additional activities undertaken alongside child care. Finally, as Ironmonger and Sonius intend to do, there is a need to disaggregate so as the productivity of different types of household can be analysed at one point in time and also over time. My comments suggest how important this is between households with and without young children but also according to the extent of paid activity of the home manager.

Further research on the economics of home activities is important. Much policy work could benefit from a concept of economic welfare that encompasses not only money income but also some measure of the value of the output of home activity. The research is also important because it is likely that the ratio of market to non-market activity will change markedly over the next decade or so and there is a need to measure that change if there is to be a true assessment of growth in our economy. For these as well as other reasons I am delighted to see that a major three-year project on the household economy has been embarked on at the University of Melbourne.

3
JACQUELINE J. GOODNOW
Work in households: an overview and three studies

This chapter has two goals. One is to describe some of the current research on work in households that my colleagues and I are conducting. The other is to provide a brief overview of material related to household work, with the intention of using that as a background both for the description of our research and for many of the chapters of this volume.

An overview of household work

I shall start with the background material, organising it around three large questions: (1) What is household work? (2) Why the increased interest in household work? (3) What gives rise to or sustains particular patterns of work?

What is household work?

At the start, everyone assumed that they knew what 'housework' or 'household work' meant. As research progressed, people began to argue both for clean definitions and for setting aside the notion that the work was all-of-a-piece, recognising instead that it consisted of a number of activities that differed in a variety of ways.

Definitions At issue are the features that distinguish work in households from other forms of work. Suppose, for instance, we

---

I take the opportunity to acknowledge the financial support of the Australian Research Grants Committee. More personally, I wish to acknowledge my debt to several others who have worked on the Macquarie studies. Susan Delaney has been involved in the study of children's household work. Jenny Bowes, Lesley Dawes and Robyn Townsend have been involved in the study of work distributions and request patterns. Lesley Dawes, Michelle Merrington and Robyn Townsend have been involved in the study of couples showing innovative distributions of work. Without these colleagues and without the people who have generously agreed to be interviewed, the research would not have been possible.

start with the notion that the main feature is the site of the work. It is done in households (house or garden) rather than in factories or offices. Emphasising the site of work has the advantage of bypassing tortuous arguments about whether the work is 'productive' or not. In the sense that nothing is being produced for sale and exchanged for money, the work is not 'productive'. As many have pointed out, however, this is a very restricting definition of 'productive' and, even if money is the critical feature, it seems odd to count as 'non-productive' the making of food or clothes that would otherwise have to be bought.

If the site of work is the critical feature, should one then count paid domestic work in other people's households, or unpaid work in the home of an elderly relative? Such cases bring out the need to add further features. The work is usually unpaid. It is not traditionally a 'money job'. It is also mostly done by women, although that need not always be so. Men can do work inside the house, and their handyman or gardening activities 'outside' the house must surely count as within the household.

Over time, the recognition has emerged that no single feature will define either work in households or that particular section labelled housework. The definition has to be in terms of a set of features. Housework, for instance, is distinguished from other forms of work by the fact that it is done in households, usually unpaid, usually done by women, invisible, repetitive, undervalued, often undone shortly after being completed, likely to expand to fit the time available, resistant to change, and oddly difficult to pass on to others.

Which particular features are the most important? I would suggest that the salient features vary with one's purpose in looking at particular forms of work. At Macquarie, for instance, one special interest has been in the bases of satisfaction and discontent about housework. Why do people have such strong feelings about it? This particular interest has led us to be very sympathetic towards the feature that Delphy (1984) emphasises: namely, that work in households is usually done for others in the family. It is, to use her phrases, not 'domestic work' but 'familial work'. This feature, she argues, is more important than the work being unpaid, and would remain as a hallmark even if people were paid a wage for time spent in child rearing or familial support.

We would emphasise a further feature, one that occurs partly in consequence of the work usually being familial. This is that work in households is often interwoven with interpersonal relationships. It is this interweaving that makes household work more than a means of producing goods and services. It allows the work to be as well a vehicle for expressing love and affection, for claiming rights (the right to be 'looked after'), and for negotiating equity. It also makes the work an especially ready base for many a negative feeling: feeling uncared for (in the literal and emotional sense), exploited, unappreciated, and treated as if one were a taken-for-granted 'servant' rather than a person who has exercised some choice and some degree of thought in the work undertaken. One may feel appreciated or unappreciated in any work situation. The more personalised the service, however, and the less opportunity there is for rewards in money terms, the more a potential exists for people's feelings to become strongly involved. Housework contains these two features—work done for others, without any direct pay—in abundance.

Distinguishing among pieces of work   We need to move beyond the notion that household work represents a single activity. The notion of single activity lends itself easily to the use of single measures: the total amount of time spent by one person rather than another, for instance. It can, however, disguise the fact that the work covers a variety of tasks or activities, and downplay the need to find appropriate ways of distinguishing among them.

The recognition of differences among activities has given rise first of all to a useful distinction between labour and responsibility. There is a difference between doing the work and having responsibility for it. The distinction has been emphasised by Oakley (1974a) and is also prominent in Harper and Richards' (1979) analysis of satisfaction. What women often wish for, Harper and Richards point out, is that someone else will take over the complete task: both doing it and being responsible for noticing that it needs doing and seeing that it gets done. What they are often given is an offer of help, or a willing response if asked, with the expectation of grateful acknowledgement and the implication that the task is still the woman's province.

The recognition of differences among activities has also led to marking out some large areas within work in households. An example of particular interest is the proposal by England and Farkas (1986) of three large areas: child rearing, housework, and 'emotional labour' (e.g., making others feel loved, secure, understood, or competent). All three activities, England and Farkas point out, count as work on the grounds that all three carry opportunity costs: that is, they involve forgoing some activity one might have preferred to do. The three, however, are not identical. To single out one aspect of difference, the likelihood of men becoming more involved in household work seems to be highest in the area of child rearing and possibly lowest in the area of emotional labour.

Finally, the recognition of variety has given rise to a spate of research exploring a variety of dimensions: asking, for instance, which tasks are most likely to be gender-marked during childhood, to show variations by social class or historical period, to be rated as labour versus leisure, or to elicit particular forms of bias in reporting. Worth particular note, in my view, is the argument that some tasks come to have high symbolic value when any estimate is made of whether tasks are truly shared. Both Backett (1982) and Gullestad (1984) note, for Scots and Norwegian couples respectively, that young couples committed to an ideology of 'sharing' may vary in their estimate of how far each has contributed towards equal shares. Men, for example, readily see the occasional diaper change or the willingness to help as a sign that they are sharing in the work, and women may accept as especially valuable the performance of tasks that men once 'wouldn't be caught dead doing'. Each partner may also be amused by the value placed by the other on a symbolic contribution that is actually small on any measure of time or effort.

There are clearly many ways in which one could differentiate among the tasks or activities that make up household work. The question now to be faced takes the form: *What aspects of difference among tasks should one work on?* The answer undoubtedly depends again upon one's general purpose. At Macquarie, for instance, we have been especially interested in the nature of change: asking how change in household work patterns comes about as a function of shifts in family structure, commitments to paid work, or social climate, and asking why household work has not shown the changes that have occurred in paid work patterns. That general interest has led to giving particular attention to the 'moveability' of pieces of work. How easy or how difficult is it to move a particular piece of work from one family member to another? Which pieces of work are the easiest or the hardest to ask someone else to do? Who does a piece of work if the first owner wishes or needs to have less responsibility for it? Who is the last person to be asked? Above all, what are the underlying rules or principles that make some pieces of work more moveable than others and more moveable in some directions than others?

Why the increase in interest?

When Lopata (1971) and Oakley (1974) published their groundbreaking books on housework, their material stood relatively alone. At that time, as Oakley (1974a) has pointed out, few academics were willing to supervise research on household work, or to spend time and risk reputations writing about it. There was no shortage of books on work, but the occupations considered were all in the paid marketplace, with household work set to the side as a quite different activity.

Since the 1970s, the amount of material has grown prodigiously. The sources of interest have been of several kinds, each prompting particular questions and particular lines of research. Two major lines of interest stand out: a rising concern with the position of women in society, and the recognition of household work as a form of work.

A rising concern with the position of women in society This concern will be a familiar one to readers of this volume. It takes a variety of forms, with some of these sparked especially by social changes that have particular implications for the work of women in households.

The social change that has generated most interest is the increasing involvement of women in paid work outside the home: single women, married women, women with school-age and pre-school children. This involvement has often been seen as a positive step for women: as a route to changing relationships between women and men (more respect and less abuse from male partners, less dependence upon men and increased opportunities to leave an unsatisfactory partnership), and as a route to greater happiness for women (a stronger sense of competence, higher self-esteem, and a greater opportunity to develop friendships). At the same time, reports from several countries are sounding a common theme that is less positive. Women are now usually engaged in 'a second shift' or 'a double day'. They have retained responsibility for household labour, with little increase in the contribution made by husbands or children. In the face of this new piece of apparent inequity, doubts begin to emerge about the advantages of full-time paid work for many women. Is it the optimal social policy at the present time? Does it need to be supplemented by other changes (the provision of supplemental care for children, for instance) in order to be as effective as one would hope? Why has there been so little change and what forms of action would bring a less heavy and more equitable load?

Less often noted but increasingly important as a change affecting work in households is the increase in households with only one resident parent, generally 'mother-headed' households. This shift immediately alters the number of people available to generate income or to cover household work. Perhaps because the relative positions of women and men have been such a major issue, researchers have been slow to look at the distribution of work in mother-headed households. There are some indications that children take on a larger share than in two-parent households (White and Brinkerhoff, 1981a and b) and that they often do so in positive fashion since a clear need for the work now exists (Berman, 1977) but a great deal is yet to be uncovered. One would expect that a concern with the position of women in modern society would lead to a larger sampling of households of this type, or to a focus on the shifts that occur when these households expand to include another adult.

The recognition of household work as a form of work, breaking the restriction of the term 'work' to activities rewarded by money or occurring outside the home This recognition is more conceptual in appearance than an outright concern with the position of women. Perhaps for this reason, it has been the more explicit springboard for a wide variety of research questions. I shall sketch out four.

First, why is so little known about this form of work when it is such an essential industry and is engaged in by so many? Societies often draw a distinction between 'public' and 'private' spheres, and then align with that dichotomy a number of others: male and female, instrumental and expressive, done for money or done for love, productive and reproductive, significant and trivial. This view has led to an examination of the dichotomies that often hamstring both theory and reform (Goodnow, 1985, provides a review). It has led also to rebuttals of the dichotomies, to demonstrations that they are more in the mind of the observer than in reality (e.g., Luxton, 1980). Among the latter, I find especially appealing Davidoff's (1979) historical research on the frequency of lodgers in Victorian households: an odd case of commercial practice in the midst of the family life that was regarded as so removed from the marketplace.

Second, what can be said about the nature of this form of work? Once defined as work, household work lends itself to all the questions asked about any other form of work. What, for instance, are the work conditions, work rewards, levels of satisfaction? Who does it? What is the length of the work day? What is the impact of changing technology? What prestige does the work have? What is its worth? This range of questions will be familiar to many, if only in the form of media discussions about the time people spend in various household activities and, perhaps even more salient, about the money worth of household work. What would it cost if one were to pay a wife and mother, or replace her? What should be the insurance value? Less dramatic, but of particular relevance to my own interest in change are questions about the extent to which work shows strict lines of demarcation, in the sense that some pieces of work are the exclusive province of particular people. Lines of demarcation,

demarcation disputes, negotiations over changes in demarcation: these are the familiar stuff of work in the marketplace and should be equally a part of work in households.

Third, what kind of economics would be relevant to this form of work? We may need to develop a new 'home economics', to ask about the consequences of including the value of household work and other unpaid labour in estimates of the GNP, to pay attention to the way money is actually exchanged within households, and to ask seriously whether 'the family' or 'the household' is a single production unit made up of people with identical interests, or whether it is itself a microcosm of society, containing people whose interests are not always identical and who are not equally affected by marketplace conditions. The reader interested in this line of thinking and questioning would find Edwards' (1984) monograph valuable. Overall, it is the challenge to standard ways of defining income and income units that underlies much of the emergence of interest among many economists in household work and the drawing together of economists and sociologists (England and Farkas' [1986] book is a particularly good example). It has also led to some nicely focussed research on issues that were often rendered invisible by the assumptions that money was a feature of marketplaces but not of households and that 'the family' was a single unit. The analysis of how money is actually exchanged or distributed among family members is a classic case of early invisibility that has given way to a search for specific data, with Hartmann's (1981) studies in the United States and Edwards' work in Australia being especially prominent (Edwards, 1984).

Fourth, what are the connections between this sphere of work and the sphere represented by the marketplace? Now that we have two forms or spheres of work, we must surely turn to considering their interconnections. One possibility is that *the marketplace drives the household.* Is it the inaccessibility of reasonably paid work for women, for instance, that gives the occupation of housewife some attraction? Is it the low status of most women's paid work that generalises to the low status of all they do? Or is it their lack of involvement in paid work that justifies the expectation that in all fairness they should be responsible for household labour? The alternate possibility is that *the household drives the marketplace.* Is it, for instance, women's greater involvement in child bearing and child rearing that restricts their movement into the marketplace, or makes sporadic their engagement in paid work? Or is it the operation of a 'while you're there' principle that adds to the work of childbearing a set of associated activities that can be fitted in and are then drawn away from the public sphere: producing food and clothing for the family, looking after the elderly or the unfit, taking in piece-work? The direction of the arrow varies from one theoretical position to the other. I shall draw out from the debate the point emphasised by England and Farkas (1986), namely, that both points of view are challenged by the reports of change in one sphere (women's increasing involvement in paid work) *not* being accompanied by anything like equivalent change in the other (involvement in household work). This odd phenomenon, as they point out, amounts at best to weak connections between the two spheres and, regardless of the direction of the arrow one sees as the essence of the connection, must be regarded as a major puzzle for all theoretical positions.

What conditions prompt or sustain particular patterns?

The answers are again many and various. They contain an emphasis on the interests of both men and women: men, for instance, as resisting (e.g., Goode, 1982), women as interested in retaining an area of activity that offers them some degree of autonomy (e.g., Bryson, 1983) and an identity that is readily available and conventionally acceptable (Finch, 1980). The answers also contain an emphasis on factors that may be structural, personal, or relational: structural in the sense of conditions such as the presence of flexi-time or childcare centres; personal in the sense of conditions such as the individual's attachment to a traditional or egalitarian view; relational in the sense of conditions such as relative bargaining power or relative tolerance for dirt and disorder, or in the sense of the couple being made up of two people of the same rather than the opposite sex.

The recognition of several kinds of condition (structural, personal, relational) has brought about two lines of research. One has to do with attempting to determine the relative contributions of the three types of condition to a particular outcome, such as the extent to which work becomes specialised along traditional male–female lines. Peplau (1983) provides a review of most of this research. Coverman (1983) provides a specific empirical example.

The other line of interest has to do with interconnections among the several factors, with ways of bringing 'micro' and 'macro' conditions together. How, for instance, can differences in power or relative earning capacity be translated into face-to-face or interpersonal terms? Patterns of negotiation represent a particularly interesting form of such translations. Negotiations are prominent in many analyses of household work, ranging from Backett's (1982) and Gullestad's (1984) ethnographic, in-depth accounts of some small samples of low-income couples to

Scanzoni's (1979) larger-scale survey of the arguments that women might offer to a partner if they wished to see an increase in their partner's participation. I shall single out one result from Scanzoni's study that strikes me as of particular interest. Collectivist justifications (e.g., 'for the good of the family' rather than more individualist justifications such as 'I need help or a break') were most frequently used by women with the least bargaining power as measured by relative earnings. I note that result because it suggests that perhaps we are in error when we concentrate our search for an effect of women's paid work on the amount of work that women and men do. It may be better to look first at the justifications offered rather than at the possible final outcome.

Negotiations bring out as well an aspect of work to which attention was drawn earlier, namely, the way in which work patterns are interwoven with relationships between people. The sharpest illustration comes from Ball's (1983) analysis of the way couples approached a recent problem of their naming (most often a problem in the division of labour). The difficulty, many reported, lay in bringing the topic up for discussion, getting it on the agenda. The source of the difficulty lay in concern that the other person would interpret the comment as a personal criticism or as an indication that the relationship was no longer as positive as it once was.

Ball's report brings up the final aspect of prompting or sustaining conditions that I wish to note before turning to a description of our own research studies. This has to do with the meaning of work to various family members, an issue that has surfaced earlier in the notion of symbolic value, and in the comment by Bryson (1983) that household work is for some women an important area of autonomy, rather than exclusively a form of drudgery. It surfaces also in analyses of children's household work. That area of work has always been a challenge to any simple theory of labour, since the cost in time and effort of getting the work done often exceeds the value of the labour finally contributed (Goodnow, 1988a). The explanation, it has been argued, lies in the meaning that adults attribute to children's participation: perceiving it as an introduction to the dignity of labour, a way of avoiding the production of a 'useless' or 'spoilt' child (Zelizer, 1985), or as a way of teaching children a sense of responsibility and a sense of being part of a family (White & Brinkerhoff, 1981a). In effect, there is no shortage of reminders that the study of household work should endeavour to bring out the meaning and significance of work rather than stop at measures of the amount done. The research question then becomes: How are we to elicit meaning?

Three research studies

I have provided a general picture of research on household work, offering it as a frame both for our own research and that of others in this volume. It will be clear that the area contains a large number of research gaps, related both to the measurement or description of work and to the conditions that promote or sustain any particular pattern. Where is one to start?

We decided to start from the phenomenon that has surfaced at several points: namely, the finding that work often does not move easily from one person to another, even under conditions that would seem to warrant it. That particular phenomenon seemed a happy junction of social and conceptual interests. It is integral to the questions of social change and the reduction of women's loads. It also brings out with particular sharpness the need to find ways of distinguishing one piece of work from another, and for making additional progress in the analysis of meanings, negotiations and justifications.

In all, we have concentrated so far on three pieces of research. The issues often overlap, and the studies may most easily be distinguished by reference to the samples interviewed:

- a group of mothers, with interviews concentrating on children's household work and on the significance of this work to mothers;
- a group of relatively traditional couples, with interviews concentrating on differentiating tasks in terms of (a) who participated in them (fathers, mothers, sons, daughters) and (b) whether one would ask another person to do them (together with a statement of why this would be so); and
- a group of less traditional couples, chosen as a way of exploring how patterns marked by a fair degree of sharing come about, especially when the social background is not one of high levels of affluence, education, or exposure to new ideologies of gender.

Apart from overlapping theoretical issues, two aspects of method unite these studies. One has to do with the use of in-depth interviews rather than structured questionnaires. That approach limits the size of the sample but gives us a better guide to the meaning of work for family members. The other uniting aspect of method has to do with socio-economic background. In each sample, the bias has been towards gathering samples that were not highly educated or affluent. Studies of two-paycheque families and of innovative household arrangements tend towards a heavy representation of the well educated. These are the families most readily tapped by turning to university samples, or by sending notes home via school children, appealing for volunteers. We have aimed at a spread of educational and income groups, using market survey assistance and word-of-mouth. The end result—one we are happy with—has been a rare bias towards families where the father is in a skilled trade. The mother's occupation has been left to swing free. Half were in paid work in the first sample, all but one in paid work in the second, and about two-thirds in the third sample.

Study 1: children's household work

Why start with children, especially when an issue such as the 'double day' suggests that the phenomenon to understand is the relatively small contribution of a competent adult partner? The reasons were several. One was the sense that ultimately divisions of labour must be dealt with in family terms. At some point, research on divisions of labour between adults and research on divisions between parents and children (normally two separate research topics) need to come together. Without a greater understanding of the less-studied areas, however (children's work), the merger would be difficult.

A second reason for starting with children's work was the likelihood that this area might be particularly useful in bringing out the significance of household work to at least one pivotal family member (mothers). In straight labour terms, children's work is often worth less than the effort and time spent in gaining the contribution. Ideologies seem especially likely to be involved. In addition, children's work is not often set in the taken-for-granted patterns that usually characterise adult arrangements. Children themselves often force reflection on why one seeks to set up a particular pattern. Finally, the emotional investment is often major, with both satisfaction and dissatisfaction closer to the surface and more sharply felt than with a spouse whose participation—large or small—is likely to be less variable. In sum, feelings, interpretations, and justifications may all come more readily to the fore than if we start with arrangements between adults.

I shall organise what we learned from 45 'Anglo' mothers under three headings: what we learned about differentiating among tasks, about the significance of relationships (the interweaving of work and love), and about the justification people offer for their own approach.

Differentiating tasks We began with a distinction borrowed from White and Brinkerhoff (1981a), namely, a distinction between 'self-care' and 'family work'. The former covers activities such as making your own bed, cleaning your room, putting away your own things, ironing your own clothes. The latter covers activities such as setting or clearing the table, washing or drying dishes (other than your own), vacuuming family space, helping in the garden.

This general distinction appealed to us because it seemed to have a particular link to the familial quality of housework and to have promising connections to the analysis of differences among cultural groups. In White and Brinkerhoff's Nebraska sample, for instance, self-care work was set at an earlier age than was family work. Self-care work, however, need not be easier than family work, suggesting that the work may have a special meaning to American or 'Anglo' parents.

We have now found that self-care work and family work vary on several dimensions. They vary in the amount done (more self-care), the extent to which gender differences occur (pronounced on family work, not significant on self-care), the routes by which children become involved (self-care work is usually based on direct delegation as 'your job', family work more often involved requests for help or volunteered help), and the values perceived (self-care promotes necessary skills and competence, family work gives more often a sense of sharing and belonging) (Goodnow and Delaney, in press).

Of particular relevance to our interest in change were results dealing with the ease with which self-care and family work could move from one family member to another. We wanted to know not simply who usually does a job, but also who the work could pass to if it were not done by the usual owner. That goal led to several questions about what happens when a child did not do its usual jobs, and I shall concentrate on two that were asked about a number of tasks: 'Do you do it? Would a brother or sister do it, or be asked to?'

All families made special arrangements for exceptional circumstances (e.g., a child was ill, or away). Apart from this, however, self-care tasks turned out to involve only two alternatives if a job was left undone by the original owner. The task either stayed with the child (the mother insisted) or moved to the mother. Mothers did not ask a sibling to put away another's things, make another's bed, clean another's room, etc. Some did not ask because 'It wouldn't do any good'. More commented spontaneously that 'They wouldn't ask', implying a moral barrier to the question. In contrast, mothers rarely took over family work tasks from a child. They more often moved them over to another child.

In effect, in this 'Anglo' group the rule of ownership with no third parties applies far more strictly to some tasks than to others. These are, in the strongest sense, 'your own'. They move back to the mother, one assumes, because they were once 'hers' or because she sees them as still basically 'hers' even though the work itself is expected to be done by the child. The difference in ownership between the two types of work, we suggest, is relevant to all work. Whenever people work together, there is an underlying expectation that the jobs people have most obligation to keep are those that represent looking after one's 'own' possessions and, most sharply, taking care of any disorder one has created (usually labelled as 'clearing up after yourself', or 'cleaning up your own mess').

The interweaving of work and family relationships Interweaving was most sharply brought out by questions about money and questions about mothers' 'good' and 'low' moments. The most interesting question about money—can one child pay another to do his or her job?—brought out not only the presence of ownership principles but also their moral aspects. To pay a sibling to do your job was regarded as wrong on several counts. It's shirking. It's 'palming off your job' on to another person. It's undermining the family relationship (e.g., 'Then they're not just brothers'; 'you don't pay your sister'; 'that's not family'). In effect, you can do things 'for love' or 'for money', but the two should be kept as separate as possible.

To bring out 'good' and 'low' moments, mothers were asked to think back to an occasion when the child had done something without being reminded: 'How did you feel? What did that mean to you in terms of what you are trying to achieve?' Mothers were also asked to think back to an occasion when they felt taken-for-granted and either said, or were tempted to say, that they felt they were being treated like the family drudge or that the home was being treated like a hotel (a line of questioning prompted by phrases that mothers spontaneously used in the pilot interviews).

The accounts of good moments brought out frequent references to the work being an indicator of the mother 'finally getting through' (49 percent of mothers) and of the child's caring for the mother (79 percent of mothers). The accounts of low moments were especially revealing. All but one mother agreed that she did indeed have such moments, and they contributed a variety of favourite sayings: 'The maid hasn't come, has gone on strike, hasn't been paid; this is not a laundromat, restaurant, delicatessen, guest-house; who was your last servant or slave?' The episodes reported all dealt with actions that the mothers felt violated their particular distinctions between being treated like a servant or like a mother. Since the activities of servants and mothers are often identical (that is, it is the spirit of the work rather than the activity itself that is the differentiating factor), it is not surprising that boundaries are often violated. The ambiguity, and the deeply felt links between work and family or interpersonal relationships, went a long way towards explaining why mothers' feelings often run high. At base, the themes of love and work are for most of them not separate but inextricably intertwined.

The use of particular justifications In this first study, we asked no direct questions about justifications, but noted the ones that spontaneously occurred. One frequent reference was to paid work. This did not correlate with the amount of work done by children. Twenty-one of the 45 mothers, however, spontaneously commented that 'things would be different' if they worked or that they had pointed out to their children that 'things are different now that I'm working'. Paid work may not alter what is actually done so much as it alters the mother's way of justifying her requests and the sense on all sides that her requests are now more legitimate.

A second reference was to the nature of children. For nine mothers, childhood was a time to be enjoyed (that is, a time of being without tasks). The more frequent references, however, were to competence. In some cases, the reference was to the recognition that children were old enough to be competent. In one mother's words, 'I just said to myself one day, why am I doing this? They're as able to do it as I am'. More often, the reference was to the need for children to become competent. It is taken for granted that girls need to become competent in many household tasks. Ten of our 45 mothers, however, went out of their way to point out that boys needed to become competent for their future good. First, they will probably be 'flatting' with other people and will be misfits if they are 'completely useless'. They will, in effect, no longer go from mother's care to wife's care. Second, boys need to be taught so that they are reasonable partners and so that the patterns of past generations are not repeated. You would not want to see your sons, to use some mothers' phrases, grow up to be 'one of those awful men who never pick up anything', 'one of those slobs that bring everything home to Mum', 'waited on by some unfortunate woman like my father was by my mother'.

This theme of a new future was not mentioned for girls. It might have been if we had asked about girls learning to replace light bulbs and replace fuses, but the prevailing social pressure seems stronger for boys to move into tasks once tagged as women's work rather than the reverse. The two directions of movement, it is important to note, are not identical, and we suspect that social change, occurring even in this relatively conservative sample, is taking the form of moving boys into 'girl's work' under the acceptable umbrellas of need (boys now need to learn) and equity (people should not expect others to clean up after them).

Study 2: the flow of work in traditional households
At this point we wanted to continue looking at the way work passes from or stays with particular people, but to broaden the scope to taking both generations into account. We also wished to take a closer look at justifications and to ask for them more explicitly rather than wait for them to emerge spontaneously.

We have met the first goal by asking both parents in a family (mothers and fathers) to nominate for us the degree of responsibility taken for each of 18 jobs by their partners and by a teenage child (twelve to sixteen years). For the second goal, we have gone through the same set of tasks asking how each parent would feel about asking either partner or child to do each task: whether they would ask without second thoughts, would have second thoughts but still ask, would not need to ask (the job would be done), or would decide to do it themselves. For each comment on request behaviours, we asked also why that would be so. The basic interest, it will be clear, still lies in the conditions that constrain or facilitate the movement of work among family members, concretised in terms of involvement and in terms of a high or low likelihood of being asked to take on a job.

Differentiating pieces of work As in the first study, pieces of work can be clustered in terms of the distribution net, and the extent to which a job stays with one person or can pass to another. Some jobs—cutting the grass, taking care of major repairs—were almost exclusively the province of the father, with one going so far as to lock up his tool kit. Some jobs (in particular sewing and cleaning the toilet) were almost exclusively the province of the mother. A third set of tasks could be characterised as 'floating' among family members, with the float being sometimes between parents but not across the generation line (e.g., shopping), sometimes across generation line but not across gender line (e.g., mothers and daughters both involved in vacuuming, but not sons or fathers), and sometimes inviting the participation of all or most family members (e.g., doing the dishes). If one were to select tasks that could most readily be subject to change, it is clearly the ones that float most readily to which one should turn. If the aim is to provoke a radical change in thinking, however, confrontation with a task that does not easily move (e.g., cleaning the toilet) would seem to be the best choice.

Justifications and dynamics We have scored explanations in terms of whether people offer a rationale rather than simply repeat a description of their pattern (e.g., 'I wouldn't ask because we have always done it that way'). Approximately half the reasons contained rationales and these turned out to be of three kinds: references to competence or incompetence (e.g., I'm hopeless'; 'he does it so much better'; 'they're not able to do it properly'); efficiency (e.g., 'I might as well do it while I'm there'); and affect (e.g., 'he likes that job'; 'she can't stand sewing'; 'it would just start an argument or be too much hassle'). We are now in the process of analysing how these justifications break down in terms of their frequency as a function of the person asking and being asked. The indications to date are that (a) both parents refer heavily to competence when discussing requests to children, (b) that the highest frequency of references to affect come from mothers when talking about asking fathers to do a range of jobs, and (c) that the jobs that elicit most references to affect (by the parents) are the jobs that appeared in the first study as having almost moral overtones (tidying one's own things and tidying or putting away anyone else's). We are also now in the process of developing ways to differentiate among families in terms of the extent to which it is easier to cross gender or generation lines, the degree to which each partner has a 'hold fast' or a 'divesting' attitude toward the possible flow of particular jobs, and the extent to which one or both parents are partial to justifications in terms of competence, efficiency, or affect.

Two points are already abundantly clear, with both holding implications for further research on justifications and negotiations. The first has to do with the need to ask when negotiation and change are ever likely to arise. If negotiations are essential to change, then one party has to make an initial move, with the most likely form being a request to some other family member to take over a task on an occasional or regular basis. What happens then when people do not make requests? For this group the very notion of asking one's partner appears to imply either that no satisfactory pattern has been established or that intrusions are being made into someone else's domain. Requests to children are in principle easier to make, but their competence is severely questioned, so that they also may not in practice be asked.

The second clear point is that justifications are not always to be taken at face value. Competence is a case in point. Competence is often a more acceptable justification than unwillingness. That is, it is often easier to say 'I can't' or 'I don't do that well' rather than 'I don't want to do that job, you do it'. The presence of a facade is not our interpretation alone. Several of the sample made it clear that competence was a surface excuse (e.g., 'He's all butterfingers, at least that's what he says'; 'she always says she can't and she couldn't learn; of course she could, she's a smart woman, she just doesn't want to'). All seemed, however, happy to accept competence or incompetence as a reasonable social motive, an acceptance that probably reflects general socialisation into ability being a more tactful justification than reluctance may be. This type of social move may mean that one has to avoid even the occasional signs of competence ('never admit you can type', for instance), and makes one wonder when it becomes permissible or productive to be open about preference rather than manoeuvre behind competence. Negotiations and justifications would clearly repay further research work, but that research will need to proceed with an alert eye to the relative acceptability of various statements.

Study 3: innovative work patterns

We have been accumulating a collection of couples who are not 'role reversals' (wife in paid work, husband at home) but have blurred the gender line. They may end up with a specialist pattern (each taking care of particular domains) but the domains are not the traditional women's work and men's work. The collection proceeds slowly because of our wish to avoid the sample closest to hand (university couples — staff or students). We are convinced, however, that the move outside this group is worth the effort.

Why do we feel that the effort to build this sample is worthwhile? At base the reasons have to do with concern about the frequent reports of 'no change' in the distribution of household work between men and women and about some standard ways of measuring change. 'No change' is the inference frequently drawn from reports that women still retain the major responsibility for housework, or that the time spent by men on housework or child rearing has not increased since an earlier survey. Attitudes have changed, it is generally agreed, with a shift towards belief in greater equality, but actions remain unaltered.

The inference of 'no change' bothers me for several reasons. First of all, I am bothered by any equating of 'women still bear the responsibility' with 'no change'. A great deal of change can be occurring and still fall short of equal shares. Second, I feel unhappy about any exclusive reliance on time as the major index of change. It is helpful to ask people how much time they spend on various activities, and to improve time measures by having people keep diaries or carry around reminders to record at particular times. Time also has some particular advantages in making comparisons across historical periods (e.g., the 1970s compared with the 1980s). Time alone, however, does not yield a picture of the way people define work, or perceive work, and it is definitions and perceptions that are most likely to yield clues to the basis as well as the existence of change.

Third, the reports of 'no change' seemed to have a poor fit with what I observed around me. In daily life, as well as in the media, there appeared to be some softening of gender lines, some questioning at least of there being by some natural law 'men's work' and 'women's work'. I was for a while concerned that the sample of people I knew might be biased towards the 'trendy' end of the population, but research by Backett (1982) and by Gullestad (1984) reassured me on this point. Their samples were of young, low-income, working-class families in Scotland and in Norway and both groups had shown a change away from strict gender demarcation and towards a belief in 'sharing the work', with some accompanying actions.

The way to proceed seemed to lie in attention to couples who had achieved some degree of innovation, some degree of moving away from strong gender lines in their distribution of work. Couples who display 'role-reversals' (man at home, woman in paid work outside) were not what we needed, however dramatic such cases may be. In such couples, the gender line seems to be still present (people are simply on different sides of it), and that was not the kind of social change that seemed to us desirable or, if one uses Russell's (1983) Australian data as a guide, likely to last.

We have now accumulated—largely by word of mouth and by tapping a variety of sources—a sample of 30 couples, ranging in occupation from clerical work and skilled trades to managers and academics. The interviews have come to concentrate on three aspects, over and above a description of exactly how work is organised and done: (a) the circumstances that have prompted the work pattern, (b) the responses of others, and (c) the difficulties encountered, with particular attention to what has needed to be worked out (if these couples are to be models for change, one needs to have some forewarning of where the rocks lie). From the ongoing analyses of results, I shall pick out some general points related to each of these areas.

The circumstances people emphasise have to do with practicality and fairness. There are few references to ideology or to the women's movement, but many to the simple need to work out a pattern that was convenient as well as generally 'fair'. This emphasis on practicality may seem a poor return for the women's movement, but it is worthwhile noting that a sample gathered in Michigan—all with a history of involvement in consciousness-raising groups for men or women—also cited practicality and convenience as the major reason for their particular versions of total equality (Haas, 1982). Once the justifications of women's work and men's work weaken and a commitment to some degree of sharing emerges, then considerations of practicality, convenience, and preference come to the fore. Practicality and fairness are also more comfortable, everyday banners than are statements about women's rights. With no pretence to being heroic or to starting new trends, and with no criticism ever implied about the past or current treatment of women, change can occur under the flag of simply getting on with the jobs that have to be done.

The responses of others emerge as of varying significance The responses of others (mainly negative) were noted by Graeme Russell (1983) as a major factor in couples giving up role-reversal patterns. The picture is both more positive and more complex for blurred gender lines. Some couples feel they are simply part of a new generation. They assume that most people their age are now 'sharing the work'. Others neither know nor care whether other people are dividing work in anything like the way they themselves do. This pattern seemed strange to us in the light of Russell's (1983) results. Two factors seem responsible. One is that many moves toward equity may be made in relative privacy and without the dramatic appearance of being 'different' (although men who do the ironing or the laundry and are known to do so are certainly not hiding their contributions). The other is a strong belief in the individuality of relationships: 'People have to work things out in ways that suit them.' 'What works for us mightn't work for others.' 'It doesn't matter to me what other people do; that mightn't work for us.' The emphasis on individuality seemed strange to us, and it has been reassuring to find it noted by Backett (1982) as a prominent theme in the comments made by her Scots sample, a sample not chosen for any innovation in pattern. The individuality of family arrangements, Backett (1982) proposes, is one of the strong 'family myths' that permeate many a discussion within and between families. It is certainly a theme that allows for change and variation without inevitably inviting criticism, or that can be used to counter criticism or amazement.

The two most pervasive difficulties have to do with how to define 'sharing' and how to deal with differences in standards For some, sharing means that one person should not sit and relax while the other works. For others, the balancing of books can be far less immediate. What counts, and can be counted on, is that the workload will even out over time. For a few, sharing and fairness have become carefully thought about and articulated. 'To us, fair means that no one gets stuck all the time with the jobs neither of us likes to do' is an example.

The issue of standards is partly bound up with estimating fair shares. If one person, for instance, cares deeply about a spotless bathroom or kitchen and the other does not, is it fair to expect that both will carry the work needed to sustain one person's standards? Standards are bound up also with how to maintain the relationship and its implication of each partner admiring and respecting the other. How can that picture be maintained if the work pattern one person proposes implies that the other is not particularly clean or is obsessionally fussy? The answer appears to be that, in order to avoid the implication of being negative towards one's partner, people attribute weaknesses or foibles to themselves. 'I can't stand a kitchen that isn't totally clean: it's a bug in my system' is one woman's version. 'I can't stand a window that doesn't close smoothly, I have to work on that and let other things go' is one man's. Foibles and eccentricities that call for amused tolerance rather than anger from one's partner smooth over the difference and justify what could otherwise be seen as simple incompatibility or forthright criticism.

Future studies and final comments

I have sketched out three studies that are relatively well in hand. They clearly do not fill all the research gaps noted in the overview. They do not, for instance, cover all the samples one would wish to cover: households where only one parent is resident, or social groups that are not 'Anglo', to take two obvious gaps. Nor do they cover all the conceptual issues that the overview has brought to the surface. We have, for instance, concentrated on the distribution of work among the available people within households, aiming at an effective description of distribution, at bringing out the principles that underlie what people regard as a fair, reasonable, or natural distribution, and at a statement of the conditions that facilitate or constrain the flow of work from one family member to another. We have not begun pilot work on two neglected aspects: children's views of a family's distribution of work, and adults' views about distributions outside the family (paying people, for instance, to take over some of the work of child rearing, indoor housework, or external house maintenance).

A great deal still remains to be done, however, especially on topics such as the nature of negotiations, the complexities of practices and attitudes about money in relation to work in households, the organisation of work in households where people share space but are not couples, the nature of emotional labour in any relationship, and attitudes across generations as to the form of help that is appropriate and expectable. That shortlist comes from a psychologist. Economists, sociologists, and social workers would undoubtedly add others. On all sides, however, we have some distance to cover before we know as much about work in households as we do about the paid activities that were once exclusively regarded as 'work'. A form of work once invisible despite its being engaged in by so many and despite its essential quality is beginning to come into its own and can only continue to attract increasing attention.

MERLE THORNTON

Commentary

One central theme of Goodnow's chapter is a concern with the ways in which housework is defined and measured. A second theme has to do with the rationales people offer in justifying an existing pattern of work or in negotiating a change. Both themes could well be expanded. The first raises a series of questions about the use of time measures. The second raises questions about social change in the form of shifting justifications.

Definitions and measurement

In particular, there are the following questions: Is housework definable in a unitary way or is it an aggregation of different tasks to be separately identified? How does the concept of *household work* relate to the concept of *housewifery*? How useful is the idea of timing household work? The questions are related.

Unitary and aggregative definitions
Under the rubric of distinguishing among pieces of work Goodnow says, 'We need to move beyond the notion that household work represents a single activity'. The unitary approach lends itself to the use of single measures such as the total time spent by one householder rather than another, she believes, but it can disguise the fact that the work covers various activities that need to be distinguished.

Goodnow approves of Oakley's important distinction between doing a task and being responsible for it. But she does not mention the central presumption of Oakley's work, namely that it is possible to add together the work of performing tasks from various categories (child care, ironing, etc.) and finish up with a sum that constitutes the work of being a housewife. In parallel, for Oakley, the time spent on one of each of the categorised tasks can be added to the time spent on the others to arrive at a sum total of the time spent on the work of being a housewife.

It is precisely the distinguishing of various household tasks which Oakley takes to be the key to measuring time spent in housewifery (contrast Goodnow's position that the unitary approach assists the use of a single, that is to say time, measure). Oakley adopts what I call the aggregative approach. The aggregative approach could be schematised as 'housework equals task *a* plus task *b* plus...', in parallel 'housework time equals task *a* time, plus task *b* time, plus...'

Timing household work

When Goodnow turns explicitly to the question of timing household work, she is 'unhappy about any exclusive reliance on time as the major index of change'. It is helpful, she believes, to get as accurate a picture as possible of how much time various householders spend on various activities, but time measures alone do not tell us how people define work or perceive work and 'it is definitions and perceptions that are most likely to yield clues to the basis as well as the existence of change'.

So Goodnow is sceptical both about the unitary approach and about the single time measure she believes sits well with it. She attaches importance to distinguishing various activities within household work, but she does not make it clear how far she means this to commit her to an aggregative position like Oakley's.

The difficulties of the aggregative approach need further consideration. One practical problem from the data-gathering point of view is that while tasks performed in the household may be conceptually differentiable, they are not necessarily performed separately, so that time spent by a householder in sewing may also be time spent watching the pot, time spent in tidying may also be spent in planning the optimum order for paying the accounts, time spent in ironing may also be time spent in child care, as manifested in simply overseeing the children or in something as positive as telling them a story. Do you count the time twice so as to get more than 24 hours in a person-day?

A hierarchy of distinctions

Another problem is that the rubrics under which tasks fall will themselves be arranged in a conceptual hierarchy. Each category will have lesser categories nested under it (as child care, covering nappy changing, supervising children, reading stories, etc.; nappy changing involving wiping bottoms, dealing with soiled nappies, etc.; wiping bottoms covering fetching the wipes and lotion — and so on). At the top of the hierarchy will be very broadly conceived tasks.

Take for example household management or monitoring and promoting the smooth flow of affairs in the household. The tasks to which these higher-order concepts belong are the most demanding and highly skilled and the most central and definitive of household tasks. It would seem, moreover, that they must leave the list of lower-level chores that will realise them essentially open-ended, rather than a closed list as in the aggregative model. Further, they have a controlling influence on time spent on any particular lower-order chore (though some households will be better than others at this regulation of their affairs).

Further, the higher-order or cover concepts are unitary with respect to household work, or at least with respect to the responsibility for household work. Not only so, but it is these concepts or ones like them that designate the central responsibilities of those who do the main work of households. This is so whether these individuals conceive them as duties, rights, impositions or whatever. If being on call (for child care, say, and for other less than predictable household essentials) is included as it should be, then in the case of the traditional housewife, household work will cover all her time, not just discrete bits of it. From this point of view, discriminable household tasks constitute strands (often concurrent strands from the point of view of measuring time spent) in the realisation of the overall objectives of household work.

Timing may thus be more useful in studying the history of some particular strand (such as ironing or cooking or dishwashing) than in studying the time taken by household work as a whole. But even in the case of the strand, the overall context in which it is set at particular times, and the concurrent responsibilities it must be offset against, need to be borne in mind when assessing the times. A paid ironer may do more ironing in a given time than a housewife, not because of greater efficiency but because of less dilution of ironing work. When ironing the housewife may also be making assorted contributions (possibly each individually small) to the ongoing of other household projects. If her responsibility for these other household projects is lessened, she may spend more time ironing—so as to get better results or so as to lessen stressful intensity of work, for instance.

In general, intensity of work is a dimension which would always need attention when considering work timings.

Shifting ideological presumptions

Goodnow seeks to understand change in the allocation of responsibility for household work in terms of the rationales actually used in negotiating the shift. This seems to me an interesting approach, which is likely to be fruitful.

A problem with the way she pursues this strategy, though, is her failure to analyse the presumptions of the various 'practical' ploys she reports. A more direct acknowledgement of the presumptions of social and political ideology underlying these rationales is needed.

Consider the following key expository passage:

> Once the justifications of women's work and men's work weaken and a commitment to some degree of sharing emerges, then considerations of practicality, convenience, and preference come to the fore. Practicality and fairness are also more comfortable, everyday banners than are statements about women's rights. With no pretence to being heroic or to starting new trends, and with no criticism ever implied about the past or current treatment of women, change can occur under the flag of simply getting on with the jobs that have to be done.

But 'once the justifications... weaken' condenses a great deal of history. This process of weakening, which is one of the major social shifts of our time, changes the framework within which there can take place negotiation to move areas of responsibility for household work from one householder to another, or from one place in the familial tableau to another. Practical considerations of efficiency, convenience, and so on may make better grounds of appeal at the surface, but they do so partly because if successful they secure tacit agreement about what the dispositions are on the higher ground of ideology. It may be true as Goodnow says that people emphasise practicality and fairness while making little reference to ideology, but it is uncritical to assume that because there is no explicit invocation of ideology, no ideology is at work.

Fairness, which Goodnow treats on a level with efficiency, convenience and suchlike, is a more directly ideological word. What counted as fair in the Victorian household is clearly different from what counts as fair among Goodnow's respondents. The reasons are not neutral with respect to statements about women's rights. Appeals to fairness in the distribution of household work as between family members will only work where the negotiators share common presumptions about, for instance, how far equity for women is similar to equity for men — or in other words what rights women have. Many householders will not be able to frame their presumptions abstractly, but the arguments they advance or accept will imply the presumptions they work with.

Similarly the 'strong belief in the individuality of relationships' is not something that could in Victorian times have been advanced as a successful counter to criticism of the blurring of gender lines within a household. The whole force of this appeal to the individuality of relationships, and presumably of the persons in them, is something that rests on major historical trends including the ideological work that has been done on gender in recent times. Our society has moved in the direction of ceasing the ascription to women at birth of an inalienable special relationship to a certain order of household and child care support work.

So emphasis on practicality in negotiating who in the family does what household work does not (as Goodnow fears it may) 'seem a poor return for the women's movement'. It is something that can only take place in the way Goodnow describes it against a background of tacit concurrence with beliefs about the standing of women in relationship to men that were little held before the women's movement.

ADAM JAMROZIK

4 The household economy and social class

This chapter aims to identify certain issues of relevance to the future of family household economy. The term 'family household' is used advisedly, as most households in Australia are family households. The chapter considers a number of factors that may facilitate, or inhibit, the functioning of family households in the foreseeable future. Among these, importance is attached to the capitalist market economy and the class structure of Australian society, as well as to the allocation of goods and services provided by the state.

The argument put forward is that the household economy has to be considered in the context of community resources and informal supports and the various forms of exchange that may take place in that context. If the household economy is to be a countervailing force against the commodification pressures of the market, its value should not be assessed on the criteria used in the measurement of production and consumption in the market.

A number of references from Australian and overseas literature indicate that the role of the family household economy is one of the important issues in the debates about the future of industrialised 'welfare state' societies.

The household economy and the formal/informal market

The boundaries of the 'household economy' are not precise, and the meaning of the concept needs some clarification. In current definitions the household economy may be taken to mean what is produced and consumed 'in the household', or 'outside the formal market', i.e., production and consumption that is not included in the calculation of the GDP. For example, Mandeville defines the household economy as 'unpaid work for one's own use' and includes in the definition

> ...raising and caring for children, food production, working and cleaning, gardening, do-it-yourself (DIY) activities, hobbies and voluntary work in the community. Community oriented voluntary

work may or may not be conducted from home. It includes not only the voluntary sector, unpaid welfare work, but also participation in citizen movements such as women's movement, environmental movement, anti-war movement...

The household economy, then, comprises the sum of all goods and services produced by households for themselves or voluntarily for the community. (1986:258)

Mandeville includes voluntary work for the community but then extends the definition to most activities outside the formal market, such as the activities that take place in the 'black', 'informal', or 'shadow' economy. The boundaries of the household economy thus become 'fuzzy', as many activities in the 'black' or 'shadow' economy are really market activities, the only difference between these activities and those in the 'formal' market being that the former are not recorded in the calculation of the GDP and the receiver of rewards for goods supplied or services rendered does not pay income tax. Thus, once the definition of the household economy extends beyond the household, it is difficult to distinguish between activities in which money actually changes hands and those based on barter, (i.e. exchange of goods or skills) or reciprocity and friendship. The economic unit of production/consumption may thus mean the household or a large number of households. Such forms of exchange of goods and services have been the feature of community life and are still practised to varied degrees in most communities.

Three other aspects of Mandeville's observations are worth noting. First, he points out that in the household economy there is no clear distinction between production and consumption, and for this reason he refers to 'prosumers'. It may be argued that the distinction between production and consumption is not always clear in the formal market either, as pointed out by some analysts (e.g., Westergaard and Resler, 1975). Second, Mandeville sees the household economy as a form of interaction with the market, in that people produce services for themselves through purchase of consumer durables and other 'raw' materials in the market and then add their own labour—the feature of the do-it-yourself industry. Third, he notes that the capacity for engaging in do-it-yourself is related to the level of people's education, as the capacity for self-help

... partly reflects the increasing education level/emphasis on human capital in advanced societies since 1950. Indeed, keenest self-sufficient householders—the alternative lifestyle movement—appear to be much higher educated than the populace as a whole. Estimates are that as many as two-thirds of alternative people have university degrees, compared to about 7 per cent possessing such in the Australian labour force. (Mandeville 1986:262)

It is important to note that Mandeville relates the capacity for self-help to the availability of information and people's ability to use this information for their own benefit. This ability depends on people's educational level, which indicates that performance of the household economy is closely related to, and dependent upon, the householders' position on the socio-economic ladder, or the class structure. In other words, to develop a degree of autonomy in the household economy one has to secure first an adequate access to the goods and services provided by the market and the welfare state.

Mandeville's example of the alternative lifestylers has to be accepted with some qualifications. He fails to mention that the feature of alternative lifestyles of the kind he refers to (i.e., educated people) is their transient character. There are not many 'permanent' alternative lifestylers of that kind; most of them have returned to 'civilisation'; others are 'part-time' alternative lifestylers, spending weekdays at relatively lucrative pursuits in the market and engaging in alternative lifestyles at weekends, thus having the best of both worlds: a good income and a weekend retreat. On that score, there are only differences to a degree between 'alternative lifestylers', 'hobby farmers' and Pitt (or Collins) Street farmers. The attraction of a 'retreat' is confined to the people who have options; for those who do not have such options a 'retreat' means an 'unfortunate necessity'.

What emerges from Mandeville's observations is an area of economic activity outside the formal market economy in which some activities centre on the household and others extend into a locality and into wider areas of the 'informal' market. However, while these activities might be carried out with some autonomy from the market, the extent of that autonomy is determined by the householders' position in the market.

The household economy and capitalism

The household in the capitalist system is essentially a unit of consumption. Based on the family unit (with some minor exceptions) the household has been almost entirely destroyed as a unit of economic production, mixed farming—rather rare in Australia—being an exception. As Oakley (1981) observes, 'Before the establishment of industrial capitalism, housework had the character of manufacture rather than service', but now housework exists to serve the consumption function of the economy (1981:163–4). The household, or rather the family, maintains the labour force, consumes goods and services produced in the market, and reproduces the future labour force and future consumers. As Bauman, among others, notes, 'Capital cannot survive without a search for an ever-increasing profit, and within the existing economic structure profit cannot be sought in any other way than extensive and intensive expansion of the markets' (1982:183).

Every time a movement takes place that potentially threatens the market, that movement soon becomes absorbed into the market and becomes another market commodity. For example, in the 1950s and early 1960s it was the emerging 'youth culture' that originally was perceived as a threat, as an 'anti-culture'. In a remarkably short period of time the youth culture became entirely commodified and became a lucrative market for capitalist exploitation—in music, fashion, sex, and even illicit drugs. The same development has occurred in 'health foods' and 'alternative medicine', not to mention various 'new' religions and 'personal development' activities.

The relentless progress of technological change, coupled with the pressures of the market, also means that the do-it-yourself activities can no longer be performed to the extent that was possible ten or fifteen years ago. Very few consumer durables can now be repaired at home, be these cars, washing machines, radios, television sets or electric kitchen gadgets. One has to call an expert, and the expert, more often than not, exchanges the faulty part rather than repairing it, or sends the whole apparatus to the workshop. Thus the dependence on the market grows daily. As Kumar says, 'The factory encroached on the productive side of the household, leaving the home a mere unit of consumption, incapable of sustaining the family out of its activities' (1978:83).

This point is made more explicitly by Gorz, who points out the interdependence of the units in the market economy on an ever-widening scale:

> No one produces what they consume or consumes what they produce... No city—even if its inhabitants were to organise into a commune—is capable of manufacturing the things necessary to cover its vital needs or of obtaining its food through exchange with the surrounding rural communities. The division of labour now exists on a transnational level. (1982:41)

In the present economic and political climate it is difficult to see how the trend towards ever-greater commodification of social life can be reversed, especially as the policies of both major political parties in Australia follow the determinants of the market. The differences between their philosophies are a matter of degree rather than substance.

The household economy and social class in Australia

Socio-economic differences in Australian society and changes that have accentuated social and economic inequalities and have deepened the class division of this society have been most evident in the structure of the labour market and in the access to services provided by the state.

The changes in the structure of the labour market over the past two decades have resulted in the decline of employment for manual labour and in a rapid growth of employment for professional, technical and other white-collar workers. The largest increase, both numerical and proportional, has occurred in the employment of women, especially married women, with tertiary educational qualifications who have entered employment in both public and private sectors of 'management industries', that is, finance, property and business services, public administration and community services. Of these industries, the largest increase in women's employment has been in community services, which includes health, education, welfare, and a host of related services such as recreation, culture, community development, etc. In 1985, over 60 percent of all employed women with degrees and 83 percent of women in professional, technical, etc. occupations were employed in community services (ABS 1985a and ABS 1985b).

Because of high degree of class homogamy in Australian

Table 4.1 Married couple income units, Australia, 1981–82

Income range per week $	Both husband and wife in labour force			Only husband in labour force		
	'000	%	% cum.	'000	%	% cum.
0–199	120	8.0	8.0	183	13.5	13.5
200–279	98	6.5	14.5	227	16.7	30.2
280–359	140	9.3	23.8	333	24.6	54.8
360–439	180	12.0	35.8	230	17.0	71.8
440–519	230	15.4	51.2	134	9.9	81.7
520–599	221	14.8	66.0	83	6.1	87.8
600–699	203	13.5	79.5	57	4.2	92.0
700 & over	307	20.5	100.0	108	8.0	100.0
All income units	1499	100.0	100.0	1355	100.0	100.0
Dependent children	'000	%	Mean income $ per week	'000	%	Mean income $ per week
None	593	39.5	558	406	30.0	374
One child	286	19.1	542	282	20.8	387
Two or more	620	41.4	530	667	49.2	406

Source: ABS (1984) Income and Housing Survey, Income of Income Units, Australia 1981–82; Cat. No. 6523.0

society (as elsewhere), the changes in the structure of the labour market have been a significant factor in the growth of a social stratum that has been defined in some sociological theories as the new class or the new middle class (e.g., Gouldner, 1979). The effect of these changes is plainly evident in the distribution of family incomes (Table 4.1), in consumption patterns, and in the life in the community. The new middle-class family is now predominantly a two-income family, with both partners in full-time or near-full-time employment. By contrast, a working-class family tends to be a one-income family.

Allocation of public social expenditure, the distribution of services and their usage also indicate that the new middle class has become a significant, and in some service areas the principal, consumer of welfare services, especially of the services that facilitate and enhance the recipients' social functioning, such as health, education and child care (Table 4.2). In all these service areas the new middle class figures prominently as the main consumer, higher education and child care being the best examples (Anderson and Vervoorn, 1983; Sweeney and Jamrozik, 1984). In childcare the working class, especially the one-income families and the families in which parents are unemployed, have now been virtually excluded from access except to occasional care, subject to rigid restrictions (Office of Child Care, 1986).

Table 4.2 Child care arrangements, Australia, November 1984

Family income per Week $	All families with children under 12 yrs '000 (1)	Families using formal childcare		Families using formal and informal childcare	
		'000 (2)	% of (1)	'000 (3)	% of (2)
Less than 200	266.2	37.2	14.0	11.1	29.8
201–300	251.2	43.4	17.3	12.3	28.3
301–400	318.9	59.3	18.6	19.6	33.1
401–500	284.8	58.0	20.4	20.4	35.2
501–600	165.6	37.6	22.6	15.5	41.1
601+	246.8	62.0	25.2	27.6	44.5
Not Stated	126.3	20.3	16.0	6.5	32.0
Total	1,659.8	317.8	19.1	113.0	35.6

Source: ABS (1986) Child Care Arrangements, Australia, November 1984; Cat. No. 4402.0

These developments have also led to new distinctions between social classes, and one manifestation of this is the growth of new forms of domestic service. The labour force surveys indicate the extent of domestic servants employed by private households to be 10 000 to 14 000. However, this is clearly a gross underestimate, as the 'cleaning lady' or the 'child minder' at home, or even a 'nanny' are now a frequent occurrence. This form of employment is arranged either privately on the 'informal' market or through employment agencies specialising in this form of service. Such agencies are now flourishing in all states, offering a wide range of services and, on the information received, have a large number of families and persons available for hire on their books. In child care, the *Australian Financial Review* (31 March 1987) published a six-page guide to services for executives and professional men and women. The guide lists public and private child care services, including 24-hour private services and live-in or live-out nanny services. There are now schools for training nannies in Sydney and Melbourne.

Parallel with these developments has been a change in the perceptions and interpretations of social issues. The debate on social provisions that enhance recipients' social functioning has progressively turned to middle-class interest, middle-class families being perceived as 'ordinary' or 'average' families, or even as 'disadvantaged' families. This is certainly evident in the debates on such provisions as health, education, and childcare services (e.g., Brennan, 1986). The issues tend to be presented as affecting 'all families' but arguments are formulated in such a way as to ensure the advantage of relatively affluent middle-class families.

By contrast, the concerns about poverty continue to be expressed in a perspective which places the poor outside the societal context (see Bryson and Eastop, 1980), separated from the mainstream of society by the 'poverty line'. In that 'dual perspective' the sight is lost of the fact that poor families are poor not only because they do not have sufficient income but also because they are virtually excluded from access to those social provisions that the more affluent families use to their advantage. This perspective is reflected in social policy and in the platforms of political parties, as all political parties are aware that in order to gain power or stay in power a party must secure a major proportion of the middle-class vote.

In sum, as a general trend (with some exceptions) over the past decade or so, much of the debate on social issues and social policy has shifted from the concern about inequality to concern for maintaining inequalities based on class division. There might be an inferred assumption in these concerns or even a genuine and well-intended belief that the advantages held by the new middle class will somehow extend to the working class and the 'underclass' of the market economy through a kind of 'trickle-down effect'. There is no evidence that this has been the case. On the contrary, the inequalities have in recent years increased, both through the changes in the labour market and through Government policies. While there might have been some improvement in the level of benefits that assist poor people in their survival, the benefits that enhance social functioning of the recipients have clearly favoured the middle classes.

As I have argued elsewhere (Jamrozik, 1986, 1987), the position of the family household is determined by social class. The viability of the middle- and upper-class family is maintained by pecuniary nexus—income, property, and formal and informal networks that facilitate access to resources. For example, the extended three-generation family interacts more frequently among the higher-income groups than among the lower-income groups. The members do not necessarily live under one roof but are able to provide support, personal and material, to one another. Inter vivos capital and income transfers from older to younger generations are also frequent. The pecuniary nexus does not necessarily disappear when the individuals exercise their personal freedom, through separation, divorce, single parenthood, or, in case of young people, leaving the parental home. They might experience personal traumas and some inconvenience, but there is a range of services at their disposal to lessen the pain: access to credit, the legal profession, tax consultants, and friendly counsellors in the Family Court. All these services are attuned to middle-class needs and have little to offer for the working class. In similar situations the members of poor family households have nowhere to go except to welfare agencies, where the receipt of assistance is conditional upon proving a 'deserving status', with associated humiliation and stigma and often surveillance and invasion of privacy.

It may be argued that income-support provisions for the unemployed and other 'dependent' population must have alleviated the inequalities generated in the market economy and have thus ensured at least a degree of autonomy for family households in these population strata. This, however, is not the case. On the contrary, there is considerable body of evidence to suggest that the expansion of the welfare state might have increased the autonomy of some households, especially the autonomy of middle-class families, but it has also contributed to the increasing dependence of working-class low-income families and of the 'underclass' families, not only for income support from the state but also for information and advice from the 'helping professions'.

The 'colonisation' of the working-class population by the apparatus of the welfare state is an issue of great concern to some analysts who are not against the welfare state but are concerned at the effects it produces. Despite repeated assertions by policy-makers, administrators, and especially social workers about the importance of 'self-determination' of the recipient population, the evidence indicates, by and large, the opposite affects. As Grosser observes, 'Those in need are forced to speak the language of administration (sometimes with the help of professional services as interpreters) and to accept the definition of their needs by professional helpers... [and, furthermore]... where welfare policy has intervened normal social contacts have been broken up' (1983:3–4).

Similar observations have been made by numerous analysts of social policy and welfare services in Britain and the United States, e.g., Kumar (1978), Gilbert (1982, 1983), George and Wilding (1984). In addition to identifying such problems as inequality in resource allocation, social control and the unavoidable stigma experienced by the 'dependent' recipients of services, these writers also note the loss of confidence among the recipients in their own abilities. Kumar observes, 'Nowhere is this lack of confidence of more consequence than in the field of medicine and welfare' (1978:268).

It is not difficult to conclude from these observations that services provided under the auspices of the welfare state acquire the characteristics of the market and thus further increase the loss of autonomy among the dependent population. The provision of services in the public sector has followed the path similar to that of the private sector; the commodification process is almost identical and leads to comparable outcomes. The more affluent and more socially competent middle classes use the services provided by the state to enhance their autonomy; the dependent population loses whatever degree of autonomy it might have had before accepting the services it needs for its subsistence.

Thus taking into account the current trends in the labour market, the differences in the provision of, and access to, services of the welfare state, and corresponding differences in incomes and lifestyles, family households are likely to continue functioning on two divergent paths. Some households will take advantage of the 'best of both worlds', while others will continue to be exploited by the market, and those in the dependent 'underclass' will continue at the level of subsistence living. If the current trends in the labour market and allocation of resources by the state continue in the direction evident over the recent years, the household economy of the relatively affluent middle- and upper-class families is likely to function well while the economy of the lower-class family households is likely to deteriorate further.

While the class division in Australia might not have reached the extent comparable with that of other countries, e.g., Britain and the United States, current trends certainly indicate a development in a direction of greater inequalities. Looking at the British scene, Pahl (1982) foresees that with the contraction of the public sector people will withdraw into their respective private lives, the well-off by choice, the poor by necessity. Access to some exclusive affluent areas, for example, will not be available to the general public (it is appropriate to note here that such an 'exclusive zone' was proposed a few years ago for a development project at Noosa, Queensland—see Jamrozik 1981). Pahl paints a gloomy picture of such a future. He sees 'More domestic servants for the rich; more migration for work for the poor; more activities centred in and around the home; more conflicts within households about who does what work, when and where; more fear; more private security systems; more conservatism' (1982:14).

Perhaps a less gloomy, less emotive, but nevertheless realistic picture is painted by Redcliff and Mingione in their introductory observations in *Beyond Employment* (1985). They say:

...where the effects of recession are marked, its impact may be partially concealed by a class-based tradition of self-help, a domestic orientation and, for the new middle classes, by a certain pre-existing stake in the consumer market. Here, at least, it would appear to be the middle and stable working classes which are able to derive some benefit from informalisation and the shift in service provision out of the State and into the private sector. For the unemployed, however, the ability to make use of alternative solutions to their survival needs appears to be increasingly problematic. (1985:5)

It is of interest to note these authors' comments on class differences in the function of household economies. They say:

...there are major differences in the kinds of transfers that are made in different class contexts, whether they are of money, goods, or services. The household as a residential unit may not necessarily be the most significant area. Extended family networks need not be spatially bounded...Goods and services can by definition only be exchanged by those in comparative proximity, while among the middle and upper classes, long-term and inter-generational transfers of financial resources, creating non-reciprocal investments through time, are more likely to be more important. All these have different implications for the reproduction of the household. Furthermore, these patterns have class bases and themselves contribute to processes of stratification, though the dynamics of this may be very different from traditional conceptions. (1985:8-9)

The role of women

Women, as well as men, divide along class lines. These divisions do not negate the existence of inequalities which affect all women and men, but most issues in current debate concern sex/gender inequalities *within* a class, and, as such, they do not 'interfere' in the class structure.

Notwithstanding the inequalities of class division, however, it is important to note that over the past two decades or so many important social issues have been brought into public debate and policy agenda by women. As Vaughan (1983) notes:

> ...it is an amazing truth that while men still dominate socially and politically in conventional ways (holding the majority of seats on local councils, for instance, standing for parliament, running for the service clubs and so on) it is women who overrun new groups— community action, school councils, experimental programs, classes, activities and discussion groups. (1983:131)

Vaughan's observation is undoubtedly true. At the same time, women's initiatives and activities have not overcome socio-economic inequalities and class divisions in the community. Distribution of social provisions and qualitative differences in services have favoured middle-class families and middle-class suburbs, childcare services being an example. It is to be expected that better educated, better informed, and more articulate and politically aware women are more successful in formulating their claims and in having them accepted as legitimate. As a result, social issues that arise as issues of general interest over time become middle-class issues, in discussion as well as in action and outcomes. Over a period of time, class interests always tend to take priority over 'general' interests, especially when valued resources are limited.

A similar problem now occurs in the development of welfare policies towards community care, which, in principle, is to be based on the interaction between professional services and self-help activities. Most professionals in these services are women and the actual 'carers' are also mainly women, but there are clear distinctions between the two groups. As Bryson and Mowbray have recently observed:

> Inevitably, the heaviest burden falls on working-class women. Within their families, they are not able to afford to substitute paid help for services previously provided by the state, and they are likely to feel compelled to give up their own income-earning activities to provide care. In the broader area, they are more likely to take up welfare work of the 'community care' kind such as providing foster care, family day care, or homemaking service. This is almost invariably poorly paid and has few of the industrial safeguards of the more established occupations. (1986:184)

Does the household economy have a future?

I have argued in this chapter that the household economy does not function separately from the market economy but to a varied degree it forms a part of the latter, serving mainly as a field for consumption of goods and services produced in the market. Secondly, the degree of autonomy a household can achieve is related to the social class of its members, namely, the higher their position in the class structure, the greater the household's autonomy. As a result, class inequalities in the household economy reflect rather than countervail the class inequalities of the market economy.

Given current trends, the most probable future development will be a continued expansion of the market and further commodification of production as well as consumption, i.e., more processed food, more fast-food outlets, more television and video entertainment, more commercialised sporting, cultural and recreational activities. In social provisions, a similar expansion is probable, namely, more childcare services (public and private), more professional intervention, more facilitative services for the relatively affluent middle class, and more social control and greater dependence among the poor.

That is a rather gloomy prognosis. Are there any apparent or real trends in the other direction? There is a large and diverse 'grey' area of more-or-less informal activities in which some writers see distinct possibilities of countervailing the influence of the market: cooperative arrangements, small-scale production for local consumption, contract work from home, household-based enterprises, voluntary work, or barter exchange of goods, services and skills. These writers argue that such developments can be encouraged by appropriate policy measures introduced by governments. For example, Mandeville argues:

> Measures to encourage householding could include: the introduction of permanent part-time work, a guaranteed minimum income scheme, extension of taxation benefits applying to corporate capital through to household capital, and measures to ensure both access to information and electronic information systems as well as capacity to utilise such. (1986:264–265)

While all these measures are feasible and some of them are already accepted in practice (e.g., permanent part-time work in the public service, teaching, etc.), there are significant political difficulties in their introduction on a wider scale. By and large, non-market production is tolerated only so far as it remains marginal and is not seen to threaten the market. Any potential threat meets with strong reaction from the 'free' enterprise, as, for example was the case with the workers' cooperative scheme in New South Wales (Jamrozik and Beck, 1981). In the present political and economic climate there are no signs of any consequence to indicate that this situation will change. Governments of whatever political persuasion now follow the policy of 'sound economic management' that is, policies that meet with the approval of international capital. Yet, to consider seriously the growth of household economy in terms of 'alternative production' is to challenge the capitalist system.

Development of the household economy as an alternative mode of production would depend on certain prerequisites. First, there would have to be a redefinition of the meaning of 'work', as argued by Nissel (1980) and Jones (1982), among many others. Another prerequisite would be integration, or rather re-integration of the household with the community. Hinrichs, Offe and Wiesenthal argue that the future of the household economy, indeed the future of work itself, will depend on the development of links between the family and the community. They say, '... cooperatives, clubs, private associations, voluntary networks of various kinds ... demonstrate that work outside employment can also be dramatically improved not only in its productivity, but also in the quality of goods and services it produces' (1984/85:53). They see in such activities the means for 'uncoupling work from employment', which would enable people whose hold on the formal labour market is tenuous or who are unemployed to engage in productive activities. However, they also emphasise that such activities would not be viable without active promotion and support by government.

Consideration of the household economy also raises the question of conceptualisation and measurement of value. At present, there are attempts to compare the tasks performed in the household with the value, or cost, of similar tasks performed in the market. However, it is questionable whether such comparisons are valid, or whether they should be used. First, a measurement instrument such as the GDP is itself a 'flawed' instrument because it measures gains and losses as a 'product'. It is primarily an 'accounting convention' that represents the volume of exchange, not necessarily the value of goods and services produced. Second, to measure the 'use value' of the household economy by the 'exchange value' of the market is to subjugate household economy to the criteria of the market, thereby attempting to commodify activities that are supposed to be a countervailing force against commodification. A similar problem occurs when the value of work performed in the household or the value of voluntary effort in the community is measured by the 'opportunity cost' forgone by the person who performs such tasks. As Roustang explains:

> ...in order to be able to trace production of market and non-market goods and services, our whole statistical system needs to be rethought, and, over and above the conceptualisation of our economic life, the way in which we picture it to ourselves needs to be changed. Our present conception remains based on the market sector, which makes it impossible to have adequate information on the whole of economic reality and to act both on the formal and informal economy. (1983:16)

Roustang argues that alternatives to the market economy have to be based and evaluated on non-market criteria: 'mode of production' has to be replaced by 'mode of life', and 'standard of living' has to give way to 'quality of life'. The household economy, therefore, needs to be considered not only in terms of non-market concepts of economic value but also in terms of a different social philosophy.

In conclusion, I have attempted to identify a number of factors which, in my view, need to be considered in relation to the future of the household economy. First among these is the capitalist system within which the families and households operate and, by and large, function primarily as units of consumption for goods and services produced in the market. An integral part of the capitalist system is the class structure — a structure of inequality in which some family households have certain advantage and relative autonomy because of their members' position of advantage in the market, e.g., employment in a professional occupation and corresponding income and work conditions. Family households whose members do not have a good position in the market have little autonomy and function in a precarious state of dependence on income support and other services provided by the state.

I have also argued that over the past two decades or so debates on social issues have progressively turned to middle-class interests, although arguments are often presented as if those issues affected equally all households. Yet, evidence from research on such aspects of social life as employment, income distribution, consumption patterns and lifestyles, as well as access to services provided by the state such as health, education and childcare, clearly favour the relatively affluent middle classes, especially the 'new middle class' of two-income households. Thus both the market economy and the welfare state contribute to the persistence and growth of inequality of a class society.

In discussing the future of the household economy, therefore, we need to consider whether the kind of future we might regard as desirable will, or can, reverse or at least attenuate the current trends towards greater inequality in society. Past and present indications are that such a reversal of trends is likely to be difficult to achieve.

MARGO HUXLEY

Commentary

I want to make a plea for clear conceptualisations of the terms we are using and the objects of our study because these will affect our strategies. We need to unpack the black boxes of 'formal economy', 'household economy', 'unit of consumption' and 'social class'. In such a short response I will be able to give only the most superficial indication of the sort of unpacking that needs to be done, and the implications for strategies that different conceptualisations can have.

First I would like to examine the statement that the household is, or could be, 'a countervailing force against the commodification pressures of the market'. At the same time the family household under capitalism is defined as a unit of consumption. However, this implies that the ideal household is one totally based on consuming marketed commodities—every article needed is bought on the market and every activity commodified. Even though such a situation is not inconceivable, and might well 'release' women from unpaid work into paid work, expand markets, increase employment and make the tax department happy, it is hardly autonomy from the market. The corollary is, therefore, that those households with the least money and assets are the most freed from consumerist commodification and have the most autonomy. It would thus seem that conceptualising the household as a unit of consumption cannot capture the aspects of autonomy from the market that appear to be desirable.

Perhaps identification of the household as a bulwark against commodification lies in examining the *work* done in the family unit—and the significance different conceptualisations of work have for our strategies. Does autonomy from the market consist in the fact that household work is *unpaid*? This unpaid work may be truly free from the market and potentially liberating *if it is done for oneself*. However, a 'family household' implies a traditional arrangement where women work, unpaid, for others; unpaid work for others is usually termed *slavery*. Sexual relations, and even feelings of altruism and respect may exist between the participants in a system of slavery but such a system cannot be equated with conditions of equality or autonomy.

Hence, we need to ask: What is the significance of the work done by the 'family household'? Does it constitute a separate mode of production (Delphy, 1984) or does household work serve to reproduce the workers, the class structures and the ideologies of the capitalist system? Or is there an 'informal sphere' predicated on non-economic altruism, as some contributions to this book imply?

In one sense at least, a separate 'household sphere' can be conceptualised, because this coincides with the *meanings* attached to household activities by the participants themselves. Ideology or not, most traditional households see the support and continuation of their families as the reasons for which paid employment is undertaken, money expended, work done. That is, the formal economy exists to support the household unit.

For women, work has almost always been uncoupled from employment. Jill Matthews (1984) has pointed out that women's experience of work is fluid and overlapping, involving many roles at once, not necessarily segregated by time, place or payment, nor unidirectionally progressing along an unproblematic 'career' or pay-increment path.

The meaning of 'autonomy' implicit in the idea of a 'household sphere' must be critically examined. Autonomy from the formal economy, or from commodification, sounds suspiciously like the idea of 'home as haven' from the hectic pressures or dulling routines of paid work—very much a male-centred view. Many traditional male household tasks are those with the greatest job satisfaction: lawns stay mown, windows fixed, cars washed, extensions built much longer than beds stay made, dishes washed, meals cooked or rooms tidied. Home is a place where many men can indulge in satisfying 'pottering': but few women have such a luxury.

It may be that in some households work and the responsibility for it is being renegotiated (see chapter 3), but this renegotiation is bound up in the class and gender structures of society. Renegotiations take place within and through the constraints and opportunities of these structures. By and large, the beginnings of change in gender expectations are the prerogative of the educated and the affluent, and are related to changing expectations and practices in paid employment.

One strategy might be to re-educate men—workers, unions, employers, governments alike—to provide work-based childcare, and to create flexible conditions for men and women involved in family households. This might help to overcome Jamrozik's gloomy prognosis about middle-class women's entrance into paid work being predicated on a double exploitation of working-class women as childcarers. But if work-based childcare applied only to highly-paid or middle-level white-collar jobs, then babysitting might be closed off as a way of making ends meet for the unemployed.

From examining some of the possible meanings of work and the implications for strategies, we must turn to examining the question of *class* in relation to the 'household economy'. If we see the household economy as separate from the formal market, and class as determined by stratification status (income and occupation) in the market, then indeed the class position of a family household *will* be determined by the fortunes of whoever is in the paid labour market under patriarchy, usually the male breadwinner. But what is the class (stratification) position of the households of the long-term unemployed; of households with two working adults; or of individuals *within* the household unit, whether in paid work or not? Feminists (e.g. Delphy, 1984; Garnsey, 1982) have shown that stratification studies cannot provide the ranking of a total society, as once was claimed. Particularly, in treating household class position as synonymous with the stratification position of the male wage earner, these rankings completely deny separate status to women.

Of the many conceptions of class, I can only deal with the implications of one aspect of the debate. This is the view that class is part of, and class practices create, the social totality. Without reducing the complexity of society to an economistic opposition between capital and labour, nevertheless, it is meaningful to see class as part and parcel of everyday life. The 'household economy' is also part of the social whole, and class relations are as integral to the non-market as to the market sphere (e.g., Connell, 1977; Connell and Irving, 1980).

We cannot simply lump certain activities together on the basis of their being unpaid or voluntary, undertaken on the basis of barter or for 'black' cash. Such activities are imbued with class significance. Middle-class 'voluntary work', such as joining resident action groups, school committees, anti-war movements or women's education groups, is reproducing the values and life chances of middle-class families, as well as enhancing (male and female) employment status and even improving property values. (See also Cass [1978] for a discussion of the relationship between gender and class.) Community self-help by the less affluent can provide childcare and care for the elderly in a direct communal way, albeit firmly within capitalist, patriarchal power structures (that is, the unpaid work is carried out by women). Such networks, even though they may be eroding rapidly, reproduce class situations, both socially and spatially.

Hence, an explanation for increased middle-class family networking might be found in greater levels of car ownership. In addition, with structural unemployment, not only of unskilled, but increasingly semi-skilled and skilled labour, people are able to trade these skills 'informally' for cash or kind (see Pahl, 1984). It is the 'unskilled' white-collar workers who are helpless in the face of a broken-down car or washing machine.

Nevertheless, Pahl (1984) shows that households with more money from whatever source 'get by' better, which supports Jamrozik's argument. However, Pahl does not fully analyse the implications of these changing everyday practices in terms of class or gender relations. He advocates a minimum wage *to the household*, a policy that does nothing about the internal inequalities within the household, and of course, ensures the household is not only 'self-sufficiently' active, but can actively continue to consume commodified goods.

Before policy recommendations are made, we need to examine more closely the relationships between class, gender and the household: sometimes our policies have a nasty habit of rebounding on us.

> The forced growth of informal work that Mingione describes for Italy can be appropriately described in a Marxist perspective, but there is, in fact, a remarkable congruence between such an approach and the views of some right-wing economists in Britain. They, too, see informal work as a survival strategy of the poor, although they adopt quite different policy perspectives. Patrick Minford has argued that unemployed people 'can do useful things at home and even earn some small amounts legally while claiming benefits', and he proposes that unemployment benefits be reduced in order to encourage workers to take low-paid employment. (Pahl 1984: p. 319)

This brings me to a final conceptualisation, which needs to be debated in relation to the autonomy of the household: that of the state. If the state is not altruistically concerned with providing welfare in a liberal or socialist democracy, but with providing the conditions for the continuation of capitalism; and if the 'household economy' is part of the system of capitalism and not autonomous from its divisions of power by class and gender, then we must not be surprised or dismayed if state welfare policies benefit the more powerful over the less. Rather, we must match our strategies to grapple with the implications of our conceptions.

PART 2

Women in the Household

5 Women in the home

MARY DRAPER

Over recent years changes have occurred in equal employment opportunity for women, shared parenting and the division of household tasks within families. Notwithstanding these changes, women today are still largely socialised in a manner that sees housework and associated family responsibilities as principally a female area. Accordingly, the majority of Australian women conform to a lifestyle that involves prolonged periods at home.

The Women in the Home Project

The following profile of the needs and concerns of women at home is based on the findings of a nine-month study by the Victorian Women's Consultative Council (VWCC), the Women in the Home Project, of which a report was published in December 1986. The VWCC is a body of nineteen women appointed by the Victorian Premier to consult with women in the community and advise him on issues affecting the status of women.

Initially there were some fears expressed that a project such as this might establish an artificial boundary between women in the home and women in paid employment and fail to recognise their common experiences. The VWCC was cognisant of this factor, but it also recognised that regardless of the extent of their involvement in paid or unpaid work, most women continue to have primary responsibility for childcare and domestic tasks, move in and out of the paid workforce according to the age of their children and the availability of suitable work, and face common problems brought about by the fact that in general, women are a less powerful group in our society with less access to a range of educational and employment opportunities.

As a group, women at home perform a multitude of socially necessary tasks in the course of their daily work. They rear and nurture children, maintain the home and service other members of the household. Women are responsible for the *management* of the household. By this I mean the usual range of management tasks — strategic decision making, negotiation, initiation, policy, budgeting, time management, priority setting, etc. They usually do these tasks in combination and frequently combine them with voluntary work in the community, care of the disabled or elderly and participation in the paid workforce.

Whilst the work of these women and their contribution to the family, the community and the economy, have major implications for social policies, all too frequently they fail to receive recognition in Government policies and programmes. The Women in the Home Project was designed as a discrete time-limited project aimed at collecting data on the needs and concerns of women in the home. Data were collected through the distribution of a discussion paper and questionnaire and by conducting consultative forums with 235 women in a variety of Victorian suburbs and towns.

The project had enormous breadth and necessitated an early decision to define its boundaries. Whilst it was acknowledged that women in the home comprise many disparate groups with a range of needs to be addressed by Government, it was necessary to narrow the field of study and pay particular attention to the issues of status, childcare, education, training and retraining and employment.

A discussion paper was used as a major vehicle for publicising the project, raising the issues and stimulating responses from women in the home in Victoria. In all 10 500 copies of the discussion paper were distributed throughout Victoria between July and September 1986. Both popular press and radio gave coverage to the discussion paper. The paper incorporated a comment sheet combining a series of structured and open-ended questions.

The questions were:

- Please describe how you have found your experience of being a woman in the home.
- Which of the following are difficulties which you experience as a woman in the home?
  (Please tick as many as appropriate.)
  Family poverty
  Lack of personal income
  Social isolation
  Child care
  Transport
  Lack of leisure time
  Lack of status as a woman in the home
  Other: please specify ....
  If you have ticked more than one, please enter the number of

the main difficulty affecting you.
Comments ....
• What would help you to overcome these difficulties?

Although the sample is a self-selected one, the very large number of returns (about 1000) and the wide range of sources of returns has ensured that the material can be considered as relatively representative of the views of women in the home. There are however, three kinds of bias—under-representation of non-English-speaking women, the usual questionnaire bias in favour of articulate women, and clustering in the 25–60 age group, reflecting the distribution channels.

Responses

The vast majority of returned comment sheets contained extremely detailed replies to the open-ended questions, with a significant number of respondents including additional pages. Most indicated a largely positive response to being in the home, with many suggesting that they wanted to remain in the home at least until their children were of school age. Almost all indicated that they experienced some difficulties and sought to alleviate these to make their lives easier. Only a small percentage of respondents indicated a totally positive or totally negative experience.

Of those respondents who noted a totally positive experience, most were women in the over 54 age group who believed that being in the home caring for the family was a responsibility of women which they accepted and were prepared to bear without complaint.

Despite the poor status afforded the work of women in the home, the majority of women surveyed (65.8 percent) largely enjoyed the experience. These women described their experience as important and worthwhile. The following quote is a good example of the perceived positive aspects: 'Being able to spend the time at home while my children have been growing up has been one of the most enjoyable times of my life. I would not have passed up this opportunity for anything'.

Not surprisingly, given that nurturing is one of women's major social roles, child-oriented activities were a major source of enjoyment and satisfaction for 84 percent of respondents. Of these women, 38 percent described time spent with their children as a major source of enjoyment; 31 percent observing the development and growth of their children, and 6 percent teaching their children.

Additional sources of enjoyment and satisfaction noted by these women included involvement in activities outside the home such as volunteer community work, involvement in their local playgroup, neighbourhood house or school council.

Over 6 percent of respondents noted that having a helpful husband or partner made their work in the home more satisfying. These partners usually acknowledged the importance of that work whilst also at times assisting them with aspects of their work, including child care. As stated by one woman: 'My husband has always been very active in the care and raising of our children. I know that without this, my attitude to staying at home would have been very different'.

The significance which respondents attached to these factors varied according to age, life cycle, individual circumstances and personal expectations. Certain factors had particular significance for those women whose lives are disadvantaged by their migrant status, disabilities, poverty, or care of an incapacitated spouse or relative. For example, women who experienced family poverty indicated that this was a constant source of worry, which frequently created feelings of depression and social isolation. Immigrant women were frequently cut off from extended family supports, and often denied access to sources of support and personal enrichment or services such as childcare, due to language or cultural barriers. Women with disabilities were frequently living on very low incomes and without access to sources of support and personal enrichment. Women who were caring for an incapacitated spouse or relative were frequently under great stress. Many experienced financial hardship, whilst others noted the loss of personal identity, social isolation and fatigue as particular characteristics of their circumstances.

Three areas rated particularly highly with women over all age groups and socio-economic circumstances. The lack of money, and, in particular, the lack of a personal income, was noted as a difficulty by 64 percent of respondents, lack of status of the woman in the home was noted as a difficulty by 55 percent, and the lack of leisure time was noted as a difficulty by 55 percent of respondents.

Figure 5.1 shows the number of responses to each of the areas of difficulty experienced as a woman in the home. The total number of respondents was 972.

For many respondents, being at home was a conscious decision made in order to fulfil what they saw as their parental responsibility to their children. Some women made this decision without reservation though many more noted that doing so necessitated some personal sacrifice and at times, financial hardship.

Particular mention was made of the difficulty experienced trying to survive on one income or a pension and the difficulty of

Figure 5.1 Difficulties experienced as a woman in the home

[Bar chart showing number of respondents (total = 972) experiencing various difficulties, with shaded portions indicating "Main difficulty": Family poverty, Lack of personal income, Social isolation, Childcare, Transport, Lack of leisure, Lack of status, Other, None]

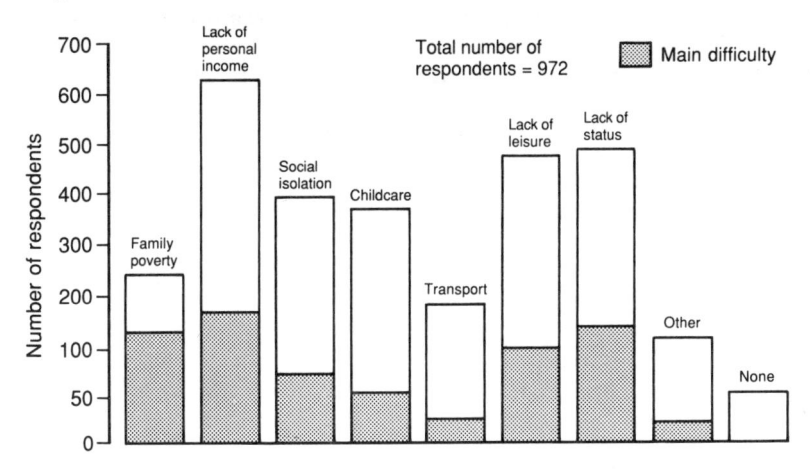

adjusting to the transition from paid employment to work in the home.

Approximately 37 percent of the sample found their experience of being at home to be a largely negative one. These women described it as tedious, repetitive, unfulfilling, isolating and demanding. One woman described it in stark terms: 'Real emotional upheaval...great loneliness and frequent boredom perpetuated by the frustrations of coping with a very dependent, demanding child...I have a dissatisfaction, a deep-rooted yearning for greater and more stimulating contact with a larger group of people'.

The suggestion that women in the home lack social standing and status is captured by the following comments:

> I enjoy my job of mothering but do feel it deserves more credit from the Government and communities in general. No sick leave for mothers, no annual leave, seven-day weeks, no unions—all of which we accept, but don't we deserve a little credit?

> I have found being a woman at home the complete opposite of what I expected, having been in the workforce for ten years...bringing up children is a demanding, self-sacrificing job with lousy pay...but [I] feel too many people are too quick to judge women at home. Our lot is not as easy as it may appear. I have never experienced such emotional and physical exhaustion, or such little recognition for what I do on a daily basis.

The significance of these views cannot be underestimated. Nor can the often-mentioned fact that women in the home were not asked for all of the details sought from other citizens in the 1986 population census. This was seen by these women to reflect the Government's and community's lack of interest or commitment to them.

The project findings confirm that occupational status is a very important consideration for women in the home. Oakley (1974a:71) notes the association between work dissatisfaction and the perception of low self-esteem in which the housework role is held. Generally, it appears that this factor impacts most profoundly on the self-esteem of the woman in the home.

Suggestions for improvements

Although the experiences of respondents varied, there was considerable similarity in the suggestions they made for improvements in the lives of women at home. Many felt that such change should commence with the early education of boys and girls on the importance of women's and men's work in the home. Others felt that it should start with women developing confidence in their role. Others felt that men, and particularly spouses and partners, should give greater respect to women in the home. Sixty-two percent of respondents felt that the community at large should develop a greater appreciation of the work of women in the home.

The need to recognise the breadth of voluntary community work undertaken by women in the home was also repeatedly emphasised. It was suggested that women's voluntary work should be recognised through the subsidisation of volunteer-related costs, for example, travel and child care and through an acceptance by both potential employers and educational institutions of the skills acquired through voluntary work.

A large number of women (64 percent) cited the lack of a personal income as a difficulty. For some this related to family poverty or a feeling of guilt associated with spending family income, which they had not earned directly, on themselves. For others it was inextricably linked with their status as women at home. Some women argued that the Government, and hence the community, should demonstrate its commitment to the work of women in the home through the payment of an allowance or wage for work done in the home.

Throughout the project a large number of women pointed out that women at home, particularly those caring for young children or people with disabilities or incapacities, rarely had time to themselves to rest, attend appointments or pursue their own interests. 'Time out' was seen to be vital to physical and emotional health. This required a range of social, recreational and educational (both vocational and non-vocational) opportunities to enable women in the home to make constructive use of their time out; facilities such as low-cost, occasional and part-time childcare at the local level in shopping complexes, neighbourhood centres and educational institutions; and further, low-cost carers to be available to relieve the primary carers of the elderly or people with disabilities.

Many women in the home are socially isolated. Much of women's work at home takes place in the privacy of the home whilst working alone. Feelings of loneliness and isolation may be accentuated by geographic isolation, financial hardship, separation from established family or friendship networks, cultural or other barriers normally experienced by ethnic women and women with disabilities, or lack of opportunities for socialising. They may also be exacerbated by a lack of immediate neighbours, given that these may be working away from their homes or may be much older or not speak the same language. The lack of recognition and status attached to this work causes many women in the home to lose self-confidence and self-esteem.

The suggestions made to reduce the social isolation of women in the home were many and varied, however the most frequently emphasised were an adequate system of both cheap and reliable public transport and community buses for women without access to private transport; and local, non-stigmatising support services, including neighbourhood centres and outreach work.

As indicated previously, more and more women today are seeking opportunities to move in and out of the workforce according to their life cycles and family responsibilities. This was true for a significant proportion of women who participated in the project. Difficulties encountered in returning to the workforce were created by the lack of suitable employment opportunities, the shortage of part-time jobs (preferred by 72 percent of respondents interested in returning to the paid workforce), a loss of confidence and out-of-date or non-marketable work skills.

It was suggested that women at home could be assisted in their return to the paid workforce by flexible employment practices and the increased availability of part-time employment opportunities; avenues of education, training and re-training that are responsive to the needs of women in the home, and recognise that in the transition from the home to education or work there is a frequent need for confidence-building; protection from exploitation (particularly of part-time and outworkers — including family day-care caregivers); and reasonably priced, good quality childcare.

In addition it was stressed that the Government should ensure that the needs and concerns of women in the home are given due recognition in the formulation of Government policies and programmes. For example, the Government's commitment to deinstitutionalisation was cited by respondents as a policy with particular implications for women. Generally it is women who are caring for people who may otherwise be in institutions. Many women give up positions in the paid labour force in order to assume the role of carer. It was argued that the women who choose to do this should receive adequate financial, domiciliary and personal support.

The project proved to be both timely and necessary. This was demonstrated by the interest the project received from women at home, policy makers and the media. Women in the home are a disparate group with a wide range of needs and experiences, who desire a greater voice in affairs, who demand that their needs be met by the community at large, and by the Government in particular, and who offer constructive suggestions for change when given the opportunity and encouragement to do so.

Conclusion

One of the strengths of the project is the lifecycle approach to the issue of women at home. The lifecycle approach describes the reality of most women's lives today. Most women today will spend some time at home, be it for six months, six years or sixteen years. Whatever the period, many women will experience the mixture of hard work, pleasure and frustration described by this study.

It is the *nature of the activity* that should be the focus of attention, and the issues that surround it—its location outside the market, the lack of social provision, and the precise nature of the devaluation (or lack of evaluation) of the activity. How much of a person's life is spent doing it is largely irrelevant. Theoretically, the same issues link it to the invisibility of workers' family responsibilities in the labour market and the devaluation of female work. Politically, most women can relate to the issue in this way.

DOROTHY BROOM

Commentary

This commentary consists mostly of questions, but in raising issues, I would not want to give the impression that my main reaction is negative. Until about a decade ago, it was routine to rely on common sense, on the world-taken-for-granted when it came to women's work in the home—if, indeed, such work was considered at all. Normal standards of social scientific research were suspended where the household was concerned; and it is still quite common for political and scientific decisions to be made about the domestic sphere on the basis of 'what everybody knows', omitting altogether systematic study of the place, the work, and the workers. So this research is a welcome addition to the (now growing) literature that is based on actual investigation of the household, and it is particularly welcome because it concentrates what women themselves have to say about domestic labour. Another recent study (undertaken by a South Australian Women's Health Centre on elderly women) was entitled—in the words of one of the respondents—'It was nice to be asked'. Similarly, in the case of Draper's study, it is appropriate and useful that women themselves should have been asked.

The Victorian Women's Consultative Council has done a lot with minimal research resources. But their resources were limited, and those limitations raise some questions. Draper's chapter would be considerably enriched if we could see exactly what was triggering such frequently strong reactions from women in the home.

One of the first things we would need to know is the definition of 'women in the home'. This definition is crucial as virtually all research on household work shows that women do the vast bulk of it, regardless of their marital, maternal, or employment status. It is also important for developing an understanding of how women see themselves: what are their salient statuses at a given time?

The discussion paper used the following statements as their definition of women in the home:

> Women in the home are also known as housewives and homemakers. They are women who assume major responsibility for the care of the

home. They may also care for children, the elderly, the sick and/or people with disabilities.

For the purpose of this project the Council has defined women in the home as women from school leaving age upwards, not engaged in full-time or regular part-time employment, nor in full-time study, who spend the major part of their time involved in domestic duties at home. Women in the home may be married, single or living with a partner and may or may not have children.

Is this definition, in fact, a negative one—based on what the respondents do *not* do (full-time paid work) rather than on what they *do* do (child care and household work)? In the end, I suspect that the definition is a subjective one, based on how women conceptualise themselves. There is, in my view, nothing wrong with such a definition, but if it is the criterion, we need to know many more details about those who identified themselves as being 'at home' in order for the results of the study to be most useful. For example, if some women at home are doing part-time paid work, it would be interesting to know which women identify as 'in the home' despite being employed, and what does this identification mean? Although it is clearly beyond the scope of the research reported here, an obvious addition to future research would be the inclusion of similar women who do not define themselves as being in the home to determine how different their overall circumstances and experience of domestic life are from women like the ones in this study.

Indeed, it seems to me that we do not, in fact, know as much as we might about the women who are included here, and there are several issues surrounding the nature of the sample that must be addressed if the conclusions drawn from this work are to be appropriately framed. For example, does the sample underrepresent mother-headed households and women who live alone? I suspect it does, but I cannot be sure. It would appear that the definition of 'women in the home' applied most directly to young women, nearly all of whom had dependent children. In turn, this suggests the possibility of an important self-selection factor favouring women from households who could afford for the wife/mother to remain at home full time, and who preferred to do so. Similarly, the study presents no information on the women's education, the amount or sources of their income, their husband or partner's occupation, or other data on which any assessment of socio-economic status might be based.

As a consequence of these omissions, it is difficult to know how far to generalise from this self-selected sample. The study surely reports on an important group of women whose voices ought to be heard, but women—even women at home—find themselves in a variety of familial and material circumstances, and if the range of those circumstances is not reflected in the sample, this should be acknowledged. Who a study does *not* include is as important as who it *does* include, particularly if the study is to be used as the basis for policy formulation.

Despite the possibility that the sample over-represents better-educated, better-off, more articulate women, it is striking that lack of personal income was the most frequently cited difficulty (mentioned by 64 percent) and that family poverty was also mentioned by 27 percent. The study, and the policy options relevant to it, must take account of the class position of families, and the possibility of maldistribution of resources within families, as Edwards (1981) has shown. Despite the cautionary note sounded in chapter 4, this study prompts me to wonder how far the state might, indeed, effect significant redistribution of resources by the provision of adequate child care.

A central theme in the chapter is the notion that women in the home suffer from 'lack of status'. I found myself puzzled as to exactly what this problem is, in view of the fact that 55 percent of the women reported it as a problem. I arrived at several hypotheses about the underlying meaning of the notion:

- Does it mean that they feel their work is not socially recognised or valued? And if it is not valued, who exactly fails to value it? Their families? Feminists? Employed women? Men? The state? And how would it be recognised? Would anything short of a living wage signal adequately the real value of their work?
- Are they concerned about a perceived lack of something akin to 'occupational prestige'? Studies of occupational prestige that have included a category such as 'housewife' or 'homemaker' generally find that respondents place the category somewhere around the middle of the prestige hierarchy. But women in the home — or these women in the home, anyway, may not perceive it in those terms.
- Are they indicating the need for some concrete help or relief from their work. Are they saying, effectively, 'This work is so low that nobody would do it unless they had to, and I'm stuck with it'? Is this really a code for asking for time off?
- Is the issue that they would like to feel somehow different — and better — about themselves and what they do? Such a feeling could involve several of the elements already mentioned in some kind of combination.

I was struck by the ambiguity and ambivalence that suffused much of what the women were saying. This is a feature of almost all the studies of domestic work with which I am familiar.

In this study, the women are mainly positive about what they do, especially caring for their children who are, after all, why most of them are *in* the home in the first place. But the majority also mention difficulties of various kinds. This impression of mixed emotions strikes me as an important element to emphasise. It is a valuable antidote to two kinds of thinking that have deflected constructive consideration of women's lives, and the policies that might grow out of such consideration. First, it provides a check to ideological 'trash the family' rhetoric that insults the vast bulk of women who will marry, have children, and make major sacrifices in their commitment to their families, regardless of a political analysis that identifies the family — however correctly — as a 'site of women's oppression'. And second, an emphasis on women's ambivalence about their domestic lives provides a needed corrective to equally ideological, romanticised statements about families, homes and the place of women in these social institutions. It would be well if we were all regularly reminded that, whatever else it is, housework is *work*, often hard work, time- and energy-consuming work; and that like most work, it has its good points and its bad points. Different women feel differently about it, and since most women do most of it, and they do it for most of their adult lives, how they feel about it is important to the quality of their lives. The fact that most women have mixed feelings about their lives at home should come as no surprise, but it is a fact that is usually forgotten in debates about women in the home.

6 Female sole-parent households

HELEN BROWNLEE

Female sole parents are a group with a high risk of having incomes below the poverty line (Gallagher, 1985). Not only is a large proportion of this group dependent on Government cash benefits as their main source of income (Cass, 1986a:3), but female sole parents tend to have low incomes even when in employment (Cass, 1986b:66).

The recent Social Security Review Issues Paper No. 3 argues that sole parents should be provided with a realistic choice as to whether to participate solely in the household economy or to combine household activities with participation in the market economy (Raymond, 1987:11). The paper argues that levels of income support should be adequate for sole parents who want to stay at home and care for their children, but that there must be more incentives and support for those who want to participate in the market economy.

Research studies have found a number of factors associated with the labour market participation of female sole parents (Cass, 1986a; Cass, 1986b; Funder, 1986b; Frey, 1986; Raymond, 1987). These include the ages and number of children, which relate to the parent's status of having the sole responsibility of caring for her children; the parent's level of skills or qualifications; her age; the length of time spent out of the labour market caring for children, which may lead to loss of confidence and self-esteem; the lower wage rates in the traditionally female occupations, particularly those in which sole parents are concentrated; the availability of paid work according to geographical location; and the disincentives for sole-parent pensioners and beneficiaries to earn income because of the combined effects of taxation and the social security income tests.

This chapter presents qualitative data from a current AIFS panel study of low-income households with children. It examines the current labour market choices of a small group of female sole parents and the factors affecting such choices.

Description of the study

This panel study is part of an evaluation of the impact of the Victorian Ministry of Housing's Loan Scheme for low-income households. The 500 households that obtained housing loans under the pilot scheme were all on very low incomes of $200 a week or less when they originally applied for a loan in 1984. Almost half of the heads of these households are sole parents. All households had to agree to participate in the AIFS evaluation study as one of the conditions of receiving a housing loan. The sole parents were first interviewed between November 1985 and June 1986, after moving into their home purchased under the scheme. The majority of households contained only a sole-parent

Table 6.1 Comparison of interview group and Australia-wide population of female sole parents

	Interview group[a] %	Australia-wide[b] %
Marital status		
Separated	23	30
Divorced	54	37
Widowed	8	13
Never married	15	20
Number of children		
One	29	51
Two	41	33
Three or more	29	16
Age of youngest dependent child		
0–4 years	28	30
5–9 years	35	26
10–14 years	21	31
15–20 years	16	13
Educational qualifications		
Left school < 16	59	46
Left school 16+	23	29
Trade or diploma	12	20
Degree	6	5
Employment status		
Full-time	5	21
Part-time	27	14
Looking for work	19	7
Not looking for work	49	59

Notes: [a] Sample of 92 in 1986 CAPIL Pilot Evaluation Study for Ministry of Housing by Australian Institute of Family Studies.
[b] Marital status for population of 238 600 in 1982; number of children, age of youngest dependent child and employment status for population of 279 000 in July 1985; education qualifications for population of 237 600 in 1981–82.
Source: *Social Security Review* 1986

Table 6.2 Labour market characteristics of sample of sole parents

	In paid work n=30	Looking for paid work n=17	Not looking for paid work n=45
Marital status			
Never married	6	1	7
Separated	5	5	11
Divorced	16	9	25
Widowed	3	2	2
Age			
20–24 years	1	—	5
25–34 years	16	9	20
35–44 years	11	7	10
45 years +	2	1	10
Level of schooling completed			
Form 3 or lower	6	9	21
Form 4	8	3	7
Form 5	5	1	5
Form 6	7	1	2
Post-school qualifications			
— degree	2	—	4
— other (e.g., business course or apprenticeship)	2	3	6
Level of schooling of youngest child			
Pre-school	5	4	18
Primary	16	8	12
Secondary	9	5	15
Number of children			
One	10	4	13
Two	14	4	20
Three or more	6	9	12

Source: CAPIL Pilot Evaluation Study for Ministry of Housing. Australian Institute of Family Studies, 1986.

family; in a very small number of cases, the households also contained boarders or relatives.

The chapter explores case study material from 92 female sole-parent households, from whom detailed occupational and employment history data were collected. Participants in the study were asked about their current circumstances and about their personal history over the preceding ten-year period, relating to their education, training, employment and housing.

Although our subjects are not representative of the entire population of female sole parents (Table 6.1) or even low-income female sole parents, the qualitative analysis provides some detailed information on female sole parents and labour market

Table 6.3 Sole parents in paid work: Occupational group and hours worked

Occupational group[a]	n=30
Para-professionals	2
Clerks	11
Salespersons and personal service workers	11
Labourers and related workers	6
Hours worked	n=30
Part-time	16
Casual/part-time	9
Full-time	4
Casual/full-time	1

Notes: [a] Australian Bureau of Statistics (1986) *Australian Standard Classification of Occupations*

Source: CAPIL Pilot Evaluation Study for Ministry of Housing, Australian Institute of Family Studies, 1986.

participation. Tables 6.2 and 6.3 show the labour market characteristics of the female sole parents included in the study.

Factors affecting sole parents' labour market participation

The following section examines the factors affecting current labour market choices of female sole parents. Women who were in paid work described their current labour market participation; those who were looking for paid work discussed the type of work they were seeking and their difficulties in obtaining work; those who were neither in paid work nor looking for paid work discussed the reasons for this situation.

The following factors emerged as affecting the choices made by this group of sole parents regarding their participation in paid employment.

The responsibility of caring for children

Having the sole responsibility of caring for their children was viewed by these women as a major factor affecting their choices regarding labour market participation. They were not simply concerned with inadequate childcare facilities, but expressed a strong desire to care for their children and emphasised the importance of their children's needs. Not only mothers with pre-school children expressed their concerns about the responsibility of caring for their children, but also mothers with only primary and/or secondary school age children.

Of those sole mothers who were in paid work, the majority were employed part-time, either in permanent or casual work. This is, of course, a characteristic of the sample selection. Those working full-time were unlikely to be eligible for the loan, unless they were very poorly paid. Many of the women said that they arranged their hours of paid employment to fit in with their children's needs. One mother, working part-time as a secretary, said, 'Now that I've moved to this area, I leave work earlier to get back to pick up my nine-year-old daughter from school'. Another woman was employed as a teachers aide in a high school, so that she could be home with her two teenage children during the school holidays.

Although these women were not asked specifically about their childcare arrangements, many of those who were in paid employment had a strong support network of family and friends who provided them with child care and other forms of assistance. Cass has noted that, unlike married mothers, sole parents do not have the child care services of a partner if they work outside conventional market working hours (Cass, 1986b:8). In this group, sole parents who were working nights and/or weekends used other family members to care for their children while they were at work. One sole parent with three primary school age children had been working as a nurse's aide on shift work at a local nursing home while her mother looked after the children. Another woman, who had a part-time casual waitressing job at a local hotel, left her teenage daughter to look after her three-year-old son while she worked on a late afternoon and evening shift.

Voysey in her study of single parents in Sydney similarly found that the most common forms of assistance received by those who were in paid work was informal childcare from family and friends (Voysey, 1986:404). Ochiltree and Amato found that children who are or have been in single-parent families tend to take more of a share in the running of the household than children in two-parent families (Ochiltree and Amato, 1984). This includes older children caring for younger children or for themselves while the parent is working.

The majority of female sole parents who were looking for paid work were looking for part-time work, where they could combine their child-rearing responsibilities with paid employment outside the home. One mother with three primary school age children said, 'I'm looking for a part-time job. It has to be close to home, so I can get back for the kids after school'.

Thirty sole parents who were not looking for paid work said that this was because of the needs of their children. Fourteen of these women had a pre-school child, but only four mentioned concerns about the lack of child care facilities or the expense of childcare for pre-school children. Only three mothers with a pre-school child said that the lack or expense of child care was the main reason they were not looking for paid work. Sixteen women with primary and/or secondary school age children only said that the responsibility of caring for their children was a reason for not seeking paid employment. One mother whose youngest child was six said, 'I can't go and look for work, not with a little one'. Six women said that they had given up looking for paid work because they had been unable to find a job with suitable hours, where they could combine paid employment with their responsibility of caring for their children.

Five sole mothers who were not looking for paid work had other specific caring responsibilities. Three women had a disabled child; one woman had a chronically sick child; another woman not only had her daughter, a sole parent, living with her, but was also responsible for the care of her elderly father.

Employment, training and labour market experience

The majority of the 30 sole parents in the labour market were employed in clerical and sales positions. Many of those with paid work were employed in traditionally female occupations, such as supermarket cashier, clerk or nurse's aide, which were low status and low paid. Other women, however, had jobs that required a level of skill or training, such as secretarial or welfare work.

Those who were in paid employment tended to have a higher level of educational qualifications or skills than those who were not working and to have upgraded those skills since they had left school. However, they were not always in employment that was commensurate with their skills. Those who were not in paid work tended to have a less consistent pattern of labour market participation and to have spent longer periods out of the labour market over the ten year period than those who were in paid work at the time of the interview.

One sole parent had left school after Form 4 and worked as a sales assistant in a department store. She had left the labour market when her son was born, but had returned to her old job on a part-time basis a year later. Another woman had trained as a bank teller when she was married with young children. She had worked full-time in this position until two years after she was separated, when she changed to casual, part-time work. Another sole parent had trained as a social worker before her child was born and had gone back to part-time paid work when her marriage broke up.

Many of the sole parents who were not in paid employment had very low levels of skills and qualifications and had been out of the labour market for several years. Seventeen women had not been in paid employment for ten years or more. One woman, who had worked as a secretary when she was first married, had not been in the paid workforce for 25 years. When she was asked why she was not looking for paid work, she answered, 'I'm afraid; I haven't worked for so long'. Four migrant women had not been in the labour market since they came to Australia. Another nine women had never had a paid job. One sole mother, a widow with a primary school age and a pre-school child described herself as a 'full-time mother'. She had married eighteen months after she left school and had her first child a year later, without spending any time in the paid workforce.

Those not in paid employment, but who had some consistent paid work experience over the ten years and/or a high level of skills or qualifications were in very diverse circumstances. Some were looking for paid work, others said they could not take a paid job because of the high costs and lack of availability of childcare, while one woman was upgrading her qualifications in order to get a better job. A single parent who had worked as a bookkeeper and accounts clerk had moved out of the labour market when her second child was born. She was later separated from her husband and went on a pension. However, now that both her children were at school and the family was settled in its own home, she was looking for a part-time paid job where she could use her skills and experience. Another mother had moved in and out of the labour market over the ten year period, employed in part-time clerical work. She was not looking for paid work when interviewed because of the expense of childcare with a pre-schooler. She had previously lost a paid job because her children were sick and there was no-one to care for them.

It is probable that a number of those with a consistent history of paid work and/or a high level of skills or qualifications will re-enter the labour market at a later date. Some of these women are in fact working in the informal economy doing home-based work such as door-to-door selling or babysitting.

Personal characteristics

Women not in paid employment felt that personal characteristics such as health, age and language difficulties prevented them from participating in the labour market. Seven women said that they were not looking for paid work because they were in poor health. A sole parent of 28, who had never had a paid job, said that she could not undertake market employment because she was nervous with people and also had back problems.

Only one sole parent, in her early fifties, felt that her age prevented her from getting a paid job. Most women felt that their health, the length of time spent out of the labour market and their lack of skills were greater barriers to paid employment.

Six single parents not in the labour market were non-English-speaking. A Greek woman who had been in Australia for two years said, 'I can't find work because of my English—it's not good enough'.

Social security benefits

Many sole parents who had paid work showed a keen awareness of how the extra income that they earned would affect their pension and related concessions. They often limited their paid working hours to stay within the parameters of the income tests.

A sole parent working on a casual basis as a part-time barmaid said, 'It doesn't matter where I work. I work as long as I get some extra income. I don't work a lot during the year—just a little bit so they don't cut off my pension'. One woman working as a part-time clerical assistant said, 'I make certain that I don't earn enough income to have my pensioner health benefit card cut off. The concessions are worth far more to me than the extra income I'd earn'. This woman worked on an hourly basis and said that she often did not claim her pay for all the hours she worked simply for this reason. Another sole parent living in a country area had taken advantage of the income-averaging effects of the earnings concession which allowed her to earn up to a specific amount of income within a set period without having her pension withdrawn. Over the past ten years, she had worked for an eight-week period every year as a full-time fruit picker while still retaining her pension.

Other women not in paid employment viewed the loss of their social security benefits as a disincentive to enter paid employment. A sole parent looking for part-time work said, 'It's a problem. If I earn too much on part-time work my pension will be cut down. If I give up maintenance I could get a job, but that would affect maintenance for the kids'.

Some women who said that they were not working appeared to be working in the cash economy in order to supplement their inadequate incomes and avoid the harsh effect of the income tests and taxation upon relatively small amounts of earned income (Brownlee, 1985).

Access to work

Sole parents' choices regarding labour market participation were affected both by the availability of paid jobs in their local area and by their access to other areas where jobs were available.

Many of those who were in paid work were employed in their local area. Four women said that they had specifically bought a home closer to their place of work. As one woman said, 'It's much more convenient living here in terms of reduced travel time and petrol expenses'. Other sole parents who were in paid work, however, had changed their employment patterns because their new home was further away from work. Since it took longer to travel to work, two women had reduced their hours of paid work so that they would not be away from their children for a greater period of time. Two other women, however, had increased their hours of paid work to cover the increased costs they had experienced since moving into a new home. The majority of women who were in paid work travelled to work by private car, four took public transport and two rode a bicycle or walked.

Many women not in paid work said that this was because there were no jobs available, particularly part-time jobs. As one woman said, 'There are just no jobs in a small country town like this. I'd have to travel to ————, 80 kilometres away, to get work. That's where the jobs are; in large country towns rather than here'. Several of those looking for paid work stressed the importance of working locally not only to minimise the costs of transport, but, more importantly, the time spent travelling. Some sole parents had bought homes in areas where they planned to find paid work. One sole parent living in a country town said, 'I want to work locally. The other towns are too far away. I bought a house where I wanted there to be the possibility of jobs of various sorts'. Six women said that they were not in paid work because of problems with transport; four of these women had no car. Another sole parent who was looking for paid part-time work said, 'I can only look for work locally, since my car isn't very reliable'. She lived in an inner urban area of the city where there was a very high rate of unemployment.

Policy implications

This brief analysis of a small group of low-income sole parents shows that the factors affecting the choices made by these women regarding labour market participation are multiple, complex and often inter-related. It is apparent that they are a heterogeneous group whose needs cannot be met by any one specific policy.

The majority of single parents in this group who wanted paid work wanted part-time work close to home where they could combine employment with their responsibilities as a sole parent who did not have the services of another partner to share in the household tasks and child care duties. Raymond notes that 'unpublished data from the ABS survey, Persons not in the Labour

Force, March 1986, showed that 75 per cent of sole mothers wanting work preferred part-time employment' (Raymond, 1987:73).

Around a third of the group had lived with parents or other members of their family for some period, and they and several other women were currently receiving assistance with household tasks and childcare from family members and friends. There was also some indication of bartering of goods and services between sole parent and family members and friends, for instance, family members would help with repairs on the house in exchange for meals provided by the sole parent. It is not clear, however, that these arrangements of informal assistance were necessarily satisfactory to the sole parent needing such assistance. Some sole mothers may have preferred to purchase these goods and services in the formal market, but have been prevented from doing so by lack of adequate services and personal financial resources.

Voysey indicates that these forms of assistance exchange were unsatisfactory to many of the single parents she interviewed, since they felt trapped in dependence on a relationship that was one of 'asymmetrical need' (Voysey, 1986:404). Ochiltree and Amato also state that the involvement of children in duties in single-parent households and childcare may not necessarily be beneficial to the child (Ochiltree and Amato, 1984). These responsibilities may lead to increased independence and competence, but may be very stressful if the child is too young to handle the experience.

A number of policy initiatives need to be implemented to give sole parents a realistic choice between participating solely in the household economy and combining paid employment with household duties and childcare.

These policy initiatives include:

- adequate levels of income support for those not in the labour market;
- availability of low-cost child care, that is, pre-school, before- and after-school care and school-holiday care 'that children will attend happily' (Voysey, 1986:405);
- availability of more part-time paid work and/or work with flexible hours;
- availability of education and training programmes, particularly on the job training programmes for sole parents who have low skills and/or have been out of the labour market for long periods; and
- making the social security system more responsive to the needs of sole parents who want to undertake part-time paid work or short periods of part- or full-time paid work. This

includes reinstating the earnings concession and ensuring that the administrative system is more responsive to changes in the employment situation of sole parents.

Implementing these policies would significantly alleviate the poverty experienced by a large group of sole parents and their children.

MARYANN WULFF

Commentary

Brownlee suggests a bleak picture of how child care responsibilities, low levels of skills and qualifications, limited opportunities for part-time or flexible paid work and concern about the potential loss of social security benefits if working, all restrict a single mother's labour market choice. In fact, it might be said that the chapter concentrates more on labour market *constraints* rather than workforce choices! This is a useful and important message to counteract any myths or preconceptions we might hold about single mothers' supposed willingness to resign themselves to living off supporting mother's benefits. Nonetheless, I feel that research of this type is limited in the insights it can provide on the labour market patterns of single mothers, in large part due to three inadequacies:

- unrepresentative sample of single mothers;
- use of cross-sectional data; and
- inadequate analysis of the data.

Before moving on to discuss each of these points in turn, I would like to say that these criticisms, per se, do not lessen the importance of the policy recommendations offered—that is, adequate levels of income support, low cost child care, more part-time and flexible paid work, and so forth—but only that these recommendations are not necessarily a by-product of this piece of research.

Unrepresentative sample of single mothers

The author does admit that the 92 women interviewed in this study are not representative of all single mothers (or even of all low-income single mothers). The sample, they point out, was drawn for a very different purpose than that found in the current paper: that is, to evaluate the recipients of a low-interest housing loan scheme funded by the Victorian Ministry of

Housing. So, as a consequence, all the single mothers in the sample are recent home purchasers. In fact, the actual percentage of home purchasers among all single mothers in Australia is much lower — 35 percent at the 1981 census. The labour market patterns of the women in the sample also differ from the national picture: in the sample group, only 5 percent were in full-time paid employment compared with 21 percent nationally. Those of the sample group in paid part-time work is nearly double the national figure: 27 percent compared with 14 percent. Nearly a third more women in the sample group were divorced compared with national statistics on the marital status of single mothers. An unrepresentative sample does not necessarily mean that we can learn nothing from the experiences of these women, but it does suggest that we cannot generalise beyond these women to the wider population of single mothers. Caution must be exercised in making policy statements based on a biased sample. As public policy is by its very nature designed for *collectives* (that is, groups of people) rather than *individuals*, then we must be careful that the information we collect on special groups accurately reflects their life situations.

A second concern with the sample of 92 women stems from the fact that they are all single mothers. You might think this is a surprising criticism given that the chapter is about the workforce choices of single mothers! But I feel that what many researchers (and certainly not just this author) often commit is 'the fallacy of the off-beat group', that is, choosing a sample that is highly selective on the very factors that we want to study. At the heart of research is the comparison of cases that fall into different categories.

Let me illustrate. When we're curious about some special group, say, drug addicts or political terrorists or single mothers, then the temptation is great to draw a sample of drug addicts or terrorists or in this case single mothers. However, such designs remove almost all the variation within the key variables. All of this means that in order to study some group you should have another group for comparison. How do we know, for example, that the labour market choices discussed in this paper are the result of single-parenthood when the entire sample consists of single mothers? Or are the labour market choices the result of receiving a home-loan from the Ministry of Housing when in fact all the women received such a loan? The precise comparison group depends on the basic questions you are pursuing in your research: in the present case, it might be, for example, a comparison of single mothers with young children to married mothers of young children or with single mothers who did *not* receive a loan from the Ministry of Housing.

Use of cross-sectional data

There are always problems and difficulties when data that are collected for a particular purpose (in this case the evaluation of recipients of a low-interest housing loan) are then used to study another issue, such as labour market behaviour. You almost always have to settle for less information than you would prefer to have (i.e., childcare information was not collected in this survey). I personally encourage any additional analysis of survey data in the belief that there is a great deal of extra information collected during a survey that can answer a number of secondary questions. So in this sense I am not criticising the author for her use of the data collected for the Ministry of Housing. What I specifically want to address is the limitations of cross-sectional data (that is, data collected at one point in time) to study questions to do with women's childcare responsibilities and labour market behaviour.

Cross-sectional data are essentially static and therefore miss out on transitions and change over the life course. Women typically experience more complex interactions with the labour market and their paid work histories show greater diversity than men's. This pattern is essentially lost in cross-sectional data. Incidentally, the author does mention that ten-year retrospective information was collected on these women, but unfortunately little of that information is reported. When it is, it is quite insightful: for example, the mention that women who were not currently in paid work had spent longer periods out of the labour market during the previous ten years than those women who were currently in paid jobs. This suggests perhaps the loss of either market work skills or self-esteem that accrues with a long period spent outside paid employment. We need more longitudinal studies that tell us about change and transition over the life cycle, that highlight, for example, the intermittent pattern of market work experience by women as they try to balance family and work responsibilities. Movement in and out of the labour market, from full- to part-time paid work or part- to full-time paid work, are closely interlinked with changes in a woman's marital status, age, and birth of children.

Marital status is not a static state either. The Institute of Family Studies survey of the Economic Consequences of Divorce shows that the single state is, for many, a temporary phenomenon. Between 40 and 50 percent of divorced mothers interviewed by the institute had repartnered in a three-year period. Remarriage may well have a more positive and immediate effect on the household economy of single parent families than does the labour market participation of the mother. Of course, I am not suggesting that we design policies to increase the remarriage possibilities for single mothers, but rather that we should be aware of the transitional nature of single parenthood and the way in which marital status, child bearing and rearing, and labour market decisions all interact in a woman's life. We can best do this with research designs that are longitudinal.

Inadequate analysis of the data

The author describes the data analysis as 'qualitative', yet we are given none of the richness of insight that is provided by, say, in-depth life histories or participant observation. Good qualitative research occurs when the researcher can become immersed in the life situations of small groups of individuals. Admittedly, this type of research is seldom funded as it is time consuming and sometimes limited in its generalisability. What the author seems to mean by 'qualitative' is really frequency counts of some of the key variables. To illustrate, in the section discussing the reasons given for not looking for paid work, we are told that 'four mentioned lack of child care facilities', 'six said that they were unable to find a job with suitable hours', etc. Unless we are given a much fuller picture of the situations, motives, feelings, indeed world view, of these women, then it cannot really be described as qualitative analysis. Qualitative analysis when done well can certainly yield insights unavailable in most surveys. Some qualitative studies of single parents have shown us the almost contradictory finding that women on supporting parents benefit can actually feel more financially secure than they do within marriage because for the first time they have control over the money that is coming into the household. This type of information is hard to obtain in a structured interview.

To be useful, this present study needs to either go into much more qualitative detail on individual case histories, or to move further in the other direction—that is, be much more quantitative. Specially, the data could have been analysed in such a way as to capture the interactions among the several factors. For example, what is the relationship between age of mother, age of youngest child and labour market choice? Do older mothers of pre-school children opt more frequently for part-time paid work, as some studies have shown, than younger mothers. Or what is the interaction between marital status, age and labour market choice? Are young never-married mothers different in their labour market patterns from older, widowed mothers? I presume so, but we need the kind of data analysis that will provide this information. Although a sample of 92 women is small by survey standards, it still does permit some multi-variate analysis.

Concluding remarks

Having reviewed this chapter almost completely on methodological grounds, I'd like to end on a more positive note and suggest some of the concepts and ideas in the chapter that may provoke further discussion in the context of this book on women and the household economy.

At several points the author mentions forms of assistance that were coming into the households from relatives and friends. Over a third of the mothers had lived with relatives at some point and many received assistance with household tasks, child care, and exchange of goods and services. Does this not raise the possibility of conceptualising household economy beyond the boundaries of the nuclear family unit? All of the policies recommended in this paper relate directly to the mother–child household unit. Is there a way that we can support and encourage these informal sources of support that are clearly important to single mothers?

The author refers to policies that will provide a single mother with a 'realistic choice' concerning full- or part-time paid employment or staying outside the paid labour force. Is there such a thing as a neutral policy, that is, one that neither encourages nor discourages paid work participation? Policy decisions, although informed, guided or illuminated by statistical data and research are ultimately about values. How do we conceptualise single mothers: as normal and regular wage earners (with similar patterns of labour market participation to married mothers), or as young mothers with overwhelming responsibilities for child care? Which image becomes incorporated into policy? What is the best for children living with one parent only?

The answers to these questions are not at all clear. Ultimately research only contributes to the policy-making process when it is accompanied by open and frank exploration of the many values and assumptions involved.

7

DIANNE RUDD

Older women living alone

The ageing of Australia's population has generated considerable concern in Government and among service providers in recent years. Much of this concern emanates from increasing demands for income support and the provision of health and community services. Given that further significant proportionate and numeric growth in the aged population is expected by the turn of the century (Department of Immigration and Ethnic Affairs, 1985; Australian Bureau of Statistics, 1986a; Hugo, 1986), and assuming that welfare expenditure is unlikely to expand dramatically, it is vital that research is focussed on ensuring the most equitable and efficient allocation of scarce resources to the aged. Identifying the aged population most in need, or 'at risk' is becoming increasingly more difficult as changing life cycle norms and changing family structure, together with greater affluence, have promoted a growing range of options for the elderly, particularly widowed females, with regard to living arrangements.

In Australia (as in other western societies) there is an increasing propensity of the elderly to choose to live alone and to form separate households (see, Hugo, 1986; ABS, 1984b). However, little is known about the characteristics and life circumstances (and as a consequence the choices concerning living arrangements), of elderly people living in different residential environments and service contexts.

The general lack of information about the feasibility and operation of small, single-person, household economies of the elderly, is surprising, given the shift in government policy in recent years towards keeping aged persons in their own homes (or more specifically out of institutional care) for as long as possible. This recent emphasis on non-institutional care is represented in several Government reports. The initial debate (as the title suggests) was *In a Home or at Home* (Report from the House of Representatives Standing Committee on Expenditure, 1982) and as a response, a more detailed review of nursing homes and hostels and of policy issues (Department of Community Services, 1986). However, not until very recently has any consideration been given to factors that may influence the nature and extent of resources and service delivery systems in non-metropolitan areas, which have scattered settlement and small populations. As Howe (1986:3) argues, 'Yet a basic requirement for the realisation of alternatives in care is that the range of services available in any locality present adequate options of nursing home and community care'.

This chapter addresses a number of issues that arise from the fact that increasingly older women are living alone and forming one of the major population sub-groups. These women often tend to be socially and economically vulnerable, and increasingly localised within specific regions and metropolitan areas. As with the rising number of single-parent, female-headed households, the increase in the number of single-person elderly households represents a major change in the composition of Australian households. To a large extent the increasing number of older women living alone is due to the fact that there are significant differentials between male and female mortality, which tend to be exacerbated by most women being younger than their husbands. This effectively gives females at advanced ages a much higher probability than males of spending their last years of life widowed. It is unlikely that this situation will change in the near future, so we can quite confidently predict that one of the fastest growing household types will be sole elderly females, most often widowed but, given the current nature of family trends, increasingly likely to be divorced or separated (Hugo, 1986).

There is a growing body of literature based mainly on the elderly in the United States (e.g., Michael *et al.*, 1980; Pampel, 1983; Chevan and Korson, 1972; Glick, 1977; Shanas, 1980; Krivo and Mutchler, 1986; Thomas and Wister, 1984) that shows that the shift toward more single-person households among the elderly has not simply been due to demographics, but largely a result of changing resources and norms facilitating a wider range of living choices. These include a greater range of housing and social support services provided by Government; higher levels of real income; fewer kin with whom to live resulting from changing family size and marriage breakdown; and wider acceptability of independent living among the elderly. The aim of this chapter is not to explain the trend towards more independent living among the elderly, especially older women, in Australia, but to focus on the feasibility of doing so in different economic, social and community contexts.

Data and method

One very simple way of broadening our understanding of the propensity of older women to live alone is to look at the characteristics and circumstances of aged females in different communities. More specifically, we can study the potential options that make it feasible for older women to maintain independence (particularly on the death of a spouse and/or with increasing sickness and disability), in different service and community contexts. By establishing the demographic and living arrangement characteristics of the aged in different geographic or spatial contexts, census data can be highly useful for providing an initial assessment of factors likely to influence the ability of older women to live alone.

The analysis undertaken here focusses on several dimensions for which selected variables and indicators are used to differentiate between the metropolitan and non-metropolitan aged population in South Australia at the time of the 1981 census. The variables used to measure these dimensions were chosen on the basis of research on the aged in Australia, specifically of those living in their own homes (e.g., Howe, 1981; Kinnear and Graycar, 1984; Rowland, 1982a, 1982b; Kendig et al., 1983; Australian Council on the Ageing (ACOTA), 1985; Day, 1985; Kendig, 1986). This literature shows that women at older ages are among the aged most 'at risk'. Moreover, the community resource base and the availability of various forms of public, private and informal support (to include that of family), was seen to be one of the most important determinants of the characteristics and life satisfaction of aged persons.

An analysis based on census data will be somewhat restricted due to the questions asked at the census and the availability of appropriate geographic and age–sex disaggregations. Nevertheless, it provides a basis to argue that there are significant differences in the demographic and household characteristics of the aged population in the two broadly defined living environments to warrant further research at the individual or household level in local communities.

More specifically, the chapter argues a case for research to be conducted at the local or community level. This would serve as a more appropriate basis for policy makers and service providers to plan for future service provision for an increasing number of single-person elderly households. Although the analysis is rather narrowly focussed on South Australia, the findings should have application in other contexts.

Ageing differentials

At the outset it is important to show the distinctiveness of the distribution, composition and patterns of growth of South Australia's metropolitan and non-metropolitan aged populations. Less than a quarter of the state's aged population live outside metropolitan Adelaide. Of particular note there has been an increase between 1966 and 1981 of some 2.9 percentage points in the proportion of the 'old-old' population (75+ years) resident in the metropolitan area from 74.3 percent to 77.2 percent.

In fact the increase in the metropolitan area's share of the total aged population between 1966 and 1981 is entirely due to the more rapid growth of the 'old' aged (75+ years). While the rates of growth in the 'young' aged population (65-74 years) are similar for the two areas, it was found that generally the non-metropolitan part of the state showed significantly lower levels of population at the oldest ages, resulting in a more 'youthful' overall age structure in 1981.

Shifts in age structure are well demonstrated by the dependency ratio, which is commonly considered to be a good measure of the extent to which a population is ageing. The aged dependency ratio (the ratio of the number of persons aged 65 years and over per hundred persons aged 15 to 64 years) in the non-metropolitan area of the state rose quite dramatically from 13.6 to 15.1 over the 1976-81 intercensal period, and yet remained below that recorded for the metropolitan population (14.5 to 16.5) for the same period.

Commentators (e.g., Kobrin, 1976) on the changing size of households show that demographic changes in fertility and mortality can have a dramatic impact on household composition resulting in 'the rise of the primary individual'. Moreover, Kobrin (1976:131) states: 'It would seem that the effect of the ageing of the population was unimportant for males. The increase of males in the oldest ages was either less than the gains in survivorship their wives experienced or else obscured by increases in remarriage'. Overall, the rise in single-person elderly households in the United States has been almost entirely a female phenomenon, usually associated with widowhood.

Gender differentials

Census data for South Australia show that considerable differences exist in the ratio of older males to females. Generally the ratio of males to females in the non-metropolitan area is more evenly balanced for all older age groups; however, the gap increases with age.

Table 7.1 Masculinity ratios for people over 54 years old, South Australia, 1966 and 1981

Sector	Masculinity ratios (males per 100 females)			
	55–64 yrs	65–74 yrs	75+ yrs	85+ yrs
1966				
Metropolitan	94.0	68.9	56.9	48.0
Non-metropolitan	113.4	93.1	83.0	65.9
1981				
Metropolitan	87.1	78.9	50.0	34.0
Non-metropolitan	100.4	95.5	70.8	46.5

Source: ABS, Censuses 1966 and 1981

In 1981 the even balance between males and females aged 55–64 years in the non-metropolitan area drops to 70.8 males per 100 females aged 75+ years with a dramatic further decline to 46.5 for the 85+ age group. This compares with some 50 males per 100 females aged 75+ years and a mere 34 males per 100 females 85+ years in the metropolitan area. Given the longer life expectancy of females it is not unusual to have a higher proportion of older females to males in a given area, however the discrepancy that exists between the areas needs some careful consideration, as it is of major significance for the local and regional planning of service provision. As there is no clear evidence to suggest that males in rural areas generally experience longer life expectancy compared with those in metropolitan areas, or, alternatively, that females in rural areas have lower life expectancy when compared with their urban counterparts, it can be surmised that the gender difference is mainly attributable to patterns of elderly migration.

Field studies of the aged (e.g., Prinsley et al., 1979; Radford, Badcock and Hugo, 1981; Rudd and Hugo, 1983, 1985; Hugo, 1986) and detailed analyses of elderly migration (Rudd, 1987; Hugo, 1986) suggest that the discrepancy results from the selective movement of older women from rural areas. This outmigration is often due to changes in life circumstances, such as the onset of ill health or the death of husbands, and is associated with a lack of readily available, and (most importantly) accessible support systems, health services, and specialised aged care and accommodation in non-metropolitan areas. It is difficult to judge whether this pattern of movement of older women will change as more services and accommodation become available or whether a considerable amount of the present pattern of movement is closely associated with a desire to be close to children living in metropolitan Adelaide. If the latter is the case, it can be expected that the differential between the metropolitan and non-metropolitan areas in respect to gender of the older population will to a large extent remain the same.

Differentials in living arrangements and marital status

Studies of Australia's aged population (Day, 1985; Kendig et al., 1983; Howe, 1981, Rowland, 1982a; Kendig, 1986) show that the living arrangements and marital status of those aged residing in private dwellings (the non-institutionalised aged) are a major determinant of independence and wellbeing among the aged. Generally married couples living in their own homes were seen to be in a better position than persons, especially aged females, living by themselves.

Table 7.2 shows that the proportion of aged persons living by themselves was slightly higher (30.9 percent) in the metropolitan area. However, some 19.1 percent of non-metropolitan aged females lived alone in 1981 compared with almost a quarter of the aged females in the metropolitan area. By contrast, only a small percentage of aged males were living on their own, with a slightly higher proportion doing so in the non-metropolitan area. Aged persons living with their spouses were also more dominant in the non-metropolitan area.

Table 7.2 Living arrangements of people over 64 years old living in private dwellings, South Australia, 1981

Living arrangements	Metropolitan	Non-metropolitan
	%	%
Person with spouse	46.9	49.8
Other living arrangement[a]	22.2	22.7
Living alone —		
Males	6.3	8.4
Females	24.6	19.1

Note[a] Includes: head, spouse, other adults; head, other adults, etc.
Source: ABS, Census 1981

The marital status of the aged is contrasted in Table 7.3. It is evident that a higher proportion of non-metropolitan males over 64 years have never married, a higher proportion of non-metropolitan females were currently married and a lower proportion of females were widowed in the non-metropolitan area.

Females at the oldest ages have a much higher probability than men of living the remaining years of their lives without partners. Overall, some 42.6 percent of the 75+ population living in private dwellings in metropolitan Adelaide were widowed females in 1981 while the equivalent figure for the non-metropolitan area was 36.7 percent. The corresponding

Table 7.3 **Marital status of people over 64 years old living in private dwellings, South Australia, 1981**

Marital status	Males		Females	
	Metropolitan	Non-metropolitan	Metropolitan	Non-metropolitan
	%	%	%	%
Never married	4.6	6.9	6.9	5.1
Now married	78.1	75.6	40.9	47.0
Separated and divorced	4.2	4.0	3.8	2.2
Widowed	13.0	13.5	48.4	45.7

Source: ABS, Census 1981

figures for males were much lower, with a slightly higher proportion being widowed males 75+ in the non-metropolitan area (10.9 percent) than in Adelaide (8.8 percent).

Older widowed females living alone are considered to be the most in need of support, some of which is often provided by close family members, primarily a son or daughter (Kinnear and Graycar, 1984; Howe, 1981; Kendig, 1986; Day, 1986). Unfortunately the details available from the 1981 Census are insufficient to draw any conclusions about the relative advantage or disadvantage of non-metropolitan aged women in regard to numbers of offspring to provide support. Studies (Rudd and Hugo, 1983, 1985) of small country towns have shown that a high proportion of the children of the older population live in metropolitan Adelaide, and therefore it can be assumed that relocation is often necessary for older females who wish to obtain the support of their children.

Housing and accommodation differentials

Kendig and McCallum (1986) state that:

> The housing one brings to old age has many impacts on successful ageing. Whether the aged in the future will be owning or renting will have major implications for their dwellings will have an important bearing on their ability to keep living independently. Those whose housing becomes inappropriate in old age will need to move to more suitable accommodation.

Many of the differences in the living arrangements and marital status of the aged population are a consequence of the more restricted range and availability of specialised accommodation and housing for the aged living in most country towns and rural areas.

There is little difference in the proportion of the metropolitan and non-metropolitan aged population living in non-private dwellings (institutional care) in 1981. Some 10 842 persons in the metropolitan area aged 65+ years, or 10.6 percent, were living in non-private dwellings compared to 3046, or 9.2 percent of aged persons in the non-metropolitan area. However, from a closer examination of the type of non-private dwellings occupied in 1981, it is clear that quite different situations prevail in the two areas. There is a higher proportion (46.4 percent) of the metropolitan aged in non-private dwellings resident in nursing homes compared with only 19.9 percent of the non-metropolitan aged. Conversely, 35.4 percent of the non-metropolitan aged in non-private dwellings are in hospitals, compared with only 16 percent of their metropolitan counterparts. This discrepancy is explained by a lack of suitable specialised nursing home care, which forces non-metropolitan aged people into hospital care as long-stay patients.

Table 7.4 People over 64 years old living in non-private dwellings, South Australia, 1981

Type of non-private dwelling	Metropolitan %	Non-metropolitan %
Nursing home	46.0	19.9
Home for the aged	22.0	35.4
Hospital	16.0	35.4
Mental institution	5.8	0.2
Other non-private	9.8	21.0

Source: ABS: 1985 Catalogue No 4102.4 p. 21

From a closer examination of the older aged population (75+ years) resident in the various forms of housing (Table 7.5, it is clear that a larger proportion of the metropolitan 75+ population (26.1 percent compared with only 5.8 percent in the non-metropolitan area) are in medium density housing. By contrast 87.7 percent of the non-metropolitan 75+ population were living in separate houses in 1981.

Table 7.5 People over 74 years old living in private dwellings, South Australia, 1981

Dwelling type	Metropolitan %	Non-metropolitan %
Separate house	65.7	87.7
Semi-detached house	7.0	4.3
Other medium density[a]	26.1	5.8
Other[b]	1.2	2.2

Source: ABS Census 1981 (Microfiche Cross-Classified Table 81.501)
[a] Includes terrace houses, town houses, flats and home units up to 3 storeys
[b] Includes flats and home units over 3 storeys, improvised dwellings

Table 7.6 **Housing tenure of the metropolitan and non-metropolitan aged, South Australia, 1981**

Nature of occupancy	Metropolitan %	Non-metropolitan %
Owner	60.9	68.1
Owner/purchaser	12.8	8.4
Tenant (SAHT)[a]	10.1	6.0
Tenant private	10.1	6.9
Other[b] and not stated	6.1	10.5

Notes: [a] South Australian Housing Trust
[b] Occupying dwelling rent free or borrowed
Source: ABS, Census 1981

The nature of occupancy is of particular importance in assessing the wellbeing and financial security of the aged, as the type and quality of aged housing greatly influences their financial situation (Howe, 1981; Henderson, 1975; Kendig and McCallum, 1986). From Table 7.6 it is clear that a higher proportion of the non-metropolitan aged population owned their own homes, 68.1 percent compared with 60.9 percent in the metropolitan area. Most importantly, some 20.2 percent of the metropolitan aged population rented accommodation compared with only 12.9 percent of their non-metropolitan counterparts. It is interesting that the ratio of public to private rental accommodation occupied by the aged in 1981 was the same in both areas. However, the 'other' category, which included rent free dwellings, was higher in the non-metropolitan area. It can be suggested that the relatively high number of holiday homes and farm houses, often no longer used as such in country areas, form a useful 'pool' of housing for which other less formal arrangements in respect to rental payments are made. The availability of public provided accommodation is especially important for those aged on lower incomes to continue to live in the same area and to maintain links with their families and the wider community (Kendig, 1986). This is of particular importance in country areas with few alternate housing options available, and yet it was generally found that little specialised aged housing (public or private) exists. Moreover, much of the limited public funded housing is concentrated within the non-metropolitan area, which effectively causes the relocation of those aged persons requiring such accommodation (Rudd, 1987).

Community and health service differentials

Data on the provision of community and health services available at the regional level, and specifically at the local level, are limited and unreliable. Nevertheless, some patterns can be discerned from data compiled by the South Australian Department of Community Services in 1985, which show that the level of community resources, public expenditure and the range of services available to the aged, at least in a formal way, is overall much lower in non-metropolitan areas. In 1985 some 24 of the 30 metropolitan councils (80 percent) were currently involved in the Home and Community Care Scheme (HACC), compared with only 15 (16 percent) of the 93 non-metropolitan councils. Moreover, 60 percent or 18 of the 30 metropolitan councils were involved in the operation of a community bus service, while in non-metropolitan areas, where public transport is virtually non-existent, only 12 councils did so.

A high proportion of areas in South Australia have 'senior citizens' or other social clubs specifically for the aged. However, while 50 day-care centres for the aged operated in metropolitan Adelaide, non-metropolitan areas had only thirteen such centres located primarily in the major towns and provincial centres.

Table 7.7 shows the major differences in the levels of nursing home and hospital beds between the two areas. There were 19.7 nursing home beds per 65+ population in the non-metropolitan area in 1981 compared with 65.7 in the metropolitan sector. Moreover, some 50.3 percent of the approved non-metropolitan nursing home beds were deficit funded (operated on a non-profit basis) compared with 38.7 percent in the metropolitan area. There are comparable hospital bed rates between the two areas however 95.5 percent of beds in the non-metropolitan area were in public hospitals as compared to 52.2 percent of metropolitan beds.

Table 7.7 Hospital and nursing home beds, South Australia 1986

	Metropolitan	Non-metropolitan
Approved hospital beds		
Public	3264	2011
Private	2685	94
Commonwealth	301	–
Total	6250	2105
Beds per 1000[a]	61.3	64.8
Nursing home beds		
Charitable & religious	171	111
Participating-profit making	2975	206
Government	957	–
Deficit funded	2596	321
Total	6699	638
Beds per 1000[a]	65.7	19.7

Note: [a] Per 1000 persons aged 65+ years in 1981
Source: South Australian Health Commission, unpublished data

The evidence suggests that the non-metropolitan aged population have limited access to what could be considered to be a poor and inadequate, sometimes non-existent community resource base in respect to both public and private support systems. This inevitably leads to a high proportion of older widowed females moving to areas where a wider range of services and family support is more readily available.

Summary and discussion

The cross-sectional analysis of selected characteristics suggests that the aged living in private dwellings in the non-metropolitan area of South Australia are generally more independent with higher levels of wellbeing than is the case for their metropolitan counterparts. The indicators revealing the relative advantages of the non-metropolitan aged population are as follows:

- a higher proportion of older persons living as married couples;
- a lower proportion of widowed females;
- a lower proportion of females living by themselves;
- a higher incidence of workforce participation among older males and females;
- a higher proportion of aged persons living in separate houses that they own; and
- a lower proportion of aged persons in rental accommodation, both public and private.

On the other hand, the most notable 'perceived' disadvantages of the non-metropolitan aged population are:

- a high proportion of aged (no longer resident in private dwellings) in long-term hospital care;
- an extremely low proportion and small number of aged residents in any medium density housing, representing a range of smaller accommodation types;
- a shortage of public housing, specifically specialised aged accommodation;
- low levels of home-based services to keep the aged at advanced ages in their own homes for as long as possible; and
- limited nursing home accommodation and health service provision.

For the aged in need, as opposed to the needs of all the aged, it can be concluded that there was a lower proportion of aged persons 'at risk' in the non-metropolitan area. It can be argued however, that those aged in the non-metropolitan area most 'at risk', in particular widowed females living alone at advanced ages, require different policies and programmes to cater for their rather more specialised needs. This is a result of the more dispersed nature of settlement and the more scattered and unequal resource base. In many contexts, it appears that those aged with impaired health and restricted personal mobility, or with changed life circumstances, such as the death of a spouse, have 'coped' with a deficient service environment by moving. For this reason, an analysis of the characteristics and circumstances of the aged in a specific area, at a given point in time, may be a somewhat misleading basis for the identification of the aged most in need. Nevertheless, it can serve as a useful basis for further analyses of the ways in which a variety of resources, such as housing, specialised aged accommodation and community support services, may influence the propensity of older females to live alone in different residential settings. It must be recognised, however, that the income and resources of single-person household units vary significantly — hence some older women have the ability to pursue independent living arrangements even with increasing disability or dependence.

Returning to the theme of the chapter, it is clear that the feasibility of older women living independently appears to be strongly related to the availability of, and access to, community services and family. Kinnear and Graycar (1984) show that there is considerable back-up support to older women living alone in their own homes from close family members, and they look specifically at the role of women as carers.

The problems with defining aged dependency are discussed by Gibson (1985), and it is apparent that similar difficulties are associated with the concept of independence among older women. The terms are used here in a very simplistic way. The census data suggest that there are variations in the propensity of older females to maintain independent households according to the amounts of resources devoted to housing, health and specialised aged care and the availability of a range of community or home-based services. In other words, without certain levels of support that equate with varying degrees of dependency it is often difficult for older females to achieve 'independence' — to simply mean living alone in a single-person household unit.

Increasing household assistance with the tasks of everyday living and maintenance of the home leads to the consumption of Government-funded or private services for which payment is made (e.g., gardening, home maintenance, home help, etc.). This tends to lead to decreasing personal independence. And Kendig et al. (1983:120) conclude with respect to the needs of older people and levels of assistance: 'The amount of assistance depends largely on household structure. Married couples, even when one partner is disabled, occasionally have some outside help but seldom rely principally on it'. On the other hand, older females living alone are seen to be the main 'high risk group' and Kendig et al. (1983:118) state: 'Difficulties with transport, minor home assistance, or gardening are especially common among women living alone. In addition to having higher disability rates than men, many women are further restricted by life long conditioning to gender roles'.

The next step is to investigate more fully the operation of individual household units within specific residential and service contexts if we are to provide a better understanding of the needs of older women living alone, and particularly if we are focussing on the feasibility of greater independent living based on the expansion of community-based services for the elderly. This will probably involve comprehensive survey work designed to ascertain levels of local service provision and household requirements for adequate home care provision by Government or family. Levels of assistance with essential activities outside of the home — e.g., shopping, transport and social interaction — will also need to be surveyed. More information is also required on the ability of single-person elderly household units to finance the assistance they require.

If an aim of Government is to reduce the burden of an ageing population by attempting to keep older people in their own homes for as long as possible, it is important to recognise that this effectively means maintaining older women in independent living arrangements. This often represents assistance with relatively minor tasks such as gardening, home upkeep and home help, which are easily attainable for all who can afford to pay. All too often institutionalisation is the only alternative available to some of the more disadvantaged older women, and yet if more flexible community services, housing alternatives or income support were available these women would stand a greater chance of retaining independent living conditions in a range of residential environments.

Research and policy issues

The analysis of census data suggests that the choices involved in independent living arrangements tend to be restricted for aged persons living in the non-metropolitan area. Similar analyses of data for local areas and regions *within* the two sectors (Rudd, 1987) show marked differences in the levels of community support and options for older women to make choices about independent living arrangements or about more intensive levels of care, such as hospitalisation or institutionalisation within their own communities. These differences are not simply the result of demographic and economic factors but clearly reflect variations in the location of a wide range of housing types, specialised aged care and accommodation, hospital, medical and community services, including transport and a wide range of urban amenities. Further research is needed on matching local service provision, community support and amenity with the concentration in particular localities of single-person elderly households.

Since the allocation of resources to the aged is limited, it is important that service providers and policy makers take more account of the spatial context within which ageing is occurring and recognise that the impact of longer life expectancy effectively means growth in the number of dependent females. So that more effective and efficient programmes to service their needs can be planned, it follows that more should be known about the household economies of older women living alone and about their expectations for continuing to live independently in the future.

ELIZABETH OZANNE

Commentary

The population and topic of this chapter, older women living alone, is not well served in Australia. In fact, it was very difficult, in looking around Australia, to find a contributor on this topic. This is surprising given the heralded ageing of the Australian population and present Federal Government policy initiatives targeted at supporting the aged to continue to live in their own homes. Australian research is still preoccupied with the younger household and the tasks of child rearing and workforce participation. There appears to have been little conceptualisation of the tasks of the late-life household. This situation needs to be corrected.

In that this volume is, however, focussed on women and the household economy, Rudd's chapter identifies and highlights a major shift in the composition of Australian households — the rise of the aged single-person, usually female, household — which should be a focal issue for research and analysis. As most gerontologists know, the study of the older household is largely a study of widows, particularly in the old-old age group of 80 years and more.

Despite this predominant statistical picture, there are in fact many different ways of coming at the study of older women living alone. Part of the problem of conceptualising this particular late-life household is to be able to draw together some fairly diverse literatures generated from quite different research traditions and perspectives. There are also many different areas of decision-making to be considered.

From the perspective of housing options and choices, the work of Coleman and Watson (1987), Kendig (1981), Howe (1978) are relevant, as is the work of Rosenman (1981, 1982) on the economic and filial circumstances of widows. Some specific analysis of the tasks of older single and couple households has been explored by the ACOTA (1985) study of Older People at Home and the Kendig (1983) Ageing and Family Project.

There are now a mounting number of studies on rural/urban

and regional differences focussed on older women (Dempsey, 1981; Carter, 1981; Rowland, 1982a, 1982b; Rudd and Hugo, 1983; Hugo, 1986) using both ABS cross-sectional data and case-study material, and the study of factors affecting late life migration patterns (Prinsley et al., 1979; Census of Population and Housing 1981). Presently there appear to be few time-use studies of older households from an economic perspective, though further analysis of the ACOTA and ANU data sets might prove useful.

Essentially Rudd puts an argument for the importance of spatial/locational factors in explicating the circumstances of older female lone households in terms of the structural constraints such factors place on individual choice options. She does this by an analysis of metropolitan/non-metropolitan differences on a set of indicators gleaned primarily from the ABS 1981 1% Household File. Such analysis would appear to provide an important baseline for implementation of current home and community care service initiatives in metropolitan and non-metropolitan areas and provide an important baseline of comparison for more individually focussed studies.

In furthering the analysis of metropolitan/non-metropolitan differences however, as Rudd herself acknowledges, 'the operation of individual household units within specific residential and service contexts' would need to be examined. Longitudinal studies of the household economy of late life, and exploration of specific and critical decision points would add much to our present limited knowledge.

Rudd identifies the selective outmovement of older women from rural areas, coinciding predominantly with widowhood as a significant phenomenon in rural communities. This territorial relocation in late life has been noted in numerous studies (Yawney and Slover, 1979; George, 1980) and its effect on the household economies of these women must be profound, apart from its other direct social/psychological effects—but the reasons for this relocation, both structural and individual, are not well articulated by simply relying on a spatial/locational analysis.

A critical gender analysis might look to the nature of inheritance patterns in which farm properties are bequeathed to sons on the death of a male spouse. It is also apparent that many farm wives have city origins to which they return in widowhood. Such factors are as structural as the availability of services and local family support. Whether the non-metropolitan widow is better off than her metropolitan counterpart, by virtue of 'geographic advantage' is a moot point requiring further analysis from a broader theoretical and methodological perspective.

PART 3

Income Support for Households

8 Perspectives of fifty low-income households

JENNY TRETHEWEY

As detailed in chapter 5, recent research commissioned by the Victorian Premier on women's experience of life at home (Victorian Women's Consultative Council, 1986) found that many women described their life at home in terms of enjoyment and satisfaction. They particularly appreciated their involvement in their children's development and the opportunity to participate in community work and groups. However, 'women who experienced family poverty indicated that this affected their whole lives. It was a constant source of worry which frequently created feelings of depression and social isolation' (VWCC, 1986:39).

This juxtaposition of circumstances and experiences introduces the central theme of this chapter: the importance of a financially secure household economy and choice to people's sense of well-being and to the quality of their futures. The chapter is based on the findings of the Brotherhood of St Laurence's Income and Expenditure Study. The study, conducted between July 1985 and June 1986, was of 50 households reliant on unemployment benefit, a supporting parent's pension or a low wage. Data on the study's households are drawn from the first month of the study, July 1985. Forty-two households participated in the study for the full twelve months.

Forty-five of the households had dependent children. Twenty-three of these households were sole-parent families and 21 were couples with children. Five households in the study did not have children. Four were single adults, who no longer had responsibility for dependent children, and one was a couple without children.

The respondents kept a diary of their income and spending for a fortnight in each month, and were interviewed monthly about their spending priorities and the effects on themselves and their children of having insufficient income to meet their needs. Thirty-nine women and eleven men were the study's diary-keepers and interview respondents.

One hundred and sixteen children lived in the study's households. They spanned the age range from early childhood to adolescence. The families lived in inner and outer Melbourne suburbs and a small country town. They were private and public tenants and home owners.

As this was a small sample there is no attempt to argue its representativeness. But the accounts of the 50 families provide information and insights into the struggle of families to bring up children on a social-security income or a low wage.

The chapter begins with a description of the household economy and living standard of the 50 families, as reported by the key respondent. It then reports the choices the study's participants said they would like to make for the future support of themselves and their children. As work was the preferred choice of the majority of respondents, the barriers they said they experienced to getting a job are described. The chapter concludes by arguing that without significant changes to the income security system, child care services and labour market programmes, many low-income families face a bleak future, with few choices other than a continuation of their current subsistence lifestyle.

As this volume has women as its focus of interest, the study's findings were analysed and are presented in terms of gender differences. Where the perceptions and experiences of men and women had much in common, they are presented together. The women's roles as household manager and childcarer meant, however, that the future choices they said they would make, and the barriers they perceived to work, were different from the men's responses. These differences are described and their policy implications explored.

The state of low-income families' household economies

In the monthly description by the respondents of their families' spending priorities and living standards, there were many shared experiences and common themes. Each month we recorded the order in which each of the households said they paid their major costs. The majority of respondents consistently said they paid their rent first. Commonplace comments were: 'Always paid the rent first—it's the first thing off the list'; 'You've got to have a roof over your head'. Respondents said that priority was then given to paying electricity and gas bills and that whatever money remained went towards the purchase of food.

Housing and energy costs absorbed a large proportion of the families' low income. For instance, one single parent with two pre-school children who lived in a privately-rented unit in an outer suburb of Melbourne said she paid $90 rent per week. This absorbed 50 percent of her income, and left her with little money to manage all other household costs. Her case was typical of the families living in private rental accommodation.

In order to manage high housing and energy costs, all the respondents said their families were forced to cut back or go without basic necessities such as food, clothing and footwear, fuel and power, medical equipment and treatment and dental care. Other 'taken-for-granted' aspects of our community's standard of living, such as use of a private car and leisure activities, also could not be afforded.

A selection of comments from the 50 respondents illustrates the severe effects of such expenditure constraints upon the families' standard of living in relation to nutrition, clothing, energy, health and leisure. They are presented as a catalogue indicative of common experiences, rather than in order of importance. One mother of six children, whose husband had been unemployed for over two years, fed her family filling foods so that she could afford enough food: 'We start the meal with bread, then when they're not so empty I serve the meal'.

The comment of another woman with two children whose husband worked, epitomised the situation of many of the families during weeks of high costs: 'Christmas was a bad time. I used Barry's holiday pay to pay hospital and electricity bills. I did without meals and made bread and biscuits for the kids with the flour I had left'.

The majority of respondents said their families had few clothes or shoes: 'I have to wear the same pair of jeans all the time. I can't go out until they're dry' (wife of couple with three children, husband employed full-time). 'The children only have gumboots. I hope it rains when school starts then no-one will know they don't have shoes' (single parent, two children, widow's pension).

During the winter and cooler months of spring and autumn half the respondents said they cut back on heating their flats or houses to keep their gas and electricity bills within affordable limits: 'I can't afford to have the heater on when it's cold. So I never turn it on unless the kids are up' (single parent, two children, supporting parent's benefit).

Although able to use doctors and hospitals when they needed to, many respondents said they were unable to afford the medication or equipment prescribed by their doctor: 'G. needs special shoes because of his rheumatoid arthritis but these are being left until we have some extra cash' (couple, invalid pension). 'D.

is four and a chronic asthmatic. He needs a 94-dollar ventolin pump but the family cannot afford it' (couple, two children, husband employed full-time).

Leisure and recreation activities were beyond the reach of all the families. This meant that they lived very home-based lives. The restrictions that lack of money place on being able to usefully and enjoyably use one's time were often severely felt: 'I did some gardening but had to stop mowing as I ran out of petrol. I also have been making a rug but ran out of wool and so was again unable to finish it. I would have visited a few more friends but couldn't afford public transport costs, so had to limit my visits' (single parent, one child, supporting parent's benefit).

Parents also spoke of the effects on their children's development of living on a low income. None of the families in the study could afford to send their children on costly school excursions or camps: 'Our oldest boy will miss out on the camp at the end of the year. He realises we can't afford it' (couple with five children, unemployment benefit).

The men's responses: work

Of the 23 men in the study, sixteen (70 percent) said they would choose to work in the coming year, fifteen full-time and one invalid pensioner part-time. One man, who was a recently arrived Polish migrant, said he wished to continue to improve his English and convert his Polish qualifications so that he could continue to practise as a doctor. One single parent said he hoped to be able to return to work when his six-year-old son became more independent.

These men spoke of their wish to work in terms of greater financial security for their families, being a better 'provider' for their wives and children, and the improved self-esteem that work would bring: 'It would keep me occupied and give me a future. I would buy the kids more stuff—I hate begging' (single parent, four children, invalid pension). 'Self-respect is a real advantage of work. You feel pretty low on a pension' (single parent, one child).

Each of the five men who would choose to continue to receive a pension was over 50 and was an invalid pensioner. They saw their working life as over. Two of these men had been unemployed for some time and during the year of the study gave up hope of returning to work and had themselves classified as invalid. This illustrates a problem with the way social security assistance payments are structured. The better levels of assistance provided by the invalid pension may be encouraging the older unemployed to seek to classify themselves as sick or invalid and to permanently withdraw from the labour force.

The women's responses: work and childcare combined

Of the 41 women we interviewed, all but four had dependent children. Their consideration of the choices they would make for the coming year was very much influenced by their childcare responsibilities. Twenty-one women (51 percent) said they would choose to work in the coming year, but eighteen also said they would prefer part-time work so that they could combine caring for their children and work. Eighteen of the twenty women who were sole parents commented that their sole responsibility for the care of their children and the functioning of the household would make full-time work impossible. The eighteen women with male partners said care of children inhibited full-time work, but they also saw part-time work more as a means of supplementing husbands' incomes rather than as a means of supporting husbands and children.

The women's comments about their choice of work for the coming year centred on the importance of being able to continue to care for their children and the added self-esteem that work would bring. 'Work would keep me sane. It has a lot to do with having your own identity instead of being someone's wife or mother' (woman with four children, husband working). 'I wouldn't take on a full-time job with the kids—I like to be here when they get home from school. But it would be nice to have some independence—money that is mine' (woman with four children, husband working).

The women's responses: childcare at home

Fifteen women (37 percent) said they would choose to stay at home and care for their children in the coming year. As a sample of their comments attest, for most of these women this choice was governed by the importance they gave to the care of their children. For three women, however, it was a choice forced because they did not have access to affordable child care. At a later interview the father reported that his son was very withdrawn. He had so often been disappointed about missing school excursions and camps.

The fact of missing out also meant that the children were marked out as different from other children. The other obvious symbols of a low family income—lack of clothing and fewer possessions—made the children targets for stigmatising comments: 'The other children are always saying that we're poor. I suppose it does affect my kids because they feel they're inferior' (single parent, two children, widow's pension).

The living standard portrayed in the respondents' perception of their families' experiences is a subsistence one. And it was in these terms that the men and women in the study spoke of their lives: the constant struggle to stretch their income to house, clothe and feed their families. In the midst of such a struggle, consideration of the future is not a major preoccupation, so we asked the respondents about the future choices they would make for the support of themselves and their children.

Choices for the future

Over the twelve months of the study many of the men and women we interviewed spoke of their desire to work and what they missed now that they were not working: a better standard of living; the pride of providing for their family; the companionship of fellow workers; a sense of belonging; and greater confidence in themselves. We decided to explore this issue further in an addendum to the study's monthly questionnaire. We asked respondents that if they could choose, what choice would they make for themselves during the coming year. The list of choices they selected from included full- and part-time work; staying at home to care for children; and continuing to receive a benefit. Table 8.1 summarises their responses. 'The children are too young to take care of themselves. They have health problems and need special care' (woman with three children, husband working). 'I don't have any choice—I have to be here for the kids' (woman with three pre-school children, husband unemployed).

Table 8.1 Choices of 50 low-income households for the coming year

	Single parent		Couple		Single over 45	
	Female	Male	Female	Male	Female	Male
Full-time work	2	2		13	1	
Part-time work	8		10	1		
At home with children						
school age	5	1	3			
pre-school	4		3			
Study/training			1	1		
Marrying	1				1	
Continue receiving						
a benefit	1			3		2
Making children						
independent			1			
Total	21	3	18	18	2	2

When asked if their choice would change in five years time, seven of these women now choosing to stay at home said they would like to work when their children were less dependent upon them. Most of the other eight women saw their time out of the workforce, and their minimal work skills, as making them unemployable: 'I'm 48, my eldest son is 29. I haven't worked for 29 years — who's going to employ me?' (single parent, two dependent children).

Further, two women strongly believed that a woman's place is 'in the home'. They both hoped they would remarry someone who would support them: 'I'd like to have somebody who'd care about me and the kids and support us' (single parent, two pre-school children).

General barriers to work

As the majority of men and half the women we interviewed said work was their preferred choice for the coming year, we were interested to explore what were the factors inhibiting their workforce participation. We asked them about the barriers to getting a job. The following were identified as 'general' barriers.

Loss of Government concessions

Twenty-four adults (38 percent of all adults interviewed) said they were concerned that if they returned to work they would lose eligibility for Government concessions. The concessions were valued as a means of reducing their living costs, for example the costs of housing, energy and health. Their fear was that they would have great difficulty affording such costs if they had to pay full price. This high level of concern about loss of concessions needs to be viewed alongside the expectation of most that the wage they could earn would not be significantly more than their present pension or benefit. Hence they believed that the loss of concessions would mean a reduction in their living standards.

Single parents who said they would like to work part-time were particularly worried that work would mean loss of eligibility for concessions. In fact, if they were to earn the wage they expected, they would continue to be eligible for a part-pension and concessions. Therefore, concern about loss of concessions not only showed the importance of concessions to the people we interviewed, but also their lack of knowledge of pension and concession eligibility criteria.

All the people we interviewed believed low-wage earners should be eligible to receive concessions: 'When you're bringing home not much more than the pension, you're still in great need' (single parent, three children).

Health and age

Ten adults (16 percent) said their state of health prevented them joining the workforce. For example, one woman and two men attributed their ill health to their long time out of work or on a pension. One 46-year-old woman had struggled for twenty years to raise three children on a widow's pension. When the last child became independent she was transferred to unemployment benefit and expected to look for work: 'I can't go out to work now, I'm totally worn out'.

Two men had each been unemployed for over two years. For both men the role of provider for the family was an important part of their identities. Without work they developed stress-related illnesses. As one man's wife commented this meant that, 'He needs a job for his health, but now it's his health that is preventing him from working'.

Five of the men and women who saw their health preventing work were aged over 45. State of health and age were very much connected in their minds. They believed that the combination of age and illness meant that their working lives was over: 'I looked for work despite my back but after five years of looking I've given in and accepted it. I'm going to be a pensioner for the rest of my days' (man in his fifties with four children).

Finally, two respondents cited physical disability as the reason they had difficulty finding work. An invalid pensioner who had lost a foot in an industrial accident noted the usual response to his requests for work: 'They see me coming with one foot and say "no!"'. One woman commented: 'I've been knocked back for a few jobs because of my weight'.

Low educational qualifications

Nine adults (14 percent) saw their low level of education as hindering their work chances. Three of the five men now invalid pensioners also believed that better education would have meant a white-collar career and the chance to still be working: 'My education is not good enough to get a decent job' (primary-educated woman with four children, husband working). 'If I had a better education when I went to school then I could possibly still work' (male invalid pensioner).

Only six households in the study had an adult who had completed secondary school. Of these six, four adults were recently-arrived migrants whose poor English prevented them working in professional jobs comparable to those they had left in their native land. Two female single parents were completing post-secondary social and youth work courses.

All the other adults in the study, both men and women, had

left school by the age of fifteen or sixteen. Four adults only had a primary-school education, two in Lebanon and two in country Victoria: 'You only went on in high school if your parents could afford it. Mine couldn't' (widow's pensioner).

Lack of English
Eight of the adults who had migrated in the last five years were from Lebanon or Poland. Their lack of English was seen as a major impediment to work.

Location
The six adults who lived in country Victoria said that there were few jobs available in their area—for either men or women: 'My husband has only had three jobs to apply for in the last three years—all mill work. The wages were $195 per week. He went for interviews but didn't get the jobs' (couple with three children). 'I've got a part-time job at the local hotel. There are no full-time jobs in a country town, particularly if you're a woman over 40' (single parent, one dependent child).

Special barriers to work: women

The 41 women we interviewed included women whose male partners were the usual study respondents. They identified three additional barriers that they saw as hindering their ability to work: lack of childcare; lack of suitable work clothes; and the time they had spent out of the workforce caring for children.

Childcare
Fifteen women (37 percent) said they were unable to work because of their lack of access to childcare. Women with pre-school children said they lacked access to affordable day-care services. Women with school-age children commented that they lacked services for their children before and after school and during school holidays: 'Where I live there is no one who runs programmes for kids in school holidays' (single parent, three children, living in a small country town). However, two women with six children said they could not imagine how, even with childcare, they would manage to both work and care for children: 'With six children it would cost a lot of money if I went to work. And I'd still have to do the cooking for all of them when I got home' (woman with six children, husband unemployed).

Lack of suitable work clothes
Eleven women (27 percent) felt their lack of suitable work clothes inhibited them from considering a job. They felt they

could afford nothing suitable to wear to job interviews and would not be able to afford clothing after starting work. Throughout the twelve months of the study, the women we interviewed recorded that clothing was one of the costs they cut to a bare minimum in order to manage to pay rent and bills and buy food. They said they felt embarrassed by their lack of clothing when asked to social occasions or the times they felt they were in the public eye. The jobs many women hoped for—such as shop assistant or hotel worker—would require them to dress well.

To elucidate this point further, two women who began part-time work during the year of the study found replenishing a depleted wardrobe a cost not calculated in their plans to move from reliance on a pension to work: 'I have to be more dressy for work as I'm in contact with the public all the time—I'll need to buy some more clothes. This will probably cost me what I earn' (single parent, one child). 'I've had to buy extra clothes to work in, particularly shoes and undies. I have to change my uniform in front of other women and I was ashamed by the state of my underwear' (single parent, two dependent children).

Time out of the workforce

Six women (15 percent) felt that the many years they had spent caring for children would make it difficult to go back to work. New job skills were required for the jobs they had experience in and their years out of the workforce had eroded their confidence in thinking of themselves as workers: 'I've been out of the

Table 8.2 Perceived barriers to work among 50 low-income households

	Single parent	Couple Female	Couple Male	Single over 45	Total
Health	3	1	5	1	10
Level of wages		1	1		2
Childcare	8	7			15
Concessions:					
— health	2	2	2		6
— transport	2				2
— public housing		1	1		2
— all	8	4	2		14
Age		1	1	2	4
Work clothes	8	3			11
Few jobs in town	1	3	2		6
Education	3	3	2	1	9
No English	1	3	4		8
Time out	3	3			6
Total	39	32	20	4	95

workforce nine years. And then I just worked in a factory. I don't think I'm employable' (27-year-old woman with two children). 'I've been a housewife for so long I'm not trained to do anything else' (single parent, two children). 'I'd prefer a job. I'd rather work for the money than have it handed to me—but it's unrealistic. I haven't worked for fifteen years and the factories where I worked have shut down' (single parent, four children).

A summary of the responses on the perceived barriers to work is given in Table 8.2.

Discussion

This chapter began with a description of the state of 50 low-income families' household economy. Whether the household was headed by a female sole parent or an unemployed male breadwinner, the families shared the experience of a subsistence living standard. Spending on basic necessities such as food, clothing and footwear, and medical treatment had to be cut back or forgone in order to meet housing and energy costs.

The Brotherhood of St Laurence has long argued that employment is the best means of improving the living standards of families with adults of working age. And the majority of men and women in our study said that work was their preferred choice for the future support of themselves and their children. Their comments that work would mean regaining a sense of purpose and self-confidence also reinforce the concept that, in our work-centred society, work is an important source of personal, as well as economic, wellbeing.

However, the respondents' perceptions of the barriers hindering their workforce participation suggest that if we are to maximise their work choices, significant change is needed. These barriers do not comprise an exhaustive or definitive list. They do, however, indicate the need for change at two levels. First, in the short term, changes to the social security system are required. Many of these are under consideration by the Social Security Review. Essentially, the social security system needs to facilitate, rather than to hinder, pensioners' and beneficiaries' transition to work. Second, in the long term, the changes required are both the most difficult and the most important: addressing the labour market disadvantage of the men and women who are currently reliant on a social security income.

The short-term priority: social security

In the constant struggle to house, feed and clothe themselves and their families, consideration of the future cannot be a major preoccupation for these people. The provision of more adequate income security payments is therefore a priority. For to provide adults and children with sufficient income to ensure a more secure and viable standard of living—to have enough to eat and wear, to be able to afford to heat their homes in winter and buy medication—is to provide a basis from which they can plan for the long term and prepare for work, rather than wondering how they will manage to feed their children tomorrow.

In response to the Social Security Review Issues Paper on income support for families with children, the Brotherhood of St Laurence has identified the following income security measures as of immediate priority in order to ensure adequacy:

- additional pension/benefit payments and the family income supplement should be substantially increased and restructured to meet the increased costs of older (including school-aged) children;
- supplementary rent assistance should be increased to assist low-income families in private rental accommodation. A structured payment providing additional increases to families with children needs to be introduced;
- the mother's/guardian's allowance, payable to sole-parent pensioners and beneficiaries, should be increased so that additional payments to a sole parent with one child are equal to the married pension rate; and
- all additional payments to families with children should be indexed in line with the CPI increases (McClelland, 1987: 3–4).

The Brotherhood has also recommended that reform of the child-maintenance system should include the introduction of an advance maintenance payment. This payment would ensure that sole-parent households where the non-custodial parent did not immediately (or subsequently) pay maintenance, or only had a capacity to pay a small amount, would receive a guaranteed minimum amount right from the beginning of their time as a sole parent.

There are also changes which could be made to the social security system in the short term, which may assist pensioners and beneficiaries to move into the workforce. For instance, the barriers to work perceived by many of our study's respondents, such as loss of concessions and inability to afford work clothes, could be substantially removed by a continuation of partial pension and concession entitlement in the first months of work (as suggested by Raymond, 1987). Such a continuation would provide an income subsidy during the crucial period of establishment in the workforce when the costs of work are high (Montague, 1987).

The Brotherhood has made additional recommendations to the Review of measures that would assist the transition between social security recipiency and the workforce (McClelland 1987: 4):

- additional pension/benefit and the family income supplement should be integrated into a payment to all children in low-income households;
- the income level above which the family income supplement is withdrawn should be raised, with priority for introducing a child-related 'free' area;
- additional consideration should be given to measures to improve the low take-up rate of the family income supplement. If substantially increased take-up rates cannot be guaranteed, serious consideration should be given to assessing the ongoing role of the family income supplement as an effective way of assisting low wage earners with children;
- the level of allowable income for pensioners and beneficiaries should also be increased again, with particular priority to increasing child-related free areas; and
- the sole parent rebate and the mother's/guardian's allowance should be amalgamated into a new sole-parent allowance.

However, even if all these recommended reforms of the social security system were to be immediately implemented, there would still be many adults in these 50 families who would be unable to fulfil their stated wish to work. The degree of labour market disadvantage that they experience cannot be addressed by changes to the social security system alone.

The long-term priority: addressing labour market disadvantage

For the men we interviewed their vulnerability to long periods of unemployment was caused by their tenuous labour market position. Nearly all had low educational qualifications, no formal post-school training or trade certificate, and a work history of unskilled, low-wage, manual jobs. Their experiences support the argument that those who experience unemployment are more likely to have had low wages when they worked than those who experienced no unemployment (Whiteford 1986b:15).

The economic restructuring that Australia is undergoing is diminishing rather than increasing the number of available unskilled jobs. Future work opportunities for men such as these lie in retraining for more skilled jobs. Given their low level of formal education, many of the men in our study would require preliminary bridging courses to improve their literacy and to build their confidence in their ability to undertake new jobs. For the migrant men (and women), literacy and fluency in English would be an essential part of this skill-development process.

For women, there are special problems. The characteristics of the women we interviewed—low educational qualifications and few job skills—reinforce the findings of other studies of female social security recipients. For instance, a recent Department of Social Security (DSS) survey of sole-parent pensioners' workforce barriers (Frey, 1986) found that two-thirds of the women interviewed had left school at fifteen and under.

To explain the low level of education and work skills of many of the 80 women receiving social security incomes in their study, Montague and Stephens (1985) noted that their status as women, rather than their family background, was a key factor in their experiences. Montague and Stephens argued that women are expected to be home and family oriented. Training for this begins in the family where daughters are expected to help at home and are often discouraged from staying at school on the grounds that education is not important for wives and mothers. For most women, their experiences in the education system and the labour market reflect this expectation. Many women are given neither the skills nor the opportunities they need to be other than family oriented.

Certainly most women in our study defined themselves as homemakers and childcarers and had spent years out of the workforce caring for children. For many the transition to work would be a long-term plan, which enabled them 'to begin an educational and a labour force entry process in a gradual manner, with basic literacy, numeracy and language skills, assertiveness training, bridging courses and general orientation to work programs' (Montague, 1987:25).

However, women's life experience and definition of self was not the major barrier to work cited by the women in our study. As already noted, child care was identified as the major requisite controlling the women's work and training opportunities. In order to work, the women in our study said they required child care services they could afford in the neighbourhood where they lived, and not just for pre-school children.

While child care responsibilities affect all women, sole parents have to bear the cost alone in terms of money, time and emotion, and so experience a significantly greater degree of labour market disadvantage and parenting responsibility (Montague, 1987). Options for sole parents must therefore include a flexible mix of income-support payments, education, training and phased re-entry to the labour force while they have sole responsibility for dependent children.

The focus of discussion thus far has been upon the means, both short and long term, of ensuring that the futures of families, such as those in our study, include employment. It is worth re-emphasising that the cause of high rates of unemployment in Australia is not primarily the labour force barriers that prevent people taking up work, it is a mismatch of jobs and potential employees and a lack of jobs. Lack of jobs as the major barrier to joining the workforce was most clearly perceived by the men and women in the study who lived in small rural towns. Thus, all the above discussion presupposes that the generation of new jobs and job training must be a central aim of all state and Federal Governments' economic policies.

The findings of our study also show that for some pensioners work is not a future choice. Their health prevents work, or the disadvantages they face in the labour market are such that for them any intervention programme or policy change would be too little too late. For people whose futures hold 20 to 30 years reliance on a pension, access to public housing and adequate income security payments are crucial.

In conclusion, this chapter has argued that if families such as those we have studied are to have a viable household economy and a future of increased choices, long-term policies that address the labour market disadvantages of men and women reliant on social security incomes are essential. In the short term such national policy and change priorities are expensive, and they are therefore very difficult to sell in the current economic and political climate. Nonetheless, the long-term effects of inaction will be extremely costly—both for individual families and for Australia as a whole.

PETER SAUNDERS

Commentary

Research of the sort reported by Trethewey has an extremely important role to play in furthering our understanding of the extreme hardship faced by low-income families and the nature of some of the longer-term consequences for families living in poverty. The chapter provides many accounts given by the families themselves of their own struggles to survive and, perhaps more significantly, their longer-term aspirations. These convey a vivid but disturbing picture of the real effects on family living standards of poverty and inequalities of income, and of access to key social services and to the labour market.

Speaking personally, I find such simple yet moving accounts do so much more to bring home the true nature of poverty than those statistical estimates of the size and incidence of poverty with which I am more familiar. For this reason I hope that the Brotherhood of St Laurence will continue to undertake such work and to ensure that their findings are spread widely in the community.

One general impression I gained on reading the chapter was the total inadequacy, indeed irrelevance to poverty issues, of many of the traditional concepts and analytical tools that economists apply to household choices and decisions. The basic theory of consumer choice emphasises that individuals will make those choices that best serve their own interests. Thus, it is argued, for example, that cash transfers are in most instances preferable to in-kind or service provision because individuals are then free to allocate these additional cash resources in order to maximise their own satisfaction. If they choose not to purchase the services that might have been provided directly, this must be because they place greater value on other items and are thus better off by purchasing these items instead. There are, of course, limits to this line of reasoning, but its central tenet, freedom of choice, remains central to modern capitalist democracies.

Compare this with the notions of choice that the chapter reveals among the low-income families interviewed. For them, there was precious little choice in any aspect of their lives. Life was a matter of survival in which choice had almost no role to play. Increased housing costs, for example, did not result (at least in the short term) in a switch in consumption towards cheaper housing but simply limited the resources available for other goods. In other words, housing costs were not the result of any notion of *choice*, but rather acted as a *constraint* on other choices. This situation is, of course, not limited to low-income families only, although its implications are that much more serious when the amount of other resources is so small. These observations serve not only to question the relevance of mainstream economic theory to such issues but they also have policy implications. Among the more important of these is the extent to which increased income support alone is really the solution to the problems of low-income families, a point which emerges in several places in the chapter.

I shall now turn to some more specific comments. The discussion of choices with regard to work raised several questions in my mind. The first of these was the precise conditions of work that respondents had in mind when indicating their preferences for work (for it is their preferences that are under consideration, rather than their choices as such). Are we to conclude, for example, that respondents would prefer to work under *any* circumstances, irrespective of wage levels or working conditions more generally? This seems most unlikely, yet without more specification of such issues it is somewhat difficult to interpret the findings. There is some discussion later in the chapter on the question of the wages and conditions of work, which could have been integrated into the discussion of work preferences and choices. The overall impression I gained was that the perceived barriers to workforce participation among respondents were such as to render their work preferences as of almost no consequence. Furthermore, it appears that the spouses in two adult families were asked for their work preferences independently, yet in practice such decisions are more likely to be inter-related, and made on a family basis, as indeed is suggested for some female partners in responses on work and childcare.

The discussion of the barriers to work raises a number of interesting issues. Amongst these was the importance of loss of government concessions as a factor hindering transition to work. What was most significant in this context was that in the majority of cases shown in Table 8.2, respondents were concerned primarily about the loss of health, transport or public housing concessions rather than of cash benefits. Although the actual losses probably arise from the interaction of social security income tests and other income tests, this observation suggests that easing the pension or benefits income test *alone* may be of limited use in facilitating the transition to work. There was in general less emphasis given among respondents to the lack of employment opportunities as a barrier to work than I would have expected. In those instances where this factor was mentioned it was attributed to location rather than the lack of jobs itself. Some of the other barriers mentioned, in particular lack of educational qualifications and English, presumably affect the kind of job opportunities that might be available, a point that relates back to my earlier comments on interpreting the findings on the overall preference for work. Finally, the lack of access to an adequate and affordable range of childcare services was clearly a major factor for female partners and all single parents.

With regard to the priorities for reform canvassed by Trethewey, it seemed to me that the long-term priorities identified were more firmly based on the findings of the research than were the short-term priorities for social security reform. It did not seem to me, for example, that the social security reform options canvassed could be derived from the findings of the survey itself. I think the reform proposals might benefit from putting much more emphasis on the longer-term priorities and stress the more limited role that the social security system can play when viewed from this perspective.

I hope that the Brotherhood will extend this line of research and continue to track the circumstances of these low-income families over time. The survey has already revealed much of interest and it would be extremely useful to complement this with more detailed study of how low-income families adjust to prolonged periods in harsh economic and social circumstances and how, if ever, they manage to escape them.

BETTINA CASS & PETER WHITEFORD

9 Income support, the labour market and the household

This chapter discusses the interaction between the market and non-market activities of family members in households and the implications of this interaction for Government income-support policies.

Income-support policies can often be largely reactive to broader social and economic processes. Nevertheless, these programmes are a fundamental institution of resource allocation and can be applied to achieving a fairer distribution of income. Nor is there anything to apologise for in a set of social programmes responsive to changing social needs. Indeed, the current Social Security Review was established in order to identify longer-term directions for change as well as short-term priorities for reform, in a period of dramatic economic and social changes, which have inspired strong ideological debates.

A number of factors have contributed to the case for the Social Security Review (Cass, 1986b:3–5). These include: rapid increases in the rate and duration of unemployment and changes in the distribution of unemployment; changes in family composition, in particular an increase in sole-parent families dependent on income security; an increase in the number and change in the composition of people in poverty; and the need to recognise the impact of demographic change on future retirement incomes policy.

These trends have had and will continue to have a significant impact on the economic circumstances of households. We provide a brief discussion of these developments, concentrating on labour market issues and their implications for welfare. The subject is potentially very broad in scope. Our object is to identify some of the relevant trends, and the implications for developments in income security policies.

We begin, however, by putting Government income-support policies into perspective, in relation to the household activities and the labour market involvement of household members. Issues such as the transfer of cash and resources within and between households are briefly touched on.

After considering the changes that have already taken place in the labour market and their implications for social security, we turn to the possible future of the relationship between the household economy, labour market participation and income support and conclude with a discussion of some relevant policy issues.

Work, the family and income support

It is not a simple exercise to disentangle the relationship between the household economy, participation in the labour market, government income support, family support and the resultant overall social welfare in the broadest sense. Some commentators have described market work and non-market work in the household economy as competing alternatives: for example, it is argued that various forms of Government provision would be unnecessary if families assumed or maintained responsibility for care of household members. It is also argued that government involvement in market activities precludes non-market activities so that public expenditure is required for services which should rightfully be provided privately, within the household (Chipman, 1981).

Conservative commentators go further by suggesting that various Government programmes designed to promote social welfare have in fact undermined welfare through their effect on incentives to paid work and on family formation and stability. These arguments have been elaborated in great detail by United States writers, especially Gilder (1981), and with more sophistication by Murray (1984).

Such debates about the respective roles of the family and the Government and the family and work have often been characterised by the lack of relevant data and by the adoption of ideological positions rather than a coherent theory. This chapter does not present a detailed theoretical framework for approaching these issues, but does identify some relevant conceptual concerns, and notes some major implications for developments in social policy.

Theories of non-market household activities

The approach adopted by the 'new theory of consumer behaviour' in economics (Becker, 1981), suggests that households make decisions about the allocation of their members' time to various activities that contribute either directly or indirectly to the welfare of household members. In a market economy, nearly all households require resources for the purchase of goods and services for consumption. The most important source of these resources is income from paid employment by one or more household members, income that is used for the purchase of commodities. Money income can of course be provided from other sources, such as Government cash transfers (pensions and benefits), unearned income from investments, transfers from outside the households, such as maintenance from non-custodial parents or charitable donations, gifts from parents and relatives, or by running down previously acquired cash assets.

An important component of this approach is the recognition that a household's welfare is not simply a matter of money income and commodities. *Time* is also allocated by households to 'investment' activities, such as education and the raising of children, to the consumption of pure 'leisure' for enjoyment, and to 'home production'. Home production involves the combination of inputs of time, members' skills and purchased goods for consumption, for example, in the preparation of meals.

In effect, this approach treats each household as a kind of little 'factory', a multi-person unit producing meals, health, skills, children and self-esteem, amongst other products, from combinations of market goods and the time, skills and knowledge of its members.

This approach has considerable problems but it is useful for analytical purposes in two ways. First, in considering the economics of household activities, apparent non-market activities should not be too sharply distinguished from market activities. The actions of household members, even those not within formal markets, can be of major economic significance and can have a profound impact on the standard of living of the household. Second, as a result, differing household activities have a high degree of inter-relationship, with many being complementary rather than competing.

We have identified two key problems with Becker's conceptualisation. First, its unit of analysis, and hence its unit of *behaviour* is the family, or the household, rather than individuals within the household and their inter-relationship. Such an aggregation of individual behaviours, interests and needs within family life neglects, even positively obscures, a number of issues that Australian and overseas studies have shown to be vital to welfare. Second, there is no sex or gender in these allocations of market and non-market work and allocations of time to production and consumption activities. Third, no distinction is made between the activities of consumption, on the one hand, e.g., the making of meals, and the activities of caring work, on the other hand, which both conservative thinkers and feminist thinkers see as the very nub of household work and household relationships.

On the first issue (the need to disaggregate individual interests and needs within the household), studies in Australia and the United Kingdom have contested the widely held assumption of a common pool of income and resources upon which all household members have an equitable claim (Edwards, 1981; Land and Rose, 1985). These studies not only demonstrate a marked complexity of financial arrangements within households and a number of different patterns ranging from complete sharing and integration of financial arrangements to those marked by extreme inequality of access to resources on the part of dependent members. It has also been noted that there is a correlation between both spouses making a similar contribution to household income and more egalitarian forms of management and control in financial arrangements.

On the second issue (the 'gendered' nature of the allocation of market and non-market work in households) various studies have noted the continuing strength of the male breadwinning/female dependency relationship, particularly in households with young children and in larger households where responsibility for caring work creates formidable barriers to women's labour market participation (Wearing, 1983; Tulloch, 1984; Cass, 1986c.)

Nevertheless, the markedly increased labour market participation rates of married women, in particular those with children, over the last fifteen years (Bureau of Labour Market Research, 1985), denote an erosion of the traditional pattern of wives' dependency. But this observation must be tempered with data on the continuing differential in men's and women's labour market involvement and hours of market work. In August 1986, the labour market participation rates of married men aged 20–54 ranged between 92 to 97 percent. In contrast, participation rates for married women ranged between 55 to 64 percent. Further, the prevailing paid employment pattern for men aged 25 to 54 continues to be full-time work, with about 97 percent employed full-time (35 hours or more per week). For women, however, the hours of paid employment are different with between 53 to 63 percent working full-time. For married women the proportions are similar, in fact, the main discriminator for women's labour market involvement and the hours of their market work is not marital status but the presence and age of dependent children.

We can now identify a well established trend in household members' allocation of their time and labour towards increased labour market participation rates for wives and mothers, a significant proportion of which is part-time, and a continuation of the pattern of women's reduced labour market participation in the period of child care, particularly when children are young. Further, an Australian study of young women's attitudes to conjugal role relationships and their actual experiences show that sharing breadwinning and household work are strongly supported before the birth of children, but tend to be modified greatly by a significant majority after the birth of children (Glezer, 1984).

What appears to be emerging is the pattern of household arrangements composed of a so-called 'primary earner' and 'secondary earner', this somewhat disparaging categorisation denoting differentiation in the continuity of husbands' and wives' labour market involvement, the hours of their paid market activity and their respective levels of earnings (O'Loughlin and Cass, 1985; Jones, 1984).

What is also clear is that these different patterns of gender-linked labour market supply are accompanied by, indeed the correlates of, gender-linked patterns of non-market work in the household economy. It is essential to demarcate conceptually the major types of non-market work carried out in households. First, there is consumption work as Becker notes and Game and Pringle (1984) have described in the Australian context, work carried out usually, but not necessarily, by women converting the commodities purchased in the market into goods and services for household use and consumption. Second, there is 'caring work', care of children, the elderly and the disabled, which remains, both in behaviour and in ideology, the predominant responsibility of women (see, e.g., Wearing, 1983; Kendig, 1984; Kinnear and Rossiter, 1984; Finch and Groves, 1983; Broom, 1984). Caring work, while also providing goods and services, is conceptually different from consumption work because of the symbolic resonance of the 'need for care' that characterises the situation of vulnerable and dependent family members who are cared for. There is a nexus of duty and obligation involved, which is much more pervasive of family relationships and the allocation of time than mere consumption work.

It is caring work that is most highly correlated with levels of women's labour market participation, although, it must be noted, that the most common pattern is not an either/or situation (i.e., either non-market caring work or paid market activity) but combinations of both.

Turning now to the consequences of men's and women's labour market participation, various Australian studies have pointed to the crucial importance of wives' and mothers' as well as fathers' labour market participation in increasing overall family money income, and in protecting both low-income married couple and single-parent families from poverty (O'Loughlin and Cass, 1985; McDonald, 1985; Gallagher and Foster, 1986). These considerations point to the need for a theory of the domestic economy that pays attention to the fact that men's and women's patterns of market and non-market work and access to income from market work are closely correlated with the gender division of labour in domestic and family life.

Development of appropriate income-support policies that will augment welfare requires a consideration of emerging trends in the combinations of paid and unpaid market and non-market work that men and women are constructing. It also requires a clear understanding of the labour market and social security factors that constrain the opportunities of household members to take paid market work.

Sources of income support

Government income-support policies make a significant contribution to the wellbeing of households. In 1981–82, for example, cash transfers from the Departments of Social Security and Veterans' Affairs amounted to more than 10 percent of the total gross income of all households. These resources are heavily concentrated on certain types of households and particularly low-income households (Economic Planning Advisory Council, 1986a). In 1981–82, Government cash benefits were the principal source of income for nearly 1.7 million income units containing over 2.5 million persons. Cash benefits were the principal source of income for around 71 percent of couples with a head over 64 years, 69 percent of female sole parents, and 83 percent of single persons over 64 years (three-quarters of whom were women) (ABS, 1984b:48).

The most important source of monetary income, however, is the labour market activity of household members. In 1982 earnings were the principal source of money income for 90.8 percent of the 1.1 million married couple income units with husbands under the age of 34 years and 81.3 percent of the 2.1 million married couple income units with husbands aged 35 to 64 years (ABS, 1984b:48). One of the most significant developments in past decades has been the increasing labour market participation rate of women, particularly married women, who consequently have made an increasing contribution to the monetary income of households. Between 1933 and 1983, the labour market participation rate of married women of working age increased from around 6 percent to 47 percent. At the time of the 1982 Family Survey, the wife was in the labour market in 48.2

percent of married couple units. The labour market participation rate of wives with dependent children was higher (at 51.1 percent) than for those without dependent children (48.8 percent) and generally increased quite significantly with the age of the youngest dependent child. Nevertheless, as Jordan notes, 'many more people depend on than receive incomes, and the actual standard of living of the recipients depends on how much goes to the support of dependents, that of dependents on how much benefit is passed on to them' (Jordan, 1987:11).

The nuclear and the extended family are in themselves the mechanisms of very extensive transfers of services and resources; for example, the provision of informal child care and care of the aged or invalid relatives, as well as the transfer of income from employment in the formal labour market to those working or dependent at home. The 1982 Family Survey found that of the 911 600 income units living in households in which all persons were aged 60 years and over, 339 600 were receiving help of various sorts. More than twice as many were receiving help from relatives (155 600) as were receiving help from voluntary organisations (33 500) and Government organisations (31 800) combined (65 300). Similarly, of the 1.8 million income units with children aged under twelve years, some 925 000 relied on other children living in the dwelling and grandparents and/or other relatives for child care, while only 138 900 used formal child care arrangements, such as pre-schools and child care centres. That is, 60 percent of those using child care used close relatives and about 9 percent used formal care. As well, some 86 percent of families using informal child care arrangements paid nothing or less than $1 per week for that care (ABS, 1984b: 38–41). It is important to note, however, that these data do not show the relative importance of formal care to the users of Government services.

The 1982 Family Survey also provides evidence to dispel the view that growth in welfare state provisions has substantially weakened the link between family members and reduced the level of family responsibility for aged or disabled members. Historical statistics are not readily available in Australia, but it appears that in common with similar societies, there has been a trend for much higher levels of independent living for both the aged and the young—for example, in 1982 only 7 percent of persons aged 25 to 64 years with at least one parent alive lived in the same household as one or both of the parents.

This appears to represent a preference of the parents as well as the children, and probably reflects long-term, real increases in incomes, necessary to finance separate housing arrangements. Nevertheless, around 14 percent of persons whose parents lived outside their household had *daily* contact with those parents, a further 49 percent had at least *weekly* contact, and a further 27 percent had at least *monthly* contact with their parents. Fewer than 3 percent had contact less than once a year or no contact at all.

The quality and reliability of contact cannot of course be gauged from such figures, but in combination with the results cited earlier, it seems fair to conclude that for most people the family, in its various forms, remains the most significant source of social support.

It would appear that cash transfers within (intra) and between (inter) families are also extremely significant. Ironmonger's (1982) study gives estimates of transfers within Australia households that show they were twice as important as community transfers. In 1975–76 'cash benefits to persons from governments (community transfers) provided about 12.8 percent of personal disposable income whilst cash and kind benefits from other individuals (family transfers) provided about 24.0 percent of personal disposable income' (Ironmonger, 1982:22). Of a total disposable income of $50 billion, $12 billion was transferred directly within families and $6.4 billion indirectly via the taxation–welfare system.

A study for the United States shows the value of income transfers within families in 1975 was over $500 billion, equivalent to nearly one-third the size of the United States' GNP, and several times larger than total Government social security programmes (Morgan, 1978). A further United States study estimated that in 1979 transfers between families for income, food, maintenance and housing amounted to about 45 percent of total Government transfers for these purposes (Lampman and Smeeding, 1983).

Lampman and Smeeding identify the conceptual issues and methodological problems involved in analyses of this sort. They estimate and compare the levels of interfamily and Government transfers for selected years between 1929 and 1979. Their estimates are based in part upon reported gifts to persons in different households, gifts received from other households, alimony and child support, as well as other regular transfers. They reach two interesting conclusions. The first of these is that the overall level of interfamily transfers as a proportion of personal income declined after the introduction of social security programmes in the mid-1930s from 6.5 to 5.0 percent. Over the same period, Government transfers increased from 2.8 to 11.2 percent, with the net result that Government plus interfamily transfers increased by 7.0 percent.

One probable reason for the relatively smaller decline in

interfamily transfers is the significant change in the household composition of the United States' population. Between 1940 and 1980 there was a 600 percent increase in the number of unrelated individuals living alone, as well as significant declines in the number of aged persons living with relatives. These trends, in combination with higher rates of separation and divorce, would suggest that interhousehold transfers would tend to increase in significance as intrahousehold transfers would decrease.

Lampman and Smeeding argue that Government transfers are conversions of interfamily transfers, i.e., if Government social security spending had not increased, forces such as higher incomes, increased mobility of nuclear families, the reduction in significance of the extended family and increased urbanisation would have led to much higher private transfers (Lampman and Smeeding, 1983:56).

The assumption that Government transfers have substituted for broadly similar levels of private transfers has significant implications for analyses of the incentive effects of welfare state provisions, which are usually based on the counterfactual of zero transfers. Lampman and Smeeding conclude that moving from private to public transfers of the same scale should have no effect on work effort:

> The major argument of this paper is that it is inappropriate to use zero transfer as the exclusive counterfactual in the study of transfers. To do so leads people to believe that total transfers have increased more than they actually have and that the effects of government transfer, desired and undesired, are greater than they actually are. This misconception may be particularly important in the case of changes in work effort due to the growth of government transfers. (Lampman and Smeeding 1983:59)

Trends in social security

The social security system has undergone very significant developments over the past twenty years. A detailed discussion of these changes can be found in Moore and Whiteford (1987).

An important influence on the growth in the scope and cost of the social security system has been the introduction of major legislative and policy changes since 1964–65. These have included: the introduction of new payments (e.g., supporting parent's benefits and family income supplement) and extension of eligibility for existing pensions and benefits; increases in rates and introduction of automatic indexation of most basic pension and benefit rates; numerous changes in the pension's means/income test and in the taxation treatment of payments;

and changes in assistance for families with children. Apart from these policy factors, the taxation and social security systems and their clients have also been influenced by various social and economic changes.

Inflation has had a major effect on the growth in social security expenditures. While the real growth in expenditures between 1964–65 and 1985–86 has been about 350 percent, the nominal increase is 2150 percent. Most of the real growth in levels of payment occurred between the late 1960s and the mid-1970s. A most important factor has been Governments' reactions to inflation—since 1976 the basic rates of most pensions and benefits have been automatically indexed by movements in the Consumer Price Index (CPI). Because some payments (notably unemployment benefit for single adults, unemployment and sickness benefits for juniors, and additional payments for children and sole parents) have not kept pace with inflation, the distribution of real disposable incomes among pensioner and beneficiary families and others has changed significantly since 1976–77.

The external (demographic, social and economic) causes of the growth in numbers receiving social security assistance and of the real growth in expenditure are complex, but include: changing demographic structure of the population, i.e., increases in the proportion of the population of age pension age; changing family patterns, i.e., the increasing numbers of sole-parent families, following, in the great majority of instances (about 82 percent), separation and divorce after a marital or a de facto relationship; and very substantial changes in labour market conditions resulting in increased rates and durations of unemployment and decreased rates of labour force participation for certain vulnerable demographic groups, e.g., older men and sole parents.

Probably the most important influence, at least since the mid-1970s, has been changed labour market conditions and the increase in unemployment, which have led not only to substantial growth in numbers receiving unemployment benefit, but have been correlated with the increase in the numbers receiving other payments, such as invalid pensions, sole-parent pensions, age and veterans' pensions, and sickness and special benefits (Sheehan and Stricker, 1981). The growth in the scope and duration of unemployment also has had implications in terms of the growing interaction of the income tax and social security systems.

In summary, the scope and cost of social security provisions has grown significantly since 1964–65. This growth has been viewed in a number of ways, either as an indication of an unwelcome increase in dependence upon Government support, as a necessary and humane public response to changed economic and social conditions, or as an only-to-be-expected development in the maturing of the Australian welfare state, whose foundations were laid in the 1940s and earlier—a maturation comparable with that of social security systems in many overseas countries.

How ever these changes are interpreted, what cannot be denied is that the social security system in the 1980s is far more than a residual part of public policies, of limited relevance to the mainstream of Australian social and economic life. Expenditure on social security programmes is now the largest single component of the federal budget. At 30 June 1986 there were some 2.7 million pensioners and beneficiaries, plus their children. For at least some time during their lives the great majority of people can be expected to rely to some extent on the social security system. This is particularly so in retirement, where the age pension (plus the equivalent service pension) currently covers some 80 percent of the aged population. Even in cross-sectional terms, the social security system extends quite deeply into the income distribution, because of the increases in real rates of payment and the liberalisations of income tests mentioned previously.

Increased social security expenditures have of course required increases in taxation to finance social spending. The increase in tax burdens is revealed in the increasing share of total Commonwealth tax revenue in GDP, which rose from 19 to 25 percent between 1964-65 and 1985-86. As a share of average weekly earnings, Commonwealth taxation increased from 12 to 17 percent, and in the same period annual per capita Commonwealth taxation increased in real 1985-86 dollars from $1628 to $3670, a growth of 3.9 percent per year. Of particular interest is the growing Australian reliance on income taxation. As a proportion of total Commonwealth taxation revenue, income taxes have increased from 41 to 56 percent between 1964-65 and 1985-86.

The visibility of income taxation may have given rise in some quarters to misperceptions about the overall level of taxation in Australia. In 1984, total income tax revenues as a proportion of GDP in Australia were eighth highest out of 23 Organisation for Economic Cooperation and Development (OECD) countries, 16.8 percent of GDP compared to the OECD average of 14.3 percent (OECD, 1984:85). This comparison is complicated by the fact that Australia finances its social security payments entirely out of general revenue, while most other countries levy social security contributions, which are analogous to income taxes. For the OECD as a whole, social security contributions on average are

9.2 percent of GDP. On income taxes plus social security levies as a percentage of GDP, Australia ranks fourth lowest in OECD countries.

In summary, the environment to which social security provisions must react—the same environment in which families and households must operate—has changed very significantly in recent decades. As noted by Saunders:

> These changes reflect both the policies that have been employed over the period but also, and more importantly, the broader economic and social trends that have taken place. The interaction of these has seen a significant change in the nature of social security expenditure, and, most likely, in public perceptions of what the social security system is intended to achieve. Provision of income support during vulnerable periods of the life cycle, from which all families expect to benefit, where eligibility and disincentive effects are weak or non-existent, and where the arguments for (and practice of) universalism have been strongest, has declined in relative importance. Against this, expenditure has increased in relative terms on those areas most sensitive to economic and social trends, most susceptible to eligibility and disincentive problems, and from which the majority of families (however incorrectly) do not expect to benefit.
>
> In the light of these changes, it is not surprising if public attitudes to, and acceptability of, the social security system have themselves undergone change. (Saunders, 1987:25)

And this has occurred precisely at the time when an increased proportion of the population of workforce age and capacity, often with dependent children, has been drawn into reliance on social security for income support.

Labour market participation and economic welfare

As already noted, the extent of labour market participation of household members is the most important determinant of that household's standard of living. This is shown in Table 9.1, which provides details of household monetary income by family type and employment status from the 1981 Census. The table shows a clear pattern, with the incidence of low income (defined arbitrarily as less than $10 000 in 1981) decreasing as labour market involvement grows. For example, among married couples, nearly 77 percent of those where both head and spouse are unemployed had money incomes less than $10 000; this decreased to about 71 percent where the head was unemployed and the spouse outside the labour force, 30 percent where the head was unemployed and the spouse employed, around 16 percent where the head was employed and the spouse unemployed, 10 percent where the head was employed and the spouse outside the labour force, and only 3.5 percent where both spouses were employed in the market economy. Single unemployed adults were four times more likely than single employed adults to have incomes less than $10 000 and other families (mainly sole parents) who had an unemployed head were three times more likely than those employed to have had low money incomes.

Table 9.1 Percentage distribution of different types of families by ranges of household income, Australia, June 1981

Family type	Household income ($'000 per year)[a]			
	0–4	4–10	10–15	15+
Married couple, with or without dependants				
Head and spouse employed	0.5	3.0	18.4	78.2
Head employed, spouse not in labour force	0.5	9.3	40.8	41.3
Head employed, spouse unemployed	0.3	15.3	51.7	32.8
Head unemployed, spouse employed	1.8	28.2	40.0	30.0
Head unemployed, spouse not in labour force	6.6	64.8	20.8	7.8
Head and spouse unemployed	14.9	62.0	12.6	10.4
Single adult				
Employed	2.2	17.7	44.9	34.7
Unemployed	50.8	29.1	15.4	4.6
Other families				
Employed head	2.7	16.5	36.9	44.0
Unemployed head	12.6	50.4	21.0	14.3

Note: [a] In general, household income is gross weekly income annualised
Source: OECD, 1984:88. Derived from 1981 Census

Gallagher (1985:33) has also drawn attention to the importance of paid employment in reducing the risk of poverty, and Gallagher and Foster (1986:95) show that the probability of children being in poverty (as defined by the Henderson Poverty Line) increases from 5 percent for children of full-time wage and salary earners to 70.5 percent for those in families where the head is not in the labour force.

Poverty research carried out at the Social Welfare Research Centre provides further evidence of the association between poverty and unemployment. While the current incidence of poverty among all income units was 8.1 percent for all income units in 1981–82, the incidence of poverty was 2.3 percent for those where the head was employed for wages and salaries and 50.3 percent where the head was unemployed (Vipond and Bradbury, 1987).

The economic welfare of households is also significantly

affected by the presence of children, who increase the financial needs of households and generally reduce the capacity of household members, usually mothers, to participate fully in the labour market.

Over the last decade, an increase in sole-parent families, due predominantly to separation and divorce, has also occurred in a climate of economic insecurity, resulting firstly in an increase of sole-parent families from 9 to 14 percent of all families with children, and even more importantly, an increase in the proportion of sole parents dependent on social security, from 57 to 83 percent. In this period the number of children whose parents are dependent on a pension, predominantly as sole parents, increased from 284 000 to 530 000, a smaller increase than for the children of the unemployed, but still a dramatic increase of 87 percent.

Overall, the percentage of children in pensioner and beneficiary families has more than doubled from 9 to 19 percent of dependent children. A further 1 percent of children live in families where the parental income is low enough to entitle the family to receive family-income supplement. It is important to note that while sole-parent families comprise about 56 percent of all families receiving social security support, the greatest increase in families reliant on income security has been amongst those dependent on unemployment benefit.

It is important to note that neither unemployment nor other forms of joblessness are distributed randomly through the community. The rate of unemployment is highest for young people, for people who have not had the opportunity to acquire formal job skills or to complete the highest level of secondary school, and this holds across the age spectrum; for more recently arrived migrants, in particular those from non-English-speaking countries, and for Aboriginal people. Durations of unemployment are greatest for older people, people without formal job skills and those who left school early, and for Aboriginal people (Chapman and Gruen, 1984).

In addition, there is a close relationship between unemployment and receipt of low income when in employment. People experiencing a period of unemployment tend to be drawn from those whose earnings are low when they are in the workforce, and furthermore, the experience of unemployment, particularly longer durations of unemployment, tends to reduce future earnings (Whiteford, 1986).

To gain an even more comprehensive profile of the social impact of unemployment, it must be noted that labour market disadvantage tends to be concentrated. Children from low income families and particularly from families with an unemployed parent have a higher rate of unemployment than do children where one or both parents are in paid employment (Bradbury, Garde and Vipond, 1985). The wives of unemployed men have an unemployment rate which is 9 times higher than that of all wives, and a labour market participation rate which is more than one third lower (Whiteford, 1986).

The situation for sole parents is similar. Female sole parents in particular have very low rates of educational attainment: over 63 percent have not attended the highest level of secondary school; and only 28 percent have post-school qualifications. This constitutes a structure of educational disadvantage much greater than for either wives with children, or for fathers in married couple and sole–parent families. The level of sole parents' educational qualifications is directly related to their labour market participation, and hence to their capacity to become self-supporting (Cass, 1986a). On all these indicators, it is clear that unemployment and joblessness and the attendant high risk of poverty are closely associated with a number of labour market and other socio-economic disadvantages.

For many women, however, lower labour market participation is simply associated with their child-rearing responsibilities. One pattern of labour market participation of women, in relation to the family life cycle, is suggested by Tables 9.2 and 9.3. Married women without children and who are aged between 15 and 34 years are predominantly in the labour market (84.2 percent) and nearly 70 percent have full-time jobs. Those in this age group who do have children have a labour market participation rate of only 44 percent, only 15 percent being in full-time work and 25 percent in part-time work. Labour market participation for women, in both full-time and part-time paid employment, increases significantly with the age of their youngest child, as can be seen in Table 9.3. The choice between full-time and part-time work also changes, married women with a youngest child under five years being nearly twice as likely to be in part-time employment rather than full-time employment, while those with children over ten years are fairly evenly split between the two employment statuses.

It should be noted that these levels of labour market participation are of course much lower than those of males in the same age group. Up to the age of 45 males, both with and without dependent children, have labour market participation rates well in excess of 90 percent. Those over 45 with dependent children have a participation rate of nearly 89 percent, while those without children have a participation rate of 50 percent, reflecting the presence of very large numbers of retired persons, particularly pensioners.

Table 9.2 Married couple families: labour market participation of wife, Australia, July 1985 (percent)

Age of wife	Without dependent children	With dependent children
15–34 years	84.2	44.0
35–44 years	63.4	59.9
45 years and over	21.2	46.4
Total	36.6	50.6

Source: Australian Bureau of Statistics (1985) *Labour Force Status and Other Characteristics of Families July 1985*

Table 9.3 Labour market participation of women, Australia, July 1985 (percent)

Age of youngest dependent child	Married parent		Sole parent	
	Employed full-time	Employed part-time	Employed full-time	Employed part-time
0–4	10.9	19.5	12.1	10.0
5–9	22.8	30.9	18.1	17.1
10–14	28.3	29.7	27.7	15.5
15–20	30.7	26.0	31.5	16.4
Total	20.1	27.0	21.0	14.3

Source: Australian Bureau of Statistics (1985) *Labour Force Status and Other Characteristics of Families July 1985*

It is interesting to note that female sole parents, while having significantly lower participation in part-time employment than comparable married mothers, have nearly identical proportions in full-time employment. This suggests, among other things, that for those expecting female sole parents to very substantially reduce their reliance on Government income support through full-time work would require sole parents to behave very differently from other women with children of the same age.

Dependency and income support: future directions

One factor often taken into account when considering the level of social welfare spending and future calls for expenditure is the 'dependency ratio'. The usual definition of the dependency ratio is the number of persons less than fifteen years and over 65 years as a proportion of the population of working age.

In recent years there has been increasing concern both in Australia and overseas with demographic trends likely to produce increasingly unfavourable dependency ratios (Halter and Hemming, 1985). For example, Australian population projections to 2021 suggest that over this time the proportion of children under fifteen years will decline somewhat from 22.8 percent to 19.0 percent under Series A projections, and to 20.5 percent under Series D. The proportion of the population over 65 years is projected to increase over this period, from 10.7 to 15.6 percent (Series A) or 14.6 percent (Series D). The overall result of these trends is that the Australian dependency ratio is projected to increase from 50.4 percent in 1987 to either 52.8 percent (Series A) or 54.1 percent (Series D), as illustrated in Table 9.4.

Broadly similar projections are available for other OECD countries. For example, the proportion of the population over 65 years is projected to grow from 9.0 percent in 1980 to 21.2 percent in 2025 in Japan, and from 11.2 percent in 1980 to 19.4 percent in 2025 in the United States (Halter and Hemming, 1985:5). In these circumstances, failing changes in policy direction, over the long run public sector outlays as a proportion of GDP must increase.

Table 9.4 Projections of the Australian population, 1987 to 2021

		Series A		Series D	
	1987	2001	2021	2001	2021
Persons ('000)	16 094.7	18 917.4	22 029.1	19 530.4	23 902.5
Males ('000)	8 026.9	9 416.1	10 917.7	9 731.6	11 877.6
Females ('000)	8 067.8	9 501.3	11 111.4	9 798.8	12 024.9
Age (%)					
0–14 years	22.8	21.4	19.0	22.4	20.5
15–24 years	16.7	13.7	13.1	13.6	13.8
25–44 years	30.8	30.2	26.7	30.1	26.4
45–64 years	19.0	22.8	25.7	22.3	24.7
65 and over	10.7	11.9	15.6	11.7	14.6
Dependency ratio	50.4	50.0	52.8	51.7	54.1
Women aged 60–64 ('000)	360.8	393.8	670.7	397.3	690.7

Source: Australian Bureau of Statistics (1985) *Projections of the Populations of Australia, States and Territories, 1984 to 2021* ABS Catalogue No. 3222.0

Saunders (1987) provides estimates of the likely magnitude of the impact of population ageing on future social security and welfare outlays, assuming that real per capita outlays for each age group remain at their 1984–85 level. His estimates show a projected real increase in total social security and welfare outlays from $17 600 million in 1985 to $30 900 million (in 1984–85 dollars) in 2021, an increase of over 75 percent. Outlays per head for those of workforce age are projected to rise by 26 percent from $1735 to $2188, and 'by and large, it will be persons of workforce age who will be primarily called upon to finance the projected rise in outlays through increased taxation' (Saunders, 1987:38).

As noted by Saunders, however, the impact of demographic changes on social welfare expenditure depends upon the costs associated with the provision of social security support to those in different age groups. The Series D projections suggest a ratio in 2021 of 54.1 percent compared to 52.8 percent under Series A. But the composition of these ratios differs—Series D suggests there will be more children and fewer aged persons in 2021 than does Series A. As noted by the Social Welfare Policy Secretariat (SWPS, 1984:4), per capita expenditure on the aged in Australia exceeds per capita expenditure on the young. For the Commonwealth and states the ratio of average outlays on the aged to those on the young was 2.08 in 1980–81. Overseas estimates of this ratio are more commonly in the range 2.5 to 3.0.

For this reason, a higher overall dependency ratio does not necessarily imply higher aggregate calls for social expenditures. Nevertheless, the 2021 projected expenditure requirements are significantly higher than those currently. The crucial issues will be taxable capacity and whether it is perceived as life-cycle support or as support by the 'productive' for the 'unproductive'.

In this context it is important to note other ambivalent characteristics about conventional dependency ratios. The concept of dependency as usually employed implies a simple dichotomy between productive and non-productive activities. But it has already been suggested that market and non-market activities are closely inter-related. Clearly, the caring work carried out in households by members who may or may not also be gainfully employed cannot be removed from the assessment of the overall production of welfare. Calasanti and Bonanno (1986) also point out that the use of simple dependency ratios implies not only that those not in the labour market do not contribute to the maintenance of society, but that all those between the ages of fifteen and sixty-four are fully employed.

This second assumption is particularly significant, as can be shown by international comparisons of conventional dependency ratios. Table 9.5 provides demographic data for nine OECD countries in 1983, the latest year for which comparable figures are available. It can be seen that while Australia's conventional dependency ratio (52.4 percent) is around the middle of these countries, there is a relatively high proportion of children less than fifteen years and relatively low proportion of those over 64 years. In contrast, countries such as Sweden and the United Kingdom currently have the sorts of proportions over 64 that

Australia is projected to have in 2021. In this sense, these countries may be considered analogues for Australia's future.

Table 9.5 Age structure and dependency ratios in nine OECD countries, 1983

Country	Percentage of population		Conventional dependency (Ratio A)	Actual dependency (Ratio B)
	Over 64 years	Less than 15 years		
			%	%
Sweden	16.8	18.5	54.6	93.0
Japan	9.7	22.6	47.7	109.4
United States	11.7	22.0	50.8	122.0
Canada	10.0	21.9	46.8	127.1
United Kingdom	15.0	19.8	53.4	140.1
West Germany	14.8	16.2	44.9	140.9
Australia	10.0	24.4	52.4	144.4
France	13.1	21.7	53.4	152.9
New Zealand	10.0	25.6	55.3	154.5

Notes: Ratio A is the number of persons less than 15 years and the number over 64 years as a proportion of the population 15 to 64 years.
Ratio B is the number of persons less than 15, those over 64, and those 15 to 64 years either outside the labour market or unemployed as a proportion of those in paid employment.
Source: Calculated from data in OECD (1984)

However, as noted previously, one of the key issues is taxable capacity, which in itself is generally assessed in relation to incomes earned from the market. Hence a second form of dependency ratio has been calculated by expressing the number of persons less than 15 years, those over 65 years, plus those between the ages of 15 and 64 who are either unemployed or outside the labour market as a proportion of those in paid employment (Ratio B). This approach would appear more likely to produce the 'actual' measure of dependency, rather than the 'potential' dependency measure implied by the conventional ratio (Ratio A).

Apart from the fact that these 'actual' ratios are much higher, the relative positions of different countries change in significant ways. For example, the United States has a higher dependency ratio than Canada when considering the potential labour force, but somewhat lower when looking at the actual employed labour force. Germany has the lowest potential dependency ratio, and the United Kingdom one of the highest, but when looking at actual dependency ratios, their positions are very similar.

Perhaps the most spectacular position is that of Sweden. While having almost the highest dependency ratio on one measure, it has by far the lowest on the other, and is in fact the only one of these countries where the employed labour force is larger than the population it is called on to support. The reasons for this appear to be the relatively low unemployment rate and, more importantly, the higher labour market participation rates, particularly for women. Thus, while Sweden is often regarded as the archetypal 'welfare state', it is also the country that has the highest proportion of its population economically active.

Those countries that enjoy the lowest 'actual' dependency ratios do so because of their higher labour market participation rates, with their 'rankings' being affected by their unemployment levels.

These figures should be treated with some caution. For example, the retired population was defined as those over 65 years. While this is common in international comparisons, women of 60 years and over in Australia are entitled to an age pension. Unemployment rates can be quite changeable; labour market participation rates less so. It is also unsatisfactory to treat all those of working age outside the labour market as equivalent to the retired or to dependent children, particularly when they are very likely to be providing care for other dependent persons. Moreover, the inter-relationship between the different factors may be more complex than it appears. The lower proportion of children in Sweden's population in one sense allows the higher labour market participation of women. It should also be noted that nearly half the women who are in paid employment in Sweden are employed part-time, while the proportion in some other countries is not much more than one-fifth.

Despite these caveats, it is clear that it is labour market conditions once again that will be a major determinant of the course of future social security policy, affecting both taxable capacity, and the numbers of people and households of workforce age requiring income support. This, in turn, should have an effect on community perceptions of the purpose and legitimacy of income support.

Conclusions and policy implications

Our major conclusion is that trends in employment, unemployment and labour market participation have been the most important factors affecting past changes in the welfare of households and will also be the predominant influence on future levels of household welfare, as well as future requirements for social security expenditure.

What are some of the major income security policies that might facilitate adults' labour market participation, particularly for unemployed couples and sole parents dependent on income support?

The most important policies are firstly those that minimise

and alleviate the accumulation of high effective marginal tax rates, which accrue through the 'piling on' of income-tested payments, rebates and concessions at Commonwealth, state and local government levels. This is particularly important for low-income people whose labour market participation is highly sensitive to high effective marginal tax rates.

Secondly, attention must be paid to developing transition payments and supportive services (in particular labour market training and child care), which will facilitate transition to the labour market, particularly for those with dependent children for whom *security* of income support is absolutely crucial and even more so when they are encountering the initial increased costs of entering paid employment.

Thirdly, in married-couple households as well as sole-parent households, the potential labour market participation of the woman must be recognised and supported. The low labour market participation rates and high unemployment rates for the wives of unemployed men reflect not only the effects of social security income test conditions, which provide disincentives to wives' participation, but also reflect a burgeoning source of labour supply that could augment the social welfare of households. The key to sole-parent households' movement out of poverty and dependence is also a concerted combination of policies to augment the parent's earnings capacity and paid workforce participation with accompanying community services like child care.

In the longer term, and in an enduring way, the issue of facilitating and maintaining men's and women's labour market participation must bring into focus questions of the most appropriate forms of income support for children. If both men and women are to be given more equal opportunity to participate in market and non-market work, then the legitimate dependency of children and their claims on transfers through the tax/benefits system becomes a clear correlate.

BARBARA SPALDING

Commentary

I would like to start where the authors left off. The proposition is that we are going to confront a considerable amount of pressure to resolve cost problems in the social security system by 'encouraging' pensioners and beneficiaries back into the labour market. Such a move would have to be a major policy issue for Government at this point in time.

The analytic data-based research approach has limitations. Policy makers and people involved in designing programmes have to see the link between income-security provisions and the labour market in a wider context. While the descriptive material in this paper is extremely helpful in assisting us in understanding part of that context, it is only part. In order to understand some of the other elements we have to cast our minds back to the recent past and reflect on the place of women in the labour market and the gender role differentiation that prevailed (and still prevails) in the domestic economy. Indeed, arrangements to keep women 'at home', or at least marginalised in the labour market, were formally institutionalised in a very wide variety of policy areas. The premises underlying the social security system itself reflect this.

There are numerous examples of barriers, penalties and disincentives to women (and especially married women) in the labour market. For example, it was only in the early 1970s in Victoria that married women could become permanent in the State Public Service and even later before they were fully entitled to superannuation. Women were not recruited into the administrative ranks at all, whether married or single. We need only recall the history of the equal wages cases in 1969 and 1972 and certainly anybody who started working life before the end of the 1960s knows that it was common for women to be working for a different wage than men in the same job.

The tax system is another arena in which these distinctions have been institutionalised. The role and gender premises are still evident in relation to eligibility for the housekeeper rebate or the assumptions underlying the dependent spouse rebate.

The reformed divorce law, again very recent history, is still having difficulty coming to grips with the assumptions underlying the division of property within marriage. And, to revert to social security, the assumptions about the roles of women in relation to male partners and financial dependency in sexual relations were unquestioned for many years. A significant piece of work by Alan Jordan in 1981 on cohabitation rules is worth quoting in this context. It is called 'As His Wife' and explores some of the traditional precepts on the roles of women and men exemplified in the social security system.

All these things are but references to time-honoured treatment of women and their relationship to the home and the labour market. My point is that we need to recognise how wide and all-embracing are the institutionalised arrangements that have reinforced women's traditional role. We need at least to recognise that there is more to attend to than the social security system if we are to seek to change the ground rules because of empirical evidence and research findings.

A second issue I would like to comment on is the theoretical treatment by economists of the household and the market economy. The work that Ironmonger is doing will contribute to that. But in particular the labelling of household activity as consumption and the activity of the marketplace as production needs to be questioned. Few orthodox economists have questioned this and most have been (apparently) comfortable with the traditional theoretical treatment. However, there are exceptions and I am grateful to the micro-economists for their analysis of the household economy and its relationship to the marketplace.

One of the ramifications of the traditional approach is in the way subsidisation of the market is treated compared with subsidisation of the domestic economy. This becomes important when judgements are being made about priorities by politicians. Similarly assumptions about options for males and females reflect theoretical limitations. Studies of the attachment of male and female workers to the labour force are usually premised on the notion that one option for a woman when the circumstances of employment change (e.g., increased tax rates) is to withdraw from the labour market. You see a different set of assumptions in relation to male workers.

So I am saying that not only have we got the law and social policy institutionalising differences in the treatment of men and women and work but at the same time we have not yet developed an economic framework that allows us to get to grips with these differences. Perhaps this is because this issue is very much one of values and is often clouded by the fact that we avoid the question of values when we are talking about disciplines such as economics. I am reminded of the position taken by the Poverty Inquiry when the decision was made to use the household as the basis for analysing data on poverty. It was still not then fashionable to consider the position of individuals within households.

I think it is also relevant to note that the situation has changed since Whiteford and Cass wrote their chapter. As the result of the May 1987 'mini-Budget' it has become clear that we are about to change the basis of some of the assumptions to which I have been referring.

In particular it will hereafter be assumed that sole parents will be treated as unemployed workers rather than people outside the labour market, once their children reach a certain age.

In conclusion I wish to refer to the authors' recommendations. This is because in Victoria we are looking at precisely what sort of policy initiatives would need to be put into place if we are going to achieve the outcomes that have been recommended, that is, to assist people who are currently dependent on social security pensions and benefits into a situation where they can receive adequate remuneration from paid employment.

From our studies the necessary elements for achieving this objective include getting information through, providing career counselling and personal support, removing disincentives (and at the state level that relates to state concessions rather than to the poverty traps that exist with respect to Commonwealth pensions and benefits), having suitable training programmes available for people at all different levels of work readiness, help with job search and of course childcare through the training/retraining phase, through the job search phase and into employment.

All those elements have to be brought into some sort of harmony if we are going to be effective in achieving our objectives in relation to helping some of these people into (or back into) steady employment. While it is possible to have a view about what needs to be done, it is another issue altogether for the people involved in policy development and programme formulation to be able to manage to get the mechanisms in place.

10 The value of work in marriage

KATHLEEN FUNDER

Jessie Bernard (1982) speaks of the 'subtle revolution' of our time involving the movement of women, particularly married women with dependent children, into the paid workforce. This movement in turn has altered expectations and social norms from clear role divisions to more diffuse allocation of labour. Similarly, Carol Jacklin (1984) describes another 'great social experiment' in which the shibboleths of good child rearing are changing. The indications are that children thrive in many different home environments and that the golden rules of child rearing are somewhat tarnished.

The meaning of marriage has also changed. The relationship is central and is expected to provide the most important emotional support in life, to be the source of leisure and fulfilment (Rapoport, 1981). The crucible of change in work, parenting and intimate relationships is the institution of marriage. Paradoxically, one of the clearest views on these changes is through the process of divorce, which exposes their unevenness.

Family law operates and develops in this milieu of rapid and uneven change, yet the challenge of good law is that it must adapt to changing social and economic circumstances. It must be stable but not stand still. The Australian Family Law Act (1975) marked an evolution that acknowledged marriage as a mostly private partnership between freely consenting equals, able to be terminated by the wish of either party with a minimum of judicial involvement. Such a law reflects social and economic circumstances and values that are not universal in Australia or elsewhere. Along with the more private termination of the marriage, there has been a reduction in the obligations of ex-spouses to each other, despite Section 72 of the Family Law Act,

---

This chapter is based on a large empirical study of the economic consequences of marriage breakdown carried out by the Australian Institution of Family Studies in 1984. Members of the research team were: Don Edgar, Kathleen Funder, Margaret Harrison, Peter McDonald, Teresa Tucker and Ruth Weston.

which specifies terms under which spousal maintenance may be awarded. In a recent Australian Institute of Family Studies (AIFS) study, only a few short-term awards of spousal maintenance were reported—nor were they much desired except for those women who had continuing care of young children (Harrison, 1986).

We espouse the privacy of the home and family—'a person's home is his/her castle'; we value marriage as a relationship very centrally directed to the personal growth and satisfaction of the partners; and our law, which facilitates a 'clean break', places a value on the rights of the individual to take new directions in life. Up to now we have been able to afford these values.

The costs, however, are substantial and increasing. Supporting parent's benefits and allowances have risen dramatically and account for an ever-increasing percentage of the total social security and welfare budget. In 1979–80 they cost $260 million (2.3 percent); by 1985–86 they had risen to $1238 million (6.5 percent). Escalating public costs are clearly identified with women and their children who, in the case of divorce, experience a disproportionately large drop in household income. Weston (1986) reports women's adjusted, net household incomes drop by $56 per week, while men's rise by $64, three to five years after divorce.

The Family Law Act Section 79(4) directs that the discretion of the court be used to make property settlements that are just and equitable. To the extent that the law promotes or exacerbates grave inequality it is defective. These issues have been addressed by the Matrimonial Property Inquiry and by the AIFS Economic Consequences of Marriage Breakdown (ECMB) study. The latter study, of a representative sample of 825 people divorced under the provisions of the Family Law Act (1975), provides an empirical base for assessing the operation of the law. The study is used as the major reference in this chapter. Full details of sample and design of the study can be found in Funder (1986a).

Any discussion of the impact of the present law on the economic circumstances of men, women and children after divorce must distinguish between the general social and economic influences on income, which are considered responsible for the continuing differences between average earnings for men and women, and those factors that are particular to marriage and the law relating to its dissolution.

Differences in income for Australian men and women are well described. In spite of legislation phasing in equal pay since the mid 1960s, by 1984 adult women's full-time, ordinary-time earnings were still only 80 per cent of those of men. Causes of this discrepancy include sex differences in education (particularly in science and technology), sex segregation in the job market, and associated differences in opportunity for on-job training and career advancement. Moreover, although the importance of sex discrimination is debated, its presence seems beyond dispute (Jones, 1984).

These differences are also influenced by family-related interruptions to work, reflected in the broken work histories of married women with children (only four women in our sample of 429 women had uninterrupted work histories) and their common return to part-time work. In the clerical, sales and service occupations women make up about 65 percent of the workers, but almost half are part-time. Time out of work appears to depreciate human capital measured by earning capacity (Mincer, 1980), and tailoring work to children's needs seems to involve downward occupational mobility, further depressing earnings (Funder, 1986b; Joshi, 1984).

The issue of isolating marriage-related impacts on women's earnings from the general societal factors was addressed in the ECMB study (Funder, 1986b). By taking a group of divorced women with varied educational, occupational, and work histories, and with different childcare responsibilities, it was possible to analyse the impact of their time out of paid work caring for children on their standard of living three to five years after divorce. Women who had spent more than two-thirds of their married life out of the labour market were $50 per week (25 percent of the average net income for this group) worse off than those who had been out of the labour market less than one-third of the marriage. This difference existed when other factors such as education, occupational level and time since separation were statistically controlled and all income transfers between the partners included. The women's incomes were depressed in proportion to the time they had spent out of the paid workforce, mostly in caring for children. Further analysis produced no evidence that the provisions in part eight of the Family Law Act, under which property and maintenance may be counterbalanced, were used to reach a just and equitable outcome.

Past and continuing care of children was a powerful influence on earnings, yet women chose to adjust their participation to fit the needs of the children—a stance which is confirmed by Helen Glezer's (1986) findings from an AIFS study of maternity leave. Women rarely indicated that lack of job opportunity or child care provisions was the most important hindrance to their paid employment. The high value put on the quality of mothering clearly runs counter to economic independence for women. However, within a marriage it seems reasonable to assume that the partners make joint decisions about the way in which they apportion work in the household and in the market economy, that they decide the way in which their children will be reared, and that they share the costs of their decisions.

The interplay between family and paid work is a powerful determinant of the inequities observed in the settlement of the economic aspects of the marriage partnership. A wife will normally have been an integral part of the productive unit and have spent time supporting a paid worker, giving precedence to his obligations, assuming major responsibility for the children and homemaking—and sharing the costs and benefits that accrue to the partnership. It is evident, however, that the benefits that come from investing in the husband's career—his security of employment, his increasing earning capacity based on continuous employment, experience and efforts in the workplace—do not advantage the wife after separation. Conversely, the costs borne by the marriage partnership of the depreciation of the wife's earning capacity through interrupted participation, downward occupational mobility, and part-time participation (which tends to be in sectors without career paths) are not passed on to the husband after separation.

Marriage as a partnership

The Australian Law Reform Commission, in its discussion of the issues before the Matrimonial Property Inquiry, makes a basic assumption that marriage is a partnership of equals (Australian Law Reform Commission, 1985). Marriage has not always been seen in this light, however, and the implementation of the present law is not always consistent with this tenet. A stumbling block to the acceptance of a full partnership principle, which would imply that the fair resolution of the partnership be from a basis of equal shares, has been the implications this has for the discretionary facility of the court and the outcomes in the cases where property is large. Scutt and Graham (1984) demonstrate the unequal outcomes of many contested hearings, mostly in wealthy partnerships, presumably reflecting unwillingness to implement fully the equal partnership assumption. Suggestions that 50/50 division be accepted for certain property but not businesses, or that some property (for example, the home) be considered matrimonial property and other property be declared outside that province and not liable for such division, may well reflect a residual reluctance to accept equal partnership as a principle. When equal partnership involves a wife receiving half of a large property, or a business to which the husband has made a large direct contribution, it seems there is a desire to redefine the marriage partnership. Certainly, our society has no clear scales of value for work in the home, an acceptance of low salaries in those sectors in which women predominate, and an expectation that women will have less income and wealth than men. The equal partnership notion is at once beguiling and uncertain in its implications for the law; our society finds it hard to accept that a woman partner to a marriage contributes on a par with a wealthy husband.

The principle of the 'clean break', implying no continuing financial responsibilities of spouses for each other, is endorsed by current practice, advised by lawyers, and desired by a representative sample of divorced Australians (Harrison, 1986). Psychologically, people wish to put paid to their marriage; even in cases of ill-health or special need people tend not to accept any ongoing responsibility for their ex-partners. Either ex-spouses become self-sufficient or they must receive public support.

Marriages in which there are children run a course during which the dependency needs of children and demands on carers change dramatically. The effects of marriage breakdown on earning potential will thus be closely related to family life-cycle stage of the carer. A clean break is not so costly in a marriage in which the woman is re-established in the workforce after her children are all at school. It is potentially ruinous for a woman with several young children who has spent eight years in full-time housemothering. There is a clear conflict here between the practical and psychological desire to cut free and avoid conflict, and the economic wellbeing of the woman who will usually receive little alimony, have responsibility for young children, and have reduced earning capacity.

In two very common circumstances women do not easily become economically independent. Women who have had prime responsibility for children and who continue to assume this role after marriage breakdown are the first group, and older women who have been long out of the labour market the second. Unless they repartner, such women are likely to be poor, to have a very large drop in income, and to live at a standard of living much below that of their ex-spouse (Weston, 1986). Many, unable to get paid work, and unsupported after the clean break, become the responsibility of the Government, generating the blowout in the budget for supporting parent's benefits and allowances. For them, self-sufficiency is more a hope than a reality, since spousal maintenance provisions are frequently not used, and then only for short periods. Poverty is the common outcome.

Provisions for property division and support

In directing the fair and equitable settlement of the economic aspects of the marriage partnership the Family Law Act applies two modes of consideration. The first looks to the maintenance responsibilities of ex-spouses for each other, and the other relates to the disposition of tangible property. These two sets of provisions are to be coordinated to reach the overall result which, in contested cases, the judge uses to inform a decision. However, detailed reference to the weight applied to each possible factor in reaching the judgement does not need to be given.

Recent precedents have shown the law to be at an interesting crossroad in interpreting the provisions relating to the disposition of property. In Mallet's case (1984), FLC 91-507, a starting point of equality in dividing property was not upheld by the High Court. The implication is that, in determining the way property was to be divided, the Court should start from an assumption, not of equality, but of the necessity to establish the extent of each contribution under section 79(4). This may thus represent an area of considerable tension within the law, given the assumption of equal partnership proposed by the Australian Law Reform Commission.

If marriage is a partnership of equals, one of the key concepts in the Family Law Act, subjective assessments of contributions appear to be unwarranted except in circumstances where fraud is suspected or alleged. In addition to being generally unwarranted, such assessment will also be at best imprecise, since no scales of value exist for assessing contributions related to the welfare of the family and children. It is impossible to dispute the net sum of a series of values that are taken into account in arriving at a global judgement.

Moreover, any enquiry into contributions made as a spouse and parent comes perilously close to an investigation into the conduct of parties to the marriage. Even if this were to be considered appropriate, which I do not believe to be the case, the ECMB study has shown it to be unreliable (Funder, 1986c).

In coming to a decision on the just and equitable apportionment of property, the court may also balance contributions against a set of considerations as outlined in section 75(2), many of which are needs-based. Consideration of needs of the ex-spouses appears, however, to run counter to the concepts of both an equal partnership and the widely preferred clean break. Since women are most often the partners in need, these considerations risk enshrining women in their role as dependants. Practically, however, the results of the ECMB study on property distribution showed that the presence of dependent children was the only needs-based factor that significantly affected the apportionment of property (McDonald, 1986).

The demonstration of need depends on changing circumstances and may rightly arouse resentment if a lump sum is allocated at the time of settlement, but circumstances rapidly change for better or worse. In addition, changes of circumstance are not all related to the marriage and ex-partners may not see any relevance to them of subsequent illness or unemployment. The possibility of manipulation and pressure is considerable. Women with dependent children in their care would be advised to have the property settlement concluded before they repartner, retrain or enter the labour market. Men would be in a stronger position the longer the proceedings were delayed, so that the ex-wife is retrained, re-employed or repartnered.

In general it is difficult to say what values are put on individual contributions or needs, since judges do not have to give any account of the way in which they have assessed each factor in arriving at their final decision. With or without the assumption of equality of contribution, the system is producing results with a definite bias in favour of men in terms of standard of living. Another approach based on different considerations may have the seeds of a fairer and more predictable law.

Opportunity costs

Differences in earnings between men and women are multiply-determined but consistently described. Some differences exist even when education, occupation and continuity in paid work are held constant. Figure 10.1 shows a schematic representation of the lifetime earnings of men and women who have had continuous paid work experience.

When women withdraw from the labour market to care for children, the opportunity costs they incur from child rearing may be expressed in terms of life-time earnings vis-a-vis women of similar background who have had continuous paid work experience. It would not be appropriate to calculate these costs by comparison with the earnings of men, since there are structural differences that explain at least some of the differences in earnings between men and women, shown in Figure 10.1.

Opportunity costs of women who withdraw from the labour market to care for children may be calculated by comparing the earnings of a woman who withdraws from or amends her labour market participation to raise children with those of like women who do not interrupt their paid work. Figure 10.2 shows how these opportunity costs may be determined.

Opportunity costs are shared during the marriage partnership

Figure 10.1 Gender differences in earnings

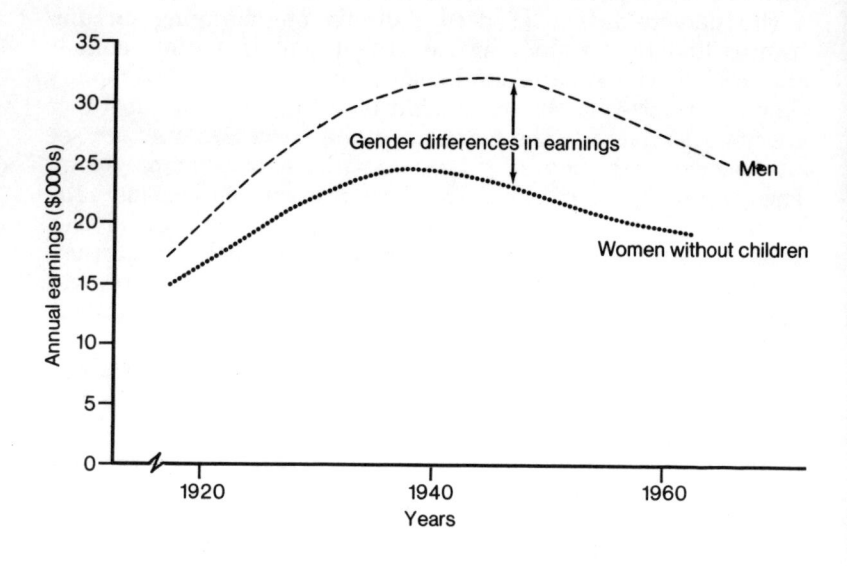

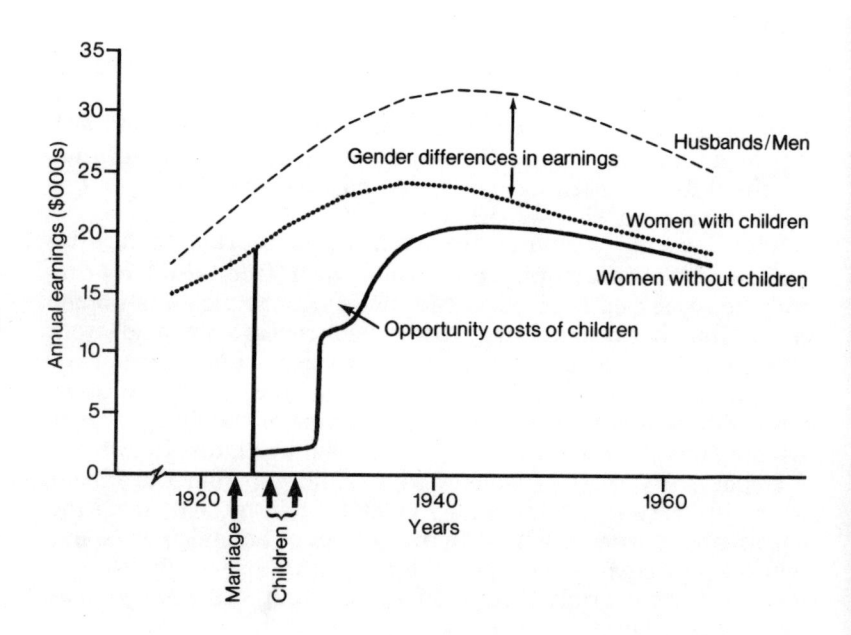

Figure 10.2 Opportunity costs of children

WORK IN MARRIAGE

Figure 10.3 Opportunity costs shared and debited

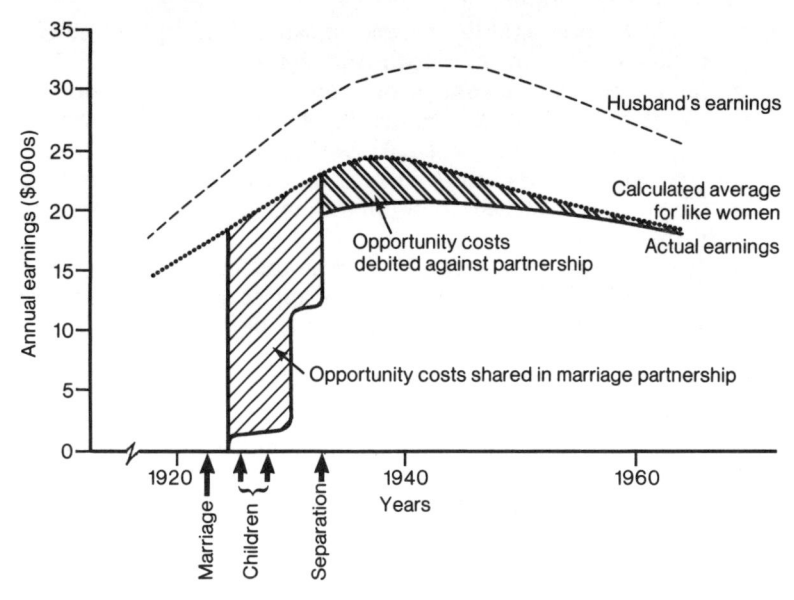

[Figure 10.3: Graph showing annual earnings ($000s) from 1920 to 1960. Curves shown: Husband's earnings, Calculated average for like women, Actual earnings. Hatched regions indicate "Opportunity costs debited against partnership" and "Opportunity costs shared in marriage partnership". Time markers on x-axis: Marriage, Children, Separation.]

and losses of income are counted against the quality of life for all family members and the parents' investment in the children. But when the partnership is dissolved, the costs that were once shared are borne by the individual whose income-earning capacity has been eroded by withdrawal from the labour market. Opportunity costs that must be carried by one partner after the dissolution of the marriage are the source of much of the inequality observed after settlement.

Figure 10.3 shows how opportunity costs, calculated against the life-time earnings expected for like women, may be calculated. Also shown is the apportionment of these opportunity costs into those that were shared within the marriage and those that are borne solely by the woman who has taken the primary role in rearing the children. It is these costs which should be considered as a debt against the marriage partnership.

An alternative approach

Any alternative approach to settlement of the marriage partnership should conform with a number of principles:

- It should produce just and equitable outcomes.
- It should be consistent with the principle of marriage as a

partnership of equals that does not exploit one partner at the expense of the other.
- It should be predictable and accountable, making public the principles and means of calculating shares.
- It should include a means of putting a dollar value on one of the most significant determinants of present inequalities — the depreciated earning capacity of women who have assumed the primary responsibility for rearing children and who have withdrawn or modified their labour market participation to fulfil this role.
- It should cover most cases in a fair and equitable way but allow the right of appeal against the application of the system to unusual cases where outcomes would be unjust.

At the heart of this proposal is the concept that labour invested in raising children and making a home detracts from efforts in the paid workforce. Withdrawal from the labour market has immediate costs to the marriage partnership in terms of lost earnings, which are shared during the marriage, as are the attendant advantages of having happy children, a secure income and a certain quality of life.

In the following discussion it is assumed that it is the woman who withdraws from the labour market and who incurs the loss in earning capacity. In our ECMB study we had no case of the reverse. The sex of the carer, however, is not important to the argument.

When a marriage ends the costs of the depreciated earnings that were previously absorbed by the partnership are carried by the partner whose paid work has been interrupted and whose individual earnings are reduced. The partner who has stayed in a paid job has typically an increased earning capacity through experience, extra training, earning increments that come with years of service, reputation as a worker, good will in business, etc. This means that instead of the assets (increased earning capacity) and the losses (depreciation in earnings) being shared, since they were in part or whole acquired during the marriage, the husband is left with the asset and the wife with the loss.

Fairness demands that the loss, in terms of continued depreciated earnings, be claimed against the assets of the partnership, since the loss was incurred while in the partnership and while contributing services to it. The loss should not be claimed against the husband inasmuch as both parties decided to apportion their roles on the tacit understanding that the benefits and costs be shared. The loss is thus a debt to be claimed against the marriage partnership at the time of settlement. The principle suggested here differs from the current thinking in several important ways.

It assumes that ex-wives, among whom are many poor and welfare recipients, have earned the right to some deferred payments against the losses they incurred in making their contributions to the marriage. They are thus reclassified as creditors asserting their claim against the marriage partnership rather than as being in need of support (either from the ex-spouse through maintenance or from public benefits). This approach is a powerful endorsement of marriage as a partnership between equals.

It does not require a tallying of contributions during the marriage, but assumes that the partnership was a shared enterprise. When the partnership is dissolved, however, debts that were carried in unison cannot be allocated to one party. Similarly, the whole orientation of the approach is retroactive, and not directed to guessing at future needs and circumstances; the debt once assessed and paid cannot be claimed again. The approach is thus consistent with the desire of people for the swiftest severing of financial ties.

Calculating the debt against the marriage partnership

There are several econometric models for calculating the opportunity costs of children. Opportunity costs may be broadly defined as 'the earnings that a woman might have had, but had to forgo, because of the need to care for her children' (Reed & McIntosh, 1971). Estimates are needed only for that portion of the costs borne by the woman after the marriage ends.

Costs are estimated by comparing the life-time earnings of groups of women who have had no children, and no child-induced interruptions to their labour market participation, with those of women who have borne children. The bases for these estimates are large nationally representative samples of women and the collection of statistics on their labour market participation, earnings and fertility. Two recent studies, in the United States (Calhoun and Espenshade, 1986) and in Great Britain (Joshi, 1984), are interesting examples. The United States study, based on the National Longitudinal Surveys of Labor Market Experience, used the Markov chain model variant of the state life table techniques to estimate family and paid work transitions of women in different categories. This approach provides the basis for describing the paid work-inhibiting effects of children on men and women over the whole working life. The use of longitudinal data permits estimates to be made of the opportunity costs for different cohorts, and to then predict future expenditure on a cohort basis.

The British study was based on cross-sectional data collected at interview from a nationally representative sample of women. This study measured the effect of dependent children on mothers' participation in the labour market and the differential in earnings associated with time out of the labour market, part-time participation and downward occupational mobility. Joshi demonstrates that interruptions to women's paid work are primarily associated with children and that the cost of these interruptions, measured by gross cash earnings forgone as a result of family formation, is about double the loss of actual woman-years in the labour market.

Both approaches can provide statistical estimates of the opportunity costs of children that lessen women's earning capacity in comparison with childless women of similar educational, occupational and regional characteristics; both suffer from a number of limitations. Predictions made from a group to an individual will contain errors. The predictions in both examples are based on observation of particular cohorts of people; those for whom the predictions are to be used as guides will have variously different individual histories. This is a weakness shared by all insurance tables and compensation estimates. For example, recent estimates of the life expectancy for young men aged eighteen in 1985 have been revised upward to 73.63 from 71.97 years in 1970–72 (ABS Lifetables).

These approaches to calculating opportunity costs might thus be used to generate tables of costs under a range of demographic, socio-economic, family formation and family dissolution circumstances. Such tables could then be made available to the public and used by the court as standards against which to assess the outstanding opportunity costs to be borne by the carer of the children. As with all insurance and compensation tables, each set of circumstances would be assessed within a band of values. The band would be set to cover about 96 percent of cases, outside of which there could be a system of appeal. Negotiations would be possible on the basis of individual variations, but the parameters would be set.

The allocation of opportunity costs to the partnership

To be both effective and equitable the following principles in compensating for lost earning capacity might be considered:

- Compensation is for prospective loss of income post-separation, to compensate for the cumulative loss following the lowered

WORK IN MARRIAGE

point of entry back into the labour market. It is *not* for the retrospective losses during the marriage; both losses during the marriage and the prospective cumulative loss post-separation are similar, however, in that they are a charge on the joint finances of the marriage.
- Compensation is calculated and finite, since ideally the compensation should be levied as a once-and-for-all debit against the net joint property of the marriage at the time of separation.

An outline of the procedures for the payment of compensation for opportunity costs might be as follows:

- Determine the net property of the partnership after all other liabilities have been accounted for.
- Deduct from that net amount another debt—that of the opportunity costs, payable in this case to one partner.
- Divide the remaining property equally between the partners.

An example of this process, constructed for an average case in the ECMB study, might be as follows: total value of net property assets before calculating opportunity costs was $50 000. Time out of the work force for a woman married ten years with two children aged seven and nine at the time of separation was about five years. For future opportunity costs of a clerical worker from the time of separation through the normal working life there are no scales, but on the basis that these costs would be diminishing over the working life between the ages of 34 and 60 years this is estimated at $20 000. On the assumption that these costs would be based on the difference between her full-time earnings and those of a matched woman without children, the calculation would be as follows:

	$	$
Total net assets:	50 000	
less opportunity costs	20 000	
remaining net assets	30 000	
	husband	wife
50/50 shares of remainder	15 000	15 000
outcome of property division and compensation payment	15 000	35 000

In the ECMB study, the average net annual income differential between men and women after tax and maintenance payments was $7800 in favour of the man at the time of interview, three to five years after separation. This difference comprises both an amount attributable to the general income differences between men and women and an amount attributable to support in the labour market by the marriage partnership and the opportunity costs of children on the carer. In this hypothetical case, the man would recoup in three years through the earnings differential the amount of compensation paid out of the marital property to compensate the wife for her continuing costs expressed in lowered earnings. In this example, there are clearly resources to pay the compensation entirely out of assets or to charge some of the debt against the husband's earnings in the years immediately following separation.

These rough estimates of a model cannot be taken much further without an Australian data base from which a scale of opportunity costs of children can be developed. With this scale and the data from the ECMB study, the limits of this proposition could be tested. In addition, possible conflicts between compensation claims and child maintenance responsibilities could be explored, together with the ambiguities about the opportunity costs and advantages of marriage *per se*. Calhoun and Espenshade (1986) report a slight earnings advantage to married men with children and Joshi finds that marriage *per se* has little effect on women's life-time earnings.

A study of 3000 women currently being undertaken at the Australian National University may provide a suitable data base for developing a working scale of values for the opportunity costs of children. Such a scale would have wider application than the context of divorce settlements. It would have implications for the ways in which household economies are organised. Within the present framework, however, the ultimate test will be whether this approach will result in more equitable outcomes than the present system and whether the logic of opportunity costs and their distribution will find acceptance in Australian society.

Any scheme for ameliorating the inequities in economic circumstances observed in the present system of finalising the economic partnership of marriage must logically and practically involve both private and public responsibility. If marriage is to be seen as a partnership of equals then its resolution should endorse that. Any other outcome implies an exploitation of one party. Each party must have the right to have debts against the marriage partnership honoured as far as possible. Conversely, not to honour such debts, and to leave a party in need because of that failure, is to create a dependency that unfairly stigmatises that party. Where there are resources, as there are in many cases, it is quite unfair that they not be tapped since not to do so spreads that debt to other tax-payers who are already absorbing similar costs in their own families.

On the other side, public responsibility is clear. The home-makers who have supported paid workers in market production have contributed to society. The rearers of the next generation make an economic contribution to the future (though these contributions are largely unobserved and uncounted in national economies). Thus society owes them some recompense for their work when the marriage partnership has insufficient funds. Moreover, since we accept the values of individualism in determining marriage relationships and their end, we must accept the public cost. Finally, as there is no possibility of individual marriage partnerships covering all the accumulated debts to the carer, it behoves the society to support the dependants and those who are their carers. As Edgar (1986) points out, all families are supported by public and private contributions. Families after divorce have particular needs, not categorically different needs.

ROSS A. WILLIAMS

Commentary

In this chapter families are treated as productive units operating in an intertemporal context. Income is generated from paid work. In order to generate that income adult labour must not only engage in paid activity but must carry out household activities such as cleaning, preparation of meals, and childcare. Non-labour inputs include purchases of food, clothing and shelter. The net monetary surplus each year is saving and assets are the sum of past surpluses.

The thrust of the argument is that, on dissolution of the partnership, assets should be distributed equally except for recognition that marriage has lowered the potential earning capacity of any adult household member, typically the wife, who has taken time off to care for children.

There is merit in the general approach adopted. A life-cycle approach to social issues is, in my view, nearly always to be preferred to just looking at current circumstances. The concept of income forgone after separation has much merit as a measure of compensation. It has the advantage of treating arrangements that held during the marriage as being mutually agreed upon and not requiring investigation. It is very difficult to measure interpersonal financial and barter arrangements over the length of a marriage. Any attempt to do so involves an investigation of past activities, which is likely to be distasteful for both partners.

The specific proposal for a lump-sum payment to cover future lost income has a number of weaknesses, however. Most importantly, there is no allowance for the discounting of future income in calculating the lump sum. A dollar received now is worth more than a dollar in ten years time, even with no inflation. More generally, Funder ignores the difficulties involved in converting expected future income flows into a lump sum payment. Assumptions need to be made about inflation, movements in earnings in different occupations, life expectation and so on. In addition, presumably compensation should cease or at least be re-examined after remarriage. The methodolgy also makes no allowance for initial holdings of wealth by each partner, at either first or subsequent marriages.

Because of all these difficulties it would seem preferable to pay income compensation annually rather than in a lump sum, with provisions for some borrowing to take place against future compensation. This would require assets to be held in a state-administered fund, say a Partner Dissolution Fund (PDF). At dissolution of the marriage the expected value of the equivalent lump sum compensation could be transferred to the PDF. Actual payments to the compensated partner may be greater than or less than anticipated. In the former case the PDF would need to be topped up, in the latter case a residual would remain at retirement age or on remarriage. These deviations around the average on expected values could be left to cancel out in the aggregate or require transfers between the fund and the partner whose career was not interrupted.

The proposal outlined by Funder appears to be designed primarily to deal with what might be called mature-marriage dissolution, that is, where the children are of an age that permits the wife to work. In the case of young couples with young children the assets of the household would generally be insufficient to cover lost earnings. This would be particularly so if lost earnings were defined as full-time earnings where children were under school age. Substantial modifications would be required to deal with this problem and any proposals would need to incorporate existing Government support schemes.

Two final comments. First, the ideas presented are most applicable to households where both adults are wage and salary earners. The issues are more complex when they relate to the self-employed and entrepreneurial classes. Secondly, the proposal is most feasible in the situation where one partner stops work for a few years to rear children. But increasingly the pattern is for both husband and wife to move in and out of the workforce—sometimes working full-time, sometimes part-time, sometimes not working at all. The practical difficulties of estimating forgone incomes are immense.

Bibliography

Anderson, D. S. and Vervoorn, A. E. (1983) *Access to Privilege: Patterns of Participation in Australian Post-Secondary Education* Canberra: Australian National University Press

Australian Bureau of Statistics (1976) *Wage Rates and Earnings* Canberra: ABS Catalogue No: 6312.0

—— (1977), Household Expenditure Survey (1975–6) *Bulletin Two: Expenditure Patterns for Households of Differing Characteristics and Compositions* Canberra: ABS Catalogue No. 6517.0

—— (1978) *1976 Census of Population and Housing* Canberra: ABS Catalogue No. 2401.3

—— (1983, 1984, 1985) *The Labour Force Australia* Canberra: ABS Catalogue No. 6203.0

—— (1984a) *Social Indicators* Canberra: ABS Catalogue No. 4101.0

—— (1984b) *Australian Families 1982* Canberra: ABS Catalogue No. 4408.0

—— (1985a) *Projections of the Populations of Australia, States and Territories, 1984 to 2021* Canberra: ABS Catalogue No. 3222.0

—— (1985b) *Labour Force Status and Educational Attainment* Canberra: ABS Catalogue No. 6235.0

—— (1986a) *Australian Demographic Trends* Canberra: ABS Catalogue No. 3102.0

—— (1986b) *Labour Force Status and Other Characteristics of Families July 1985* Canberra: ABS Catalogue No. 6224.0

Australian Council on the Ageing and Commonwealth Department of Community Services (1985) *Older People at Home* Canberra: Australian Government Publishing Service

Backett, K. C. (1982) *Mothers and Fathers: A Study of the Development and Negotiation of Parental Behaviour* London: Macmillan

Ball, F. L. J. (1983) *Understanding Problem Solving in Couple Relationships* PhD thesis, Berkeley: University of California

Bauman, Z. (1982) *Memories of Class: The Pre-History and After-Life of Class* London: Routledge and Kegan Paul

Becker, G. S. (1981) *A Treatise on the Family* Cambridge: Harvard University Press

Berk, R. A. and Berk, S. F. (1979) *Labour and Leisure at Home: Content and Organisation of the Household Day* Beverley Hills: Sage

—— (1983) 'Supply-side sociology of the family: The challenge of the new home economics' *Annual Review of Sociology* 9: 375–95

Berman, E. (1977) *The Cooperating Family* Englewood Cliffs: Prentice-Hall
Bernard, J. (1982) *The Future of Marriage* New Haven: Yale University Press
Boulding, K. E. (1978) *Ecodynamics: A New Theory of Societal Evolution* Beverley Hills: Sage
—— (1981) *A Preface to Grants Economics: The Economy of Love and Fear* New York: Praeger Publishers
Bradbury, B., Garde, P. and Vipond, J. (1985) *Bearing the Burden of Unemployment Unequally* SWRC Reports and Proceedings No. 53, Kensington: University of New South Wales
Brennan, D. (1986) 'Rights—at a price' *Australian Society* 5(6) June 38–40
Broom, D. (1982), 'Out of the frying-pan: Technological change and domestic work' *Women and Technological Change* Melbourne: Status of Women Committee, Sybylla Co-op Press and Publications Limited
—— (1984) 'Natural resources: health, reproduction and the gender order' in D. Broom (ed.) *Unfinished Business: Social Justice for Women in Australia* Sydney: Allen and Unwin
Brownlee H (1985) 'Poverty traps' *Australian Tax Forum* 2: 161–72.
Bryson, L. (1983) 'Thirty years of research on the division of labor in Australian families' *Australian Journal of Sex, Marriage and the Family* 4: 125–32
Bryson, L. and Eastop, L. (1980) 'Poverty, welfare and hegemony, 1973 and 1978' *The Australian and New Zealand Journal of Sociology* 16 (3): 61–71
Bryson, L. and Mowbray, M. (1986) 'Who cares? Social security, family policy and women' *Social Security Review* 2 (86): 186–200
Bureau of Labour Market Research (1985) *Who's in the Labour Force? A Study of Labour Force Participation* Research Report No. 7, Canberra: Australian Government Publishing Service
Burns, A. and Cairns, S. (1987) 'Mother-headed families: A cross-national comparison' *Australian Journal of Family Law* 1: 214–233
Burns, S. (1977) *The Household Economy: Its Shape, Origins and Future* Boston: Beacon Press
Calasanti, T. and Bonnano, A. (1986) 'The social creation of dependence, dependency ratios, and the elderly in the United States: A critical analysis' *Social Science and Medicine* 23 (12): 1229–36
Calhoun, C. A. and Espenshade, T. J. (1986) 'The opportunity costs of rearing American children', Project report, Washington: The Urban Institute
Carter, J. (1981) *Nothing to Spare* Melbourne: Penguin
Cass, B. (1978) 'Women's place in the class structure', in E. Wheelwright and K. Buckley (eds) *Essays in the Political Economy of Australian Capitalism* vol. 3, Sydney: Australia and New Zealand Book Company
—— (1986a) 'The economic circumstances of single parent families in Australia: 1974–1985. Some implications for child maintenance policies and the social security system', paper prepared for presentation at workshop on *Child Support Issues* Canberra: Social Justice Project, Australian National University

—— (1986b) 'The case for review of aspects of the Australian social security system' *Social Security Journal* June, Canberra: Australian Government Publishing Service pp. 2–8

—— (1986c) *Income support for families with children* Issues Paper No. 1, Social Security Review, Canberra: Department of Social Security

Chapman, B. and Gruen, F. (1984) 'Unemployment, the Background to the Problem' *Discussion paper No. 90* Centre for Economic Policy Research, Canberra: Australian National University

Chevan, A. and Korson, J. (1972) 'The widowed who live alone: an examination of social and demographic factors' *Social Forces* 51: 45–53

Chipman, L. (1981) 'National family policy—a concept', in The Australian Family Association *Second Annual Seminar, The Family—Education and Community Support* Melbourne: University of Melbourne

Cities Commission (1975) *Australians' Use of Time, Albury–Wodonga and Melbourne 1974: A Preliminary Report* Canberra: Cities Commission

Clark, C. (1958) 'The economics of housework' *Quarterly Bulletin of the Oxford University Institute of Statistics* 20: 205–11

Coleman, L. and Watson, S. (1987) *Women Over Sixty: A Study of the Housing, Economic and Social Circumstances of Older Women* Canberra: Australian Institute of Urban Studies

Connell, R.W. (1977) *Ruling Class, Ruling Culture* Cambridge: Cambridge University Press

Connell, R.W. and Irving, T. (1980) *Class Structure in Australian History* Sydney: Allen and Unwin

Coverman, S. (1983) 'Explaining husbands' participation in domestic labour' *Sociological Quarterly* 26: 81–97

Cowan, R.S. (1976) 'The "Industrial Revolution" in the home: Household technology and social change in the 20th century' *Technology and Culture* 17: 1–23

Davidoff, L. (1979) 'The separation of home and work? Landladies and lodgers in nineteenth and twentieth century England', in S. Burman (ed.) *Fit Work for Women* London: Croom Helm pp. 64–98

Delphy, C. (1984) *Close to Home: A Materialist Analysis of Women's Oppression* London: Hutchinson; Amherst: University of Massachusetts Press

Dempsey, K. (1981) 'The rural aged' Chapter 18 in A. Howe (ed.) *Towards an Older Australia* St Lucia: University of Queensland Press

Department of Community Services (1986) *Nursing Homes and Hostels Review* Canberra: Australian Government Publishing Service

Department of Immigration and Ethnic Affairs (1985) *Australia's Population Trends and Prospects, 1985* Canberra: Australian Government Publishing Service

Economic Planning Advisory Council (1986a) *Growth in Australian Social Expenditures* Canberra: Australian Government Publishing Service

BIBLIOGRAPHY

―― (1986b) *Trends in Employment and Unemployment* Canberra: Australian Government Publishing Service

Edgar, D. (1986) 'Marriage, the family and family law in Australia' *Discussion Paper No. 13* Melbourne: Australian Institute of Family Studies

Edwards, M. (1979) 'The economics of home activities', paper given at the conference of the Sociology Association of Australia and New Zealand, Canberra.

―― (1981) *Financial Arrangements Within Families* Canberra: National Women's Advisory Council

―― (1984) *The income unit in the Australian tax and social security systems* Melbourne: Institute of Family Studies

Eisner, R. (1978) 'Total incomes in the United States, 1959 and 1969' *Review of Income and Wealth* 24: 41–70

Eisner, R., Simons, E., Pieper, P. and Bender, S. (1982) 'Total incomes in the United States, 1946–1976: a summary report' *Review of Income and Wealth* 28: 133–74

England, P. and Farkas, G. (1986) *Households, Employment and Gender: A Social, Economic and Demographic View* New York: Aldine

Finch, J. (1980) 'Devising conventional performances: The case of clergymen's wives' *Sociological Review* 28: 851–70

Finch, J. and Groves, D. (eds) (1983) *A Labour of Love. Women, Work and Caring* London: Routledge and Kegan Paul

Frey, D. (1986) *Survey of Sole Parent Pensioners' Workforce Barriers* Background/Discussion Paper No. 12, Social Security Review, Canberra: Department of Social Security

Funder, K. (1986a) 'The design of the study', in P. McDonald (ed.) *Settling Up: Property and Income Distribution on Divorce in Australia* Melbourne: The Australian Institute of Family Studies and Sydney: Prentice-Hall pp. 15–39

―― (1986b) 'Work and the marriage partnership', in P. McDonald (ed.) *Settling Up: Property and Income Distribution on Divorce in Australia* Melbourne: Australian Institute of Family Studies and Sydney: Prentice-Hall pp. 65–99

―― (1986c) 'His and her divorce', in P. McDonald (ed.) *Settling Up: Property and Income Distribution on Divorce in Australia* Melbourne: The Australian Institute of Family Studies and Sydney: Prentice-Hall pp. 224–40

Gallagher, P. (1985) 'Targeting welfare expenditures on the poor: Work in progress on poverty in Australia 1981–82' *Social Security Journal* December Canberra: Australian Government Publishing Service, pp. 19–34

Gallagher, P. and Foster, C. (1986) 'Targeting Income Support to the Poor' *Income Support Seminar* Melbourne: Standing Committee of Social Welfare Administrators

Game, A. and Pringle, R. (1984) 'Production and consumption public versus private', in D. Broom (ed.) *Unfinished Business: Social Justice for Women in Australia* Sydney: Allen and Unwin

Garnsey, E. (1982) 'Women's work and theories of class and stratification', in A. Giddens and D. Held (eds) *Classes, Power and Conflict: Classical and Contemporary Debates* London: Macmillan

George, L. K. (1980) 'Role transitions in later life: Residential relocation' Chapter 7 in *Role Transitions in Later Life* Pacific Grove: Brooks/Cole

George, V. and Wilding, P. (1984) *The Impact of Social Policy* London: Routledge and Kegan Paul

Gibson, D. (1985) 'The dormouse syndrome — restructuring the dependency of the elderly' *Australian New Zealand Journal of Sociology* 21: 44–63.

Gilbert, N. (1982) 'The plight of universal social services' *Journal of Policy Analysis and Management* 1 (3): 301–16

—— (1983) *Capitalism and the Welfare State: Dilemmas of Social Benevolence* New Haven: Yale University Press

Gilder, G. (1981) *Wealth and Poverty* New York: Basic Books

Gillin, E. (1974) 'Social indicators and economic welfare' *Economic Papers* 46: 48–82

Glezer, H. (1984) 'Changes in marriage and sex-role attitudes among young married women: 1971–1982', in Australian Family Research Conference *Proceedings, Family Formation, Structure, Values* vol. 1 Melbourne: Institute of Family Studies

—— (1986) 'The impact of the first birth: Determinants of continuing in the workforce amongst married women in Australia', paper presented at *The Second Australian Family Research Conference* Melbourne: Australian Institute of Family Studies

Glick, P. (1977) 'Updating the family life cycle' *Journal of Marriage and the Family* 39: 5–13

Goode, W. (1982) 'Why men resist', in B. Thorne and M. Yalom (eds) *Rethinking the Family* New York: Longman pp. 131–50

Goodnow, J. J. (1985) 'Topics, methods, and models: Feminist challenges in social science', in J. J. Goodnow and C. Pateman (eds) *Women, Social Science and Public Policy* Sydney: Allen and Unwin pp. 1–31

—— (1988a) 'Children's household work: Its nature and functions' *Psychological Bulletin* 103: 5–26

Goodnow, J. J. and Delaney, S. (in press) 'Children's household work: Task differences, styles of assignment, and links to family relations' *Journal of Applied Developmental Psychology*

Gorz, A. (1982) *Farewell to the Working Class: An Essay on Post-Industrial Socialism* London: Pluto Press

Gouldner, A. W. (1979) *The Future of Intellectuals and the Rise of the New Class* London: Macmillan

Gullestad, M. (1984) *Kitchen-table society: A case study of the family life and friendships of young working class mothers in urban Norway* Oslo: Universitetsforlaget

Haas, N. (1982) 'Determinants of role-sharing behavior: A study of egalitarian couples' *Sex Roles* 8: 747–60

Halter, W. and Hemming, R. (1985) *Social Security Pension Financing in the Context of Demographic Change* Paris: Organization for Economic Cooperation and Development

Harper, J. and Richards, S. (1979) *Mothers and Working Mothers* Ringwood: Penguin
Harrison, M. (1986) 'Attitudes to lawyers and the legal process', in P. McDonald (ed.) *Settling Up: Property and Income Distribution on Divorce in Australia* Melbourne: Australian Institute of Family Studies and Sydney: Prentice-Hall pp. 241–58
Hartmann, J. (1981) 'The family as the locus of gender, class and political struggle: The example of housework' *Signs* 6: 366–94
Hawrylyshun, O. (1976) 'The value of household services: a survey of empirical estimates' *Review of Income and Wealth* 22: 101–31
Henderson, R. F. (1975) *Poverty in Australia, Commission of Enquiry into Poverty, First Main Report* Canberra: Australian Government Publishing Service
Hershlag, Z. Y. (1960) 'The case of unpaid domestic service' *Economic Inter-regionale* 13: 25–41
Hinrichs, K., Offe, C. and Wiesenthal, H. (1984/85) 'The crisis of the welfare state and alternative modes of work redistribution' *Thesis Eleven* 10/11: 37–55
House of Representatives Standing Committee on Expenditure (1982) *In a Home or at Home: Accommodation and Home Care for the Aged* Canberra: Australian Government Publishing Service
Howe, A. (1978) 'The changing distribution of Melbourne's aged population: Patterns and implications' *Australian Geographical Studies* 16: 136–48
Howe, A. (ed.) (1981) *Towards an Older Australia* St Lucia: University of Queensland Press
―――― (1986) 'Aged care services: An analysis of provider roles and provision outcomes' *Urban Policy and Research* 4: (3) 2–14
Hugo, G. J. (1986) *Australia's Changing Population: Trends and Implications* Melbourne: Oxford University Press
Ironmonger, D. (1982) 'Income security and the future', in R. Mendelsohn (ed.) *Social Welfare Finance: Selected Papers* Canberra: Centre for Research on Federal Financial Relations, Australian National University pp. 15–35
―――― (1988a) 'Statistical perspectives and economic stability', in D. Ironmonger, J. O. N. Perkins and Tran Van Hoa (eds) *National Income and Economic Progress* London: Macmillan, pp. 32–48
Ironmonger, D. and Sonius, E. (1987) 'Household productive activities' Research Discussion Number 2, Melbourne: Centre for Applied Research on the Future, University of Melbourne
Jacklin, C. (1984) 'Opening address' at The Australian Psychological Society Meeting, Perth, August
Jamrozik, A. (1981) 'Changes in the labour market and social policy', in B. Cass (ed.) *Unemployment: Causes, Consequences, and Policy Implications* SWRC Reports and Proceedings No. 11, Kensington: University of New South Wales pp. 53–72
―――― (1986) 'Social security and the social wage: priorities and options in social policy', in A. Jamrozik (ed.) *Social Security and Family Welfare: Directions and Options Ahead* SWRC Reports and Proceedings No. 61, Kensington: University of New South Wales pp. 9–41

—— (1987) 'Winners and losers in the welfare state: recent trends and pointers to the future', in P. Saunders (ed.) *Social Welfare in the late 1980s: Reform, Progress, or Retreat?* SWRC Reports and Proceedings No. 66, Kensington: University of New South Wales pp. 45-78

Jamrozik, A. and Beck, R. (1981) *Worker Co-operatives: An Evaluative Study of the New South Wales Worker Co-operative Programme* SWRC Reports and Proceedings No. 12, Kensington: University of New South Wales

Jones, B. (1982) *Sleepers, Wake! Technology and the Future of Work* Melbourne: Oxford University Press

Jones, F.L. (1984) 'Income inequality', chapter 5 in D. Broom (ed.) *Unfinished Business: Social Justice for Women in Australia* Sydney: Allen and Unwin

Jordan, A. (1987) *The Common Treasury. The Distribution of Income to Families and Households* Background Paper Social Security Review, Canberra: Australian Government Publishing Service

Joshi, H. (1984) 'Women's participation in paid work: further analysis of women and employment survey' *Department of Employment Monograph No. 45* London: Her Majesty's Stationery Office

Kendig, H. (1981) 'Housing and living arrangements of the aged', in A. Howe (ed.) *Towards an Older Australia* St Lucia: University of Queensland Press

—— (1984) 'Blood ties and gender roles: Adult children who care for aged parents', in *Australian Family Research Conference, Proceedings: Support Networks* vol. V Melbourne: Institute of Family Studies

—— (ed.) (1986) *Ageing and Families: A Social Networks Perspective* Sydney: Allen and Unwin

Kendig, H., Gibson, D., Rowland, D. and Hemer, J.M. (1983) *Health, Welfare and Family in Later Life* Canberra: Ageing and the Family Project, Research School of Social Sciences, Australian National University

Kendig, H. and McCallum, J. (1986) *Greying Australia: The Future Impact of Population Ageing* National Population Council Report, Canberra: Australian Government Publishing Service

Kinnear, D. and Graycar, A. (1984) 'Ageing and family dependency' *Australian Journal of Social Issues* 19: (1) 13-26

Kinnear, D. and Rossiter, C. (1984) 'Family care policies: Findings from a survey of carers' in *Australian Family Research Conference, Proceedings, Support Networks* vol. V, Melbourne: Institute of Family Studies

Kobrin, F. (1976) 'The fall in household size and the rise of the primary individual in the United States' *Demography* 13: 127-38

Krivo, L. and Mutchler, J. (1986) 'Metropolitan variation in household status of the elderly: A cross-sectional analysis' Paper presented at the annual meetings of the Population Association of America, San Francisco, April

Krupinski, J. and Mackenzie, A. (eds) (1979) *The Health and Social Survey of the North West Region of Melbourne* Melbourne: Health Commission of Victoria

Kumar, K. (1978) *Prophecy and Progress: The Sociology of Industrial* and *Post-Industrial Society* Harmondsworth: Penguin

Lampman, R. and Smeeding, T. (1983) 'Interfamily transfers as alternatives to government transfers to persons' *Review of Income and Wealth* 29: 45–66

Land, H. and Rose, H. (1985) 'Compulsory altruism for some, or an altruistic society for all?', in P. Bean, J. Ferris and D. Whynes (eds) *In Defence of Welfare* London: Tavistock

Linder, S.B. (1970) *The Harried Leisure Class* New York: Columbia University Press

Lopata, H.Z. (1971) *Occupation: Housewife* London: Oxford University Press

Luxton, M. (1980) *More Than a Labour of Love: Three Generations of Women's Work in the Home* Toronto: Women's Press

McClelland, A. (1987) *Investing in Our Future: A Better Deal for Children* Melbourne: Brotherhood of St Laurence

McDonald, P. (1985) *The Economic Consequences of Marital Breakdown in Australia* Melbourne: Institute of Family Studies

—— (1986) 'Property distribution: the shares of each partner and their determinants', in P. McDonald (ed.) *Settling Up: Property and Income Distribution on Divorce in Australia* Melbourne: Australian Institute of Family Studies and Sydney: Prentice-Hall pp. 171–93

Maddock, R. and Carter, M. (1983) 'Work and wellbeing', paper to the *First Spring Workshop in Economic History* Canberra: Australian National University

Mandeville, T. (1986) 'Information and the emerging self-serviced household economy', in R. Castle, D. Lewis and J. Maugan (eds) *Work, Leisure and Technology* Melbourne: Longman Cheshire pp. 256–67

Matthews, J.J. (1984) 'Deconstructing the masculine universe: the case of women's work', in Women and Labour Publications Collective *All Her Labours: Working it Out* Sydney: Hale and Iremonger

Michael, R., Fuchs, V. and Scott, S. (1980) 'Changes in the propensity to live alone: 1950–1976' *Demography* 17: 39–53

Miller, J.G. (1978) *Living Systems* New York: McGraw-Hill

Mincer, J. (1980) 'Human capital and earnings', in A.B. Atkinson (ed.) *Wealth, Income and Inequality* 2nd edn Oxford: Oxford University Press

Montague, M. (1987) A response paper to the Social Security Issues Paper No. 3

Montague, M. and Stephens, J. (1985) *Paying the Price for Sugar and Spice, A Study of Women's Pathways into Social Security Recipiency* Canberra: Australian Government Publishing Service

Moore, J. and Whiteford, P. (1987) *Trends in the Disposable Incomes of Australian Families, 1964–65 to 1985–86* Social Security Review Background Discussion Paper No. 11, Research Paper No. 31, Dec. 1986, Canberra: Australian Government Publishing Service

Morgan, J.N. (1978) 'Intra-family transfers revisited: The support of dependants inside the family', in *Five Thousand American Families —Patterns of Economic Progress, Vol. 16* Ann Arbor: Institute of Social Research, University of Michigan

Murray, C. (1984) *Losing Ground: American Social Policy 1950–1980* New York: Basic Books

Nissel, M. (1980) 'The family and the welfare state' *New Society* 7 August 259–62

Oakley, A. (1974a) *The Sociology of Housework* New York: Pantheon

―― (1974b) *Woman's Work: The Housewife Past and Present* New York: Pantheon Books, Random House

―― (1981) *Subject Women* Oxford: Martin Robertson

Ochiltree, G. and Amato, P. (1984) 'Child and adolescent competence in three family types', paper presented at seminar at James Cook University, Townsville: James Cook University, July

Office of Child Care (1986) *Child Care Handbook* (and associated documents) Canberra: Commonwealth Department of Community Services

O'Loughlin, M. A. and Cass, B. (1985) 'Married women's employment status and family income distribution', in R. Hooke (ed.) *54th ANZAAS Congress: SWRC Papers* SWRC Reports and Proceedings No. 47, Kensington: University of New South Wales

Organisation for Economic Co-operation and Development (1984) *Employment Outlook* Paris: Organisation for Economic Co-operation and Development

Pahl, R. E. (1982) 'The pockmarked road to a private life' *New Society* 7 October, 12–14

―― (1984) *Divisions of Labour* Oxford: Basil Blackwell

Pampel, F. (1983) 'Changes in the propensity to live alone: 1950–1976' *Demography* 20: 433–47

Peplau, L. A. (1983) 'Roles and gender', in H. H. Kelley, E. Berscheid, A. Christensen, J. H. Harvey, T. L. Huston, G. Levinger, E. McClintock, L. A. Peplau and D. R. Peterson (eds) *Close Relationships* New York: Freeman pp. 220–64

Pigou, A. C. (1920) *The Economics of Welfare* London: Macmillan (fifth edition 1946)

Prinsley, D., Kidd, B., Howe, A. and Cameron, K. (1979) *The Experience of Retirement Migration to Phillip Island and its Impact on the Community* Occasional Paper in Gerontology, Melbourne: National Research Institute for Gerontology and Geriatric Medicine, University of Melbourne

Radford, A., Badcock, K. and Hugo, G. (1981) *The Elderly of Port Elliot and Goolwa in South Australia* Monograph 5, Adelaide: Unit of Primary Care and Community Medicine, The Flinders University of South Australia

Ravetz, A. (1965) 'Modern technology and an ancient occupation: Housework in present-day society' *Technology and Culture* 6: 256–60

Raymond, J. (1987) *Bringing Up Children Alone: Policies for Sole Parents* Social Security Review Issues Paper No. 3, Department of Social Security, Canberra: Australian Government Publishing Service

Redcliff, N. and Mingione, E. (eds) (1985) *Beyond Employment: Household, Gender and Subsistence* Oxford: Basil Blackwell

Reed, R. H. and McIntosh, S. (1971) 'Costs of children', in E. R. Morse and R. H. Reed (eds) *Economic Aspects of Population Change* Washington: US Government Printing Office

Rosenman, L. (1982) 'Widowhood and social welfare policy in Australia' *Social Welfare Research Centre Reports and Proceedings* No. 16, Kensington: University of New South Wales

Rosenman, L., Shulman, A. D. and Penman, R. (1981) 'Support systems of widowed women in Australia' *Australian Journal of Social Issues* 16 (1): 18–31

Roustang, G. (1983) 'Changes in the relationship between work and social life', Expert Meeting on *Can There Be a New Welfare State: Social Policy Options Towards Shaping an Uncertain Future* Vienna: European Centre for Social Welfare Training and Research

Rowland, D. (1982a) 'The vulnerability of the aged in Sydney' *Australian and New Zealand Journal of Sociology* 18: 229–47

Rowland, D. (1982b) 'Living arrangements and the later family life cycle in Australia' *Australian Journal on Ageing* 1: (2) 3–6

Rudd, D. M. (1987) The Ageing of Non Metropolitan Local Area Populations in South Australia, MA Thesis, Adelaide: Flinders University of South Australia

Rudd, D. and Hugo, G. (eds) (1983) *Willunga's Ageing Population: Implications for Current and Future Service Provision* Adelaide: School of Social Sciences, The Flinders University of South Australia

Rudd, D. and Hugo, G. (eds) (1985) *Studies in the Social Geography of Northern Yorke Peninsula* Adelaide: School of Social Sciences, The Flinders University of South Australia

Russell, G. (1983) *The Changing Role of Fathers?* St Lucia: University of Queensland Press

Saunders, P. (1987) 'Past developments and future prospects for social security in Australia' pp 13–44 in P. Saunders and A. Jamrozik (eds) *Social Welfare in the late 1980s: Reform, Progress or Retreat* SWRC Reports and Proceedings No. 65, Kensington: University of New South Wales

Scanzoni, J. (1979) *Sex roles, women's work, and marital conflict* Lexington: Heath

Scutt, J. and Graham, D. (1984) *For Richer, For Poorer: Marriage and Property Rights* Ringwood: Penguin

Shanas, E. (1980) 'Older people and their families: the new pioneers' *Journal of Marriage and the Family* 42: 9–15

Sheehan, P. and Stricker, P. (1981) 'Welfare benefits and the labour market', in R. Blandy (ed.) *Understanding Labour Markets* Sydney: Allen and Unwin

Snooks, G. D. (1983) 'Household services and national income in Australia, 1891–1981: some preliminary results', paper to the *First Spring Workshop in Economic History* Canberra: Australian National University

Social Welfare Policy Secretariat (1984) *The Impact of Population Changes on Social Expenditure: Projections from 1980–81 to 2021* Canberra: Social Welfare Policy Secretariat

Sweeney, T. and Jamrozik, A. (1984) *Perspective in Child Care: Experiences of Parents and Service Providers* SWRC Reports and Proceed-

ings No. 44, Kensington: University of New South Wales
Szalai, A. (1972) *The Use of Time: Daily Activities of Urban and Suburban Populations in Twelve Countries* The Hague: Mouton
Thomas, K. and Wister, A. (1984) 'Living arrangements of older women: the ethnic dimension' *Journal of Marriage and the Family* 46: 301–12
Tulloch, P. (1984) 'Gender and dependency', in D. Broom (ed.) *Unfinished Business: Social Justice for Women in Australia* Sydney: Allen and Unwin pp. 19–37
Vanek, J. (1974) 'Time spent in housework' *Scientific American* 231: 116–20
—— (1978) 'Household technology and social status: Rising living standards and residence differences in housework' *Technology and Culture* 19 (3): 361–75
Vipond, J. and Bradbury, B. (1987) Personal communication (to B. Cass and P. Whiteford)
Voysey, E. (1986) 'Sole parents and domestic barriers to employment' *Australian Quarterly* 58 (4): 398–406
Wearing, B. (1983) *The Ideology of Motherhood* Sydney: Allen and Unwin
Welfare Rights Centre (1985) 'Tougher line on casual earnings' *Welfare Rights Centre Newsletter* December
Westergaard, J. and Resler, H. (1975) *Class in a Capitalist Society: A Study of Contemporary Britain* London: Heinemann
Weston, R. (1986) 'Changes in household income circumstances' in P. McDonald (ed.) *Settling Up: Property and Income Distribution on Divorce in Australia* Melbourne: Australian Institute of Family Studies and Sydney: Prentice-Hall pp. 100–30
White, L.K. and Brinkerhoff, D.B. (1981a) 'Children's work in the family: Its significance and meaning' *Journal of Marriage and the Family* 43: 789–98
—— (1981b) 'The sexual division of labor: Evidence from childhood' *Social Forces* 60: 170–81
Whiteford, P. (1986) 'Unemployment and family incomes', paper given at *Second Australian Family Research Conference* Melbourne: Australian Institute of Family Studies
Yawney, V.A. and Slover, O. (1979) 'Relocation of the elderly', in A. Monk (ed.) *The Age of Ageing, A Reader in Social Gerontology* Buffalo New York: Prometheus pp. 164–178
Zelizer, V. (1985) *Pricing the Priceless Child* New York: Basic Books

Index

Aboriginal people, 162
ABS, *see* Australian Bureau of Statistics
ACOTA, *see* Australian Council on the Ageing
Adelaide, 116-9, 122
adult population, 25
age and illness, 138
age structure, 167
aged, 115-19, 123, 126, 127, 165
aged accommodation, 121, 124
Ageing and Family Project, 127
agriculture, 30
Albury-Wodonga, 11, 21-5, 36
alimony, 177
alternative lifestyle, 65, 66
Amato, P., 101, 106
Anderson D. S., 69
animals, 22, 26
ANU, *see* Australian National University
Australia, 7, 8, 31, 44, 64-9, 72, 113, 115, 127, 143, 145, 151-6, 160, 161, 164-8, 173
Australian data base, 186; labour force, 65; social and economic life, 159; society, 64, 68, 186; time-use survey, ix, 8; welfare state, 159
Australian Bureau of Statistics, ix, 8, 18, 25, 28, 68, 69, 100, 105, 113, 117-21, 128, 154, 155, 164, 165
Australian Council on the Ageing, 115, 128
   Department of Science, 18
   Family Law Act (1975), 173
   Financial Review, 70
   Institute of Family Studies, 97-100, 110, 174-175
   Law Reform Commission, 176, 178
   National University, 7, 128, 186
   Research Committee, xi
   Research Grants Committee, xi, 38

automatic indexation, 157
autonomy, 45, 46, 79, 80

Backett, K. C., 41, 45, 55, 56
Badcock K., 117
Ball, F. L. J., 46
barriers to work, 137, 139
barter, 65, 81, 106,
Bauman, Z., 67
Beck, R., 76
Becker G. S., 3, 150, 151, 153
Bender, S., 7
benefits, 157
Berk R. A., 3, 20, 21, 36, 37
Berk S. F., 3, 20, 21, 36, 37
Berman, E., 43
Bernard, J., 173
boarding houses, 25, 99
Bonanno, A., 166
Boulding, K. E., 11, 3
Bowes, Jenny, 38
Bradbury, B., 161, 163
breadwinning, 152
Brennan, D., 70
Brinkeroff, D. B., 43, 46, 48, 49
Britain, 7, 72, 73, 82, 152, 166, 167, 183, 184
Broom, D., 20, 153
Brotherhood of St Laurence, 141-3, 146, 148; Income and Expenditure Survey, 131
Brownlee, H., 108
Bryson, L., 45, 46, 74, 76
Bureau of Labour Market Research, 152
Burns, S., 5, 6
business, 176

Calasanti, T., 166
Calhoun, C. A., 183, 186
Canada, 7, 167
CAPIL Pilot Evaluation Study, 99, 100

201

capital equipment, 31
capital gains tax, 17
capitalism, 66, 77, 79, 80, 82, 146
carers, 74, 92, 124, 177
cars, 6, 9, 67, 80, 82, 133
Carter, J., 128
Carter, M., 7, 8
cash benefits, 147; economy, 104; transfers, 146, 156
Cass, B., 97, 101, 149, 152–4, 163, 172
census data, 115
Census of Population and Housing, 128
changing technology, 43
Chapman, B., 162
chemists, 26, 30
Chevan, A., 114
child care, 6, 7, 15, 20, 22, 26, 31, 33, 35–7, 60, 69, 70, 85, 88, 90, 91, 94, 95, 106, 108, 110, 112, 132, 135, 139, 148, 169, 172; arrangements, 69; centres, 45; fees, 30; formal and informal, 69; inputs, 30; part-time, 91; travel, 29; services, 70, 74, 75; work-based, 80, 81
childcarers, 81, 144
child maintenance system, 142
child rearing, 14, 39, 40, 44, 54, 173
children, 20, 29, 35, 37, 46–8, 51, 52, 53, 87, 88, 90, 96, 97, 100–102, 131, 134–6, 139, 142, 143, 151, 152, 155, 161–3, 166, 169, 172, 177–9, 181–5, 189; and household work: 48; raising and caring, 64; supplemental care, 42;
children's views on work, 57
Chipman, L., 150
Christmas, 133
Cities Commission, 11, 18, 21
civic and collective 7, 15, 23, 25, 26
civic and community activities, 75, 76, 81
Clark, C., 7
class, 64, 66–70, 73–75, 77, 81; conceptions of, 01; new middle, 69; differences, 73–75; division inequalities, 68, 70, 74, 75; homogamy, 68; interests, 74; structure, 64, 66, 77
cleaning, 6, 35, 49, 52, 69
Coleman, L., 127
Collins Street farmers, 66
Commission for the Future, xi
commodification, 67, 75, 76, 82; bulwark against, 79; process, 72
commodify activities, 76
commodities, new and outmoded, 11
communications technologies, 9–11

community, 65, 90; health services, 121; care, 74; services, 126, 68; support, 125
competence, 53, 54
computing systems, 9
Connell, R. W., 81
consumer behaviour, 4, 10, 150; durables, 67; market, 73
Consumer Price Index (CPI), 142, 158
consumption, 65, 75; patterns, 77; unit, 21
contraception, 20
contract work, 75
cooking, 6, 9, 20, 22, 26, 28–31, 35, 61
cooperatives, 75, 76
councils, 122; school, 74; local, 74
counsellors, 71
country areas, 121; towns, 105; 119
couples, 41, 45, 47, 54, 55
Coverman, S., 45
Cowan, R. S., 20
CPI, *see* Consumer Price Index
credit, access to, 71
Cross, B., xi
Crossley, L., xi
cultural activities, 75; barriers, 88

data logging, 11
Davidoff, L., 43
Dawes, Lesley, 38
Day, 115, 118
day-care 74, 139
Delaney, S., 38, 49
Delphy, C., 39, 80, 81
demarcation disputes, 44
demographic change, 149
Dempsey, K., 128
Department of Community Services, 113; Immigration and Ethnic Affairs, 113; Social Security, 144, 154; Veterans' Affairs, 154
dependency ratio, 164
dependent children, 160; females, 126, 160; people care, 35
dignity of labour, 46
disabilities, 88
disabled, care of, 86
discussion groups, 74
dishwashing, 29, 37, 52, 61, 80
disposable income, 156
distribution of income, 4
distribution of work, 57
division of labour, 5, 19, 46, 48, 67
division of property, 171
divorce, 15, 16, 109, 114, 158, 173–5, 177

INDEX

do-it-yourself, 64, 65, 67
doctors, 133
domestic labour, 93; labourer, 19; servants, 69, 73; services, 28, 37, 69
Draper, M., 16, 93
duty and obligation, 153

earnings concession, 107
Eastop, L., 70
ECMB study, *see* Economic Consequences of Marriage Breakdown
ecological model, 11, 17
econometric, 11, 183
Economic Consequences of Divorce, Survey 110
Economic Consequences of Marriage Breakdown (ECMB), 174, 178, 182, 185, 186
economic inequalities, 74; insecurity, 162; management, 76; reality, 77; welfare, 37, 160
Economic Planning Advisory Council, 154
economics, 33, 44; of labour, 4
economies of scale, 32
economists, 14, 44, 58, 82, 171
economy, formal and informal, 65, 77, 79
Edgar, D., 173, 187
education, 68, 69, 70
Edwards, M., 34, 44, 152
Eisner, R., 7
elderly, 45, 81, 86, 114
electricity, 20, 26, 29
emotional labour, 40
employment: uncoupling work from, 76
employment agencies, 70
employment of opportunities, 148
energy, 11, 18, 19, 30, 132
England, P., 40, 44, 45
English, 139, 144
entertainment, 27, 29
environmental impact, 11
equal employment, 85
equality, 80
equipment, 9, 11, 30
equity, 14, 40, 52, 56, 62
equivalence scales, 11
Esponohade, T. J., 183, 186
exchange of goods, 75, 76
exclusive zone, 73
expenditure public social, 69
experimental programs, 74

familial quality, 49
familial work, 39
families, 15, 150, 156, 187, 20; affluent, 70; affluent middle class, 72; middle class, 70, 74; poor, 70; support and continuation, 80; upper class, 72; working-class, 55
family, 3, 20, 44, 114, 176, 178; arrangements, 56; dissolution, 184; formation, 184; household, 64, 77, 79, 80; household, class position, 81; incomes, 69; income supplement, 142, 143, 157; law, 173; life, 154; life cycle, 163; members, 44; middle- and upper-class, 71; middle-class, 69; myths, 56; networking middle-class, 82; networks, 73; one-income, 69; patterns, 158; poverty, 95; relationships and work, 50; structure shifts, 41; three-generation, 71; two-income, 69; work, 48, 49; working-class, 69
Family Court, 71
Family Law Act, 174, 175, 178
Family Survey, 154, 155
Farcas, G., 40, 44, 45
fares and freight, 26
farm wives, 128
fast-food, 17, 75
fathers, 48, 52
feminists, 19, 81
financial hardship, 88; management, 20; resources, 73
Finch, J., 45, 153
flexi-time, 45
flow of work, 52
food, 18, 26–9, 39, 133
food production, 64
forestry, 30
formal economy, 77, 79
formal sectors, 15
Foster, C., 154, 161
foster care, 74
France, 7, 167
Franklin Ben, 6
free time, 23, 25
freedom of choice, 146
Frey, D., 97, 144
full-time employment, 163
Fuchs, V., 114 *see* Michael *et al*
Funder, K., 97, 173–5, 178, 188, 189
furniture, 27, 29
future, 75

Galbally, R., xi
Gallagher, P., 97, 154, 161

Game, A., 153
Garde, P., 163
garden, 39, 80
gardening, 6, 22, 26, 29–31
Garnsey, E., 81
gas, 26, 29
GDP *see* Gross Domestic Product
gender, 132, 152, 53; and class, 81; differences, 180; dimensions, 16; division, 154; expectations, 80; lines, 55, 62; roles, 19, 125; 170; structures, 80
general systems theory, 11
generation lines, 53
George, L. K., 128
George, V., 72
Gibson, D., 124
Gilbert, N., 72
Gilder, G., 150
Gillin, E., 8
Glezer, H., 153, 175
Glick, P., 114
GNP, *see* Gross National Product
Goode, W., 45
Goodnow, J. J., 43, 46, 49, 59, 60, 62, 63
goods and services, 23, 26, 65, 76
Gorz, A., 67
Gouldner, A. W., 69
Government, 86
government concessions, 137, 147
government sector, 4
Graham, D., 176
Graycar, A., 115, 119, 124
Gross Domestic Product (GDP), 8, 59, 60, 64, 65, 76, 160
Gross National Product (GNP), ix, 7, 14, 21
Grosser, 72
Groves, D., 153
Gruen, F., 162
Gullestad, M., 41, 49, 55

Haas, N., 56
hairdressing, 26
Halter, W., 164
Harper, J., 40
Harrison, M., 173, 174, 177
Hartmann, J., 44
Hawrylyshun, O., 7
health, 68–70, 102, 124, 147; and age, 138; foods, 67; problems, 136
heating, 133
Hemer, J. M., 115, 118, 124 *see* Kendig *et al*
Hemming, R., 164, 165
Henderson, R. F., 121

Henderson Poverty Line, 161
Hershlag, Z. Y., 21
High Court, 178
Hinrichs, K., 76
hobbies, 64
hobby farmers, 66
holiday homes, 121
holidays, 27, 29
home activities, 33, 34, 36
Home and Community Care Scheme (HDCC), 133
home; as a haven, 80; computers, 9; economics, 44; manager, 34, 36; ownership, 9; renovations, 15; units, 25
home-based lives, 134
homemakers, 144
homemaking service, 74
hospitals, 15, 122, 126
hotels, 25
hours of work, 36
house maintenance, 6, 26
House of Representatives Standing Committee on Expenditure, 1982, 113
house-keeper wage, 35
household, x, 15, 20, 25, 28, 94; activities, 151; appliances, 26, 29; autonomy, 75, 82; based enterprises, 75; commodities, 11; domestic services, 29; equipment, 9; expenditure, 25; expenditure surveys, 18; family, 71, 79, 80; germ, 20; ideal, 79; incomes, 11; labour, 42; management, 6, 60; manager, 132; money worth, 43; minimum wage to, 82; monitoring, 60; non-durables, 26, 28; production, 7, 11; productive activities, xi, 5, 24; productivity, 8, 32, 35, 37; purchases surveys, 32; reproduction of, 73; research, 41; sector, 4; sphere, 80; supplies, 19; surveys, 11; tasks, 80, 85; technology, 8; types, 37; work, 38, 41, 43, 47
household economy, x, 4, 5, 10, 14, 64, 65, 73, 75, 76, 79, 171; definition, 15, 79; dynamic model, 11; future of, 78; performance, 66
Household Expenditure Survey, 28
households, ix, 112, 152; family, 77; late-life, 127; mother-headed, 42, 94; poor family, 71; traditional, 80; two-earner, 17; two-parent, 42
housekeeper, 170
housemothering, 177

INDEX

houses, 25
housewifery, 59, 60
housework, 22, 29–31, 38–40, 59;
 definition, 59; measured, 59
housing, 99, 114, 119, 120, 124, 132,
 137, 155; costs, 27, 28, 147; loans, 98
Howe, A., 115, 118, 121, 127
Hugo, G. J., 113, 114, 117
human capital, 65; input, 35
husband, 88, 176

identity, 45
ideology, 62
immigrant women, 88
imputed rents, 17
incentives, 170
Income and Housing Survey (ABS), 68
income distribution, 5, 15; minimum,
 75; security, 142; security payments,
 145; support, 14, 106, 149, 150, 154,
 160, 164; tax revenues, 159
income-earning capacity, 181
incomes, 69, 189
independence, 124, 125
industrial capitalism, 66
industrialisation, 20
inequality, 68, 70, 73, 74, 77, 146, 152,
 181
inequity, 42
inflation, 158
informal economy, 65, 77; market, 66;
 sectors, 15; sphere, 80
information technology, 10
input-output, 11; coefficients, 30, 31,
 37; structure, 5; tables, xi, 11, 18, 24,
 29, 32, 33, 36
Institute of Family Studies see
 Australian Institute of Family
 Studies
institutions, 25
insurance, 27, 43
inter-generational transfers, 73
interfamily transfers, 157
internal inequalities, 82
interpersonal relationships, 39
invalid pensioner, 134
investment in human capital, 6, 16
investments, non-reciprocal, 73
ironing, 49, 56, 61
Ironmonger, D. S., 21, 33–5, 37, 156,171
Irving, T., 81
Italy, 82

Jacklin, C., 179
Jamrozik, A., 17, 69, 73, 76, 81, 82
Japan, 165, 167

job interviews, 140
job satisfaction, 80
jobs, 145
Jones, B., 76
Jones, F. L., 153, 175
Jordan, A., 155, 171
Joshi, H., 175, 183, 184, 186
justifications, 47, 53, 54

Kendig, H., 115, 118, 119, 121, 124,
 127, 153
Kidd, B., 117, 128
Kinnear, D., 115, 119, 124, 153
kitchenware, 26, 28, 67
Kobrin, F., 116
Korson, J., 114
Krivo, L., 114
Krupinski, J., 8
Kumar, K., 67, 72

labour, 68, 82
labour force, 66, 145, 164
labour market, 66, 68–70, 72, 111, 141,
 150, 153, 158, 160, 168, 185;
 programmes, 132; training, 169
labour time, 4, 33
labour versus leisure, 41
labour-saving devices, 20
Lampman, R., 156, 157
Land, H., 152
language barriers, 88; difficulties, 102
laundry, 6, 9, 56
leisure, 5, 10, 23, 29, 30, 88, 134
life cycle, 91, 110, 113, 177, 188
lifestyles, 72, 77
Lindner, S. B., 10
living systems theory, 11
loneliness, 89
Lopata, H. Z., 41
low-income couples, 45; families, 132,
 141, 146–8; households, 136, 140
Luxton, M., 43

McCallum, J., 119, 121
McClelland, 142, 143
McDonald, P., 154, 173, 179
McIntosh, S., 183
Mackenzie, A., 8
Macquarie, 39, 41
Maddock, R., 7, 8
maintenance payments, 185
Mallet, 178
management industries, 68
Mandeville, T., 64–6, 75
manufacturing, 7, 30
marital property, 186

marital status, 109, 111, 118, 119
market, autonomy from, 79; commodity, 67; cost approach; 34; criteria of, 76; economy, 4–7, 14, 75, 77; dependence, 67; economies, 10; informal, 70; modification pressures, 79; place, 42, 44, 171; purchases, 35; sector, 77; threaten, 75; wage, 28
markets, 67
Markov, 183
marriage, 152, 169, 171, 173, 175–7, 179, 181–3, 185–8
Marxist, 82
masculinity ratios, 117
Matrimonial Property Inquiry, 174, 176
Matthews, J., 80
May, 1987, economic statement 16, 172
means/income test, 157
medical equipment, 133; expenses, 26, 30
medicines, 30, 133
Melbourne, 11, 21, 24, 25, 36, 70, 132, 133
men, 54, 80, 90, 179, 185; wage earning, 22, 24, 26, 36
Merrington, M., 38
Michael, R., 114
Michigan, 55
micro-economists, 171
middle class, 70, 71, 72; interests, 77; issues, 74; needs, 71; suburbs, 74; vote, 70
migrants, 88, 138, 144
Miller, J., 11
Mincer, J., 175
Minford, P., 82
Mingione, E., 73
mining, 30, 7
Ministry of Housing, 99, 100, 109, 110
money, 6, 39, 44, 50, 57, 134, 151
Montague, M., 143, 144
Moore, J., 157
Morgan, J. N., 156
mortality, 114
mother's/guardian's allowance, 142, 143
mothers, 47–9, 50, 51, 52
movement of work, 52
Mowbray, M., 74
Murray, C., 150
music, 67
Mutchler, J., 114

nanny, 69, 70
national accounts, 33; income, 34; product, *see*, Gross National Product
National Longitudinal Surveys of Labor Market Experience, 183
Nebraska, 49
negotiation, 45–7, 53, 54, 57, 61, 62, 86
new middle class, 69, 70, 73
new religions, 67
New Right, 17
New Zealand, 167
newspapers, 26, 9
Nissel, M., 76
non-market, 151; concepts of economic value, 77; criteria, 77; household activities, 150; transfer of goods, 15
non-metropolitan areas, 114
non-reciprocal investments, 73
Noosa, 73
Norway, 41, 55
nuclear families, 157
nursing homes, 113, 122
nutrition, 133

Oakley, A., 19, 40, 41, 59, 60, 66
occupational prestige, 95
Ochiltree, G., 101, 106
Offe, C., 76
old-old age group, 127
older females, 125, 127
Older People at Home, 127
O'Loughlin, M. A., 153, 154
opportunity cost, 34, 77
Organisation for Economic Cooperation and Development (OECD), 159
outreach work, 91
outworkers, 11, 15
overtime, 22
owner-built home, 16
ownership, 49, 50

Pahl, R. E., 73, 82
paid work, 51, 102, 111
Pampel, F., 114
Parent's Benefits and Allowances, 177
parental care, 35
parenting, 173; shared, 85
parents, 15, 48, 53
parliament, standing for, 74
Partner Dissolution Fund (PDF), 189
partnership, 181, 184
patriarchy, 81
Penman, R., 127
pensioners, 163
pensions, 104, 137. 138, 142, 143, 148, 157, 158, 162
Peplau, L. A., 45

INDEX 207

personal care, 26; development, 67; sacrifice, 88
physical disability, 138
physiological needs, 23, 29
Pieper, E., 7
Pigou, A. C., 21
policy implications, 14, 16; issues, 125; makers, 71, 92; questions, 11; work, 37
political parties, 70
poor 70, 71, 75
population, 90; projections, 165
pottering satisfying, 80
poverty, 70, 88, 107, 131, 146, 161, 172, 177
Poverty Inquiry, 172
practicality, 55, 56, 62
press and radio, 86
primary earner, 153
Pringle, R., 153
Prinsley, D., 117 128
privacy, invasion of, 71
private associations, 76; dwellings, 25; sector, 72
production, 44, 65, 75
productivity, 8, 20, 35, 37
professional services, 74
property, 176, 185; and maintenance, 175; division, 178; values, 81
prosumers, 65
psychologists, 14, 58
public housing, 145, 147
public responsibility, 187; sector, 72, 73; support, 177

qualifications, 102
quality of life, 181, 77
Queensland, 73

Radford, A., 117
radio, 9, 23, 67
Rapoport, I., 173
Ravetz, A., 20, 21
Raymond, J., 97, 105, 106, 142
reciprocity and friendship, 65
recording equipment, 30
recreational activities, 68, 75
Redcliff, N., 73
Reed, R. H., 183
reformed divorce law, 171
relative earnings, 46; prices, 11
relatives, 112
remarriage, 110, 189
rent, 132
rented accommodation, 121
repairs, 6, 52

replacement cost approach, 34
reproduction of the household, 73
research, 93
reservation wage approach, 34
Resler, H., 65
responsibility, 40, 52, 54, 61
retirement, 163, 189
Richards, S., 40
right-wing economists, 82
role divisions, 173
role reversals, 54–6
roles of women and men, 171
Rose, H., 152
Rosenman, L., 127
Rossiter, C., 153
Roustang, G., 77
Rowland, D., 115, 118, 128
Rudd, D. M., 119, 121, 125, 127, 128
rural areas, 117
Russell, G., 55, 56, 56

Saunders, P., 160, 165, 166
Scanzoni, J., 46
school committees, 81; councils, 74; excursions, 134, holidays, 101
Schumacher, N., xi
Scotland, 55
Scots, 41, 56
Scott, S., 114 *see* Michael *et al*
Scutt, J., 176
secondary students, 17
security, 106, 169
self-care, 48, 49
self-confidence, 91
self-help, 66, 73, 74
self-sufficient householders, 65
separate mode of production, 80
separation, 188
servant or slave, 50
service clubs, 74
sex, 67, 79
sex/gender inequalities, 74
Shanas, E., 114
sharing, 41, 49, 55, 56
Sheehan, P., 158
shopping, 6, 7, 9, 26, 29, 30, 31, 52, 125
sick leave, 89
Simons, E., 7
single mothers, 100, 106, 109, 111, 112
single-person household units, 124
skills, 32, 82, 90, 102, 108
slavery, 79, 80
sleep, 5, 23
small-scale production, 75
Smeeding, T., 156, 157
Snooks, G. D., 7

social activities, 23; class, 71, 75, 79; control, 72; interaction, 125; isolation, 88; issues, 70, 74, 77; policy, 70, 70, 72, 86, 171; programmes, 149; provisions, 92; security, 134, 142, 157, 165, 170; security benefits, 104; security income tests, 147; security reform, 148; status, 90; welfare, 166; workers, 58, 71
Social Security Review, 97, 98, 141, 142, 149
Social Welfare Policy Secretariat, 166
socialising, 91
socio-economic circumstances, 184
socio-economic ladder, 66
sociological theories, 69
sociologists, 14, 33, 44, 58
sole parent families, 131, 149, 158, 162; rebate, 143
sole parents, 100, 101, 104, 144, 97, 98, 99
Sonius, E., xi, 33–5, 37
sons, 51
South Australia, 115–23
South Australian Department of Community Services, 122; Health Commission, 122; Housing Trust, 121; Women's Health Centre, 93
special accommodation, 119
specialised aged care, 126
specialist pattern, 54
sporting activities, 75
standard of living, 77, 133, 160
State Public Service, 170
state welfare, 82
statistical system, 77
status, 90, 95
Stephens, J., 144
stratification status, 81
stress-related illnesses, 138
Stricker, P., 158
structured questionnaires, 47
subsidisation, 171
subsistence living, 72
supermarket industries, 17
support, 92, 101, 108, 114
supporting parent's benefits, 157, 174
supportive services, 169
surveillance, 71
Sweden, 166, 167, 168
Sweeney, T., 69
Sydney, 101, 70
Szalai, A., 24

tasks, 40, 41, 52

tax, 15, 16, 185; consultants, 71; department, 79; rates, 171; transfers, 16
taxation, 11, 14, 158, 4
taxpayers, 187
technology, 8, 11, 67
telegraph, 9
telephone, 9, 26
television, 9, 10, 23, 27, 67, 75
tertiary qualifications, 68
textiles, 27
Thomas, K., 114
time, 5, 6, 10, 18, 30, 33, 43, 54, 59, 60, 151
time, Australians' use of, 18; budget, 24; measures, 54; off, 95; out, 90; scarce resource, 33; series, 11; use, 32
time use, pilot survey, ix, 11; survey, x, 21, 24, 25
tools, 26
Townsend, R., 38
traditional men's work, 54; women's work, 54; couples, 47; households, 52
training, 32, 91, 99, 102, 144, 172
transport, 91, 105, 122, 125, 126, 147
travel, 6, 7, 22, 26, 90, 105
Trethewey, J., 146, 148
Tucker, T., 173
Tulloch, P., 152

underclass, 70–2
unemployed, 16, 71, 73, 81, 134, 160, 172
unemployment, 82, 143, 149, 158, 161, 168
unit of consumption, 66, 79
United Kingdom *see* Britain
United States, 7, 8, 44, 72, 114, 116, 150, 156, 157, 165, 167, 183
University of Melbourne, x, xi, 37
unpaid, 81; domestic activities, 33; work, 19, 39
use value, 76

vacuuming, 49, 52
valuation, 32
valuation method, 34
value, conceptualisation and measurement, 76
Vanek, J., 8, 20
Vaughan, 74
vehicles, 26, 29, 9
Vervoorn, A. E., 69
Victoria, x, 86, 139, 170, 172
Victorian household, 43, 62; Premier, 85, 131; times, 62

Victorian Ministry of Housing, 108
  Ministry of Housing's Loan Scheme, 98
  Women's Consultative Council, 85, 93, 131
video recorders, 9
Vipond, J., 161, 163
Voysey, E., 101, 106

wages, 28, 90, 97, 147
washing machines, 67, 82
washing up, 26, 28–31
Watson, S., 127
Wearing, B., 152, 153
Weisenthal, H., 76
welfare, 68, 151; agencies, 71; outlays, 165; policies, 74; services, 69, 72; state, 64, 71, 72, 77; work, 74
West Germany, 167
Westergaard, J., 65
Weston, R., 173, 177
White, L. K., 43, 46, 48, 49
Whiteford, P., 143, 157, 162, 163, 172
widowed females, 113, 124, 127
Wilding, P., 72
Wister, A., 114
woman's place, 137
women, 54, 68, 73, 85, 86, 88, 90, 110, 168, 175, 179, 185; employed with degrees, 68; living alone, 114; married, 42, 68; non wage earning, 22, 24, 26; non-English speaking, 87; position in society, 42; role, 73; separate status of, 81; single, 42; wage earning, 22, 24, 26, 36; with school-age and pre-school children, 42; working-class, 74
Women in the Home Project, 86
women's, experience of work, 80; initiatives, 74; movement, 55, 63; pages, 20; rights, 56, 62; studies, 5; work, 55, 56; work justifications, 62
work, 40, 47, 90, 100, 102, 104, 110, 112, 135, 136, 142, 150, 169; clothes, 139; conditions, 43; contract, 75; definition, 55, 60; informal growth, 82; meaning, 47, 76; meaning and significance, 46; measurement or description, 47; moveability, 41; organisation, 55; paid, 79, 80; patterns, 46, 54; perception, 55, 60; permanent part time, 75; place, 104; preferences, 147; rewards, 43; self-care, 49; significance of, 80; site of, 39; unpaid, x, 79
work-centred society, 141
workers, 68
workers' cooperative scheme, 76
workforce, 182
working class, 70, 71, 73
working life, 185
workload, 56

Yawney, V. A., 128
youth culture, 67

Zelizer, V., 46